The Gospel of Matthew

The Gospel of Matthew

Worship in the Kingdom of Heaven

John Paul Heil

James Clarke & Co

James Clarke & Co
P.O. Box 60
Cambridge
CB1 2NT
United Kingdom

www.jamesclarke.co
publishing@jamesclarke.co

ISBN: 978 0 227 17685 6

British Library Cataloguing in Publication Data
A record is available from the British Library

First published by James Clarke & Co, 2018

Copyright © John Paul Heil, 2017

Published by arrangement
with Cascade Books

All rights reserved. No part of this edition may be reproduced, stored electronically or in any retrieval system, or transmitted in any form or by any means, electronic, mechanical, photocopying, recording, or otherwise, without prior written permission from the Publisher (permissions@jamesclarke.co).

Contents

Abbreviations | vii

1. Introduction | 1
2. Worshiping the Infant King (Matthew 1–2) | 5
3. Foundation for Worship in the Kingdom of Heaven (Matthew 3–4) | 12
4. Teaching about Worship in the Kingdom of Heaven (Matthew 5–7) | 21
5. Inviting People to Worship in the Kingdom of Heaven (Matthew 8–10) | 34
6. Failures to Repent and Parables for Worship in the Kingdom of Heaven (Matthew 11–13) | 48
7. Worshiping in the Kingdom of Heaven (Matthew 14–18) | 68
8. Worship and the Coming Kingdom of Heaven (Matthew 19–25) | 95
9. Worshiping the Risen King (Matthew 26–28) | 134
10. Conclusion | 159

Bibliography | 175
Scripture Index | 179
Author Index | 195

Abbreviations

AcT	*Acta Theologica*
AnBib	Analecta Biblica
AsTJ	*Asbury Theological Journal*
BBRSup	*Bulletin for Biblical Research, Supplements*
BDAG	Danker, Frederick W., Walter Bauer, William F. Arndt, and F. Wilbur Gingrich. *Greek-English Lexicon of the New Testament and Other Early Christian Literature.* 3rd ed. Chicago: University of Chicago Press, 2000.
BDF	Blass, Friedrich, Albert Debrunner, and Robert W. Funk. *A Greek Grammar of the New Testament and Other Early Christian Literature.* Chicago: University of Chicago Press, 1961.
BECNT	Baker Exegetical Commentary on the New Testament
Bib	*Biblica*
BL	*Bibel und Liturgie*
BZ	*Biblische Zeitschrift*
CBQ	*Catholic Biblical Quarterly*
CBQMS	Catholic Biblical Quarterly Monograph Series
ConBNT	Coneictanea Biblica: New Testament Series
EDB	*Eerdmans Dictionary of the Bible.* Edited by David Noel Freedman. Grand Rapids: Eerdmans, 2000.
EDNT	*Exegetical Dictionary of the New Testament.* Edited by Horst Balz and Gerhard Schneider. ET. 3 vols. Grand Rapids: Eerdmans, 1990–1993.

ETL	*Ephemerides Theologicae Lovanienses*
Int	*Interpretation*
JBL	*Journal of Biblical Literature*
JSNT	*Journal for the Study of the New Testament*
JSNTSup	Journal for the Study of the New Testament Supplement Series
Neot	*Neotestimentica*
NICNT	New International Commentary on the New Testament
NIDB	*New Interpreter's Dictionary of the Bible*. Edited by Katharine Doob Sakenfeld. 5 vols. Nashville: Abingdon, 2006–2009.
NIGTC	New International Greek Testament Commentary
NovT	*Novum Testamentum*
NTS	New Testament Studies
PIBA	Proceedings of the Irish Biblical Association
PRSt	*Perspectives in Religious Studies*

1

Introduction

Worship in the Gospel of Matthew

ALTHOUGH THERE HAVE BEEN brief treatments of the theme of worship in the Gospel of Matthew, a full scale comprehensive treatment has yet to appear.[1] With this book I intend to offer a new and more comprehensive treatment by considering all of the various aspects and dimensions of worship in Matthew.[2] According to the biblical tradition worship in its broadest sense includes not only acts of cultic, liturgical, or ritualistic worship but the moral or ethical behavior, the obedient service that God desires, which is a predisposition for and complements the various forms of ritualistic worship.[3] In this book, then, I will consider both the liturgical or ritual as well as the moral or ethical dimensions of worship in Matthew, a theme that has not been fully appreciated and remains largely underdeveloped.

Worship in Matthew centers around the person of Jesus Christ, characterized as "God with us" (Matt 1:23; cf. Isa 7:14) from the beginning of

---

1. For some brief treatments of worship in Matthew, see Peterson, *Engaging with God*, 81–93; Powell, *God With Us*, 28–61; Powell, "Worship in the Gospel of Matthew," 3–17; Borchert, *Worship*, 12–23; Boxall, *Matthew*, 3–4.

2. For my treatments of worship in other NT writings, see Heil, *Letters of Paul*; Heil, *Hebrews*; Heil, *James*; Heil, *1 Peter, 2 Peter, and Jude*; Heil, *Book of Revelation*; Heil, *1–3 John*; Heil, *Gospel of John*.

3. According to Peterson (*Engaging with God*, 70), "from a scriptural point of view, worship involves specific acts of adoration and submission as well as a lifestyle of obedient service. To make this point, it may be helpful to translate words indicating service to God as 'worship.' There is always the danger, however, that readers of the English text will then understand such worship purely in cultic terms! The problem for translation and for theology is that the English word 'worship' is generally used too narrowly."

the Gospel. He is the newborn divine King of the Jews (2:2) who becomes the object of reverential worship (2:11; 14:33; 28:9, 17) as well as supplicatory worship (9:18; 15:25; 20:20). Jesus teaches about prayer (6:5-15), about ritualistic worship such as fasting (6:16-18), and about the ethical worship that complements cultic worship (5:23-24; 9:13; 12:7; 23:23). The miraculous healings Jesus performs are "good deeds" that inspire others to acts of doxological worship of God (5:16; 9:8; 15:31). Jesus institutes and promotes such ritualistic or sacramental forms of worship as the Eucharist (26:26-28) and baptism (28:19). Finally, Jesus himself worships God with prayers of thanksgiving (11:25-26) and supplication (26:36-46; 27:46-53), engages in ritualistic worship (3:13-17; 14:19; 15:36; 26:26-30), and performs ethical worship (9:10-13; 12:1-14).

Preliminary Overview of the Theme of Worship in Matthew

The notion of Jesus as "God with us," which implies that he is worthy to be an object of divine worship, forms a literary inclusion that embraces the entire Gospel of Matthew. At the beginning of the Gospel, Jesus, before his birth, is designated as one whose name they will call Emmanuel, which means "God with us" (1:23). In the final scene of the Gospel the risen Jesus, after being worshiped by women (28:9) and by his disciples (28:17), declares, "I am with you all days, until the end of the age" (28:20).

Within the Gospel various forms of the divine presence of Jesus are indicated. His divine presence is closely associated with the disciples he sends out: "Whoever receives you receives me, and whoever receives me receives the one who sent me [God]" (10:40). Whoever receives a child in the name of Jesus receives Jesus himself (18:5). Where two or three are gathered together for prayer in Jesus' name, he is there in the midst of them (18:19-20). Most provocatively, Jesus identifies himself with the least of his brothers, so that whatever is done for one of them is done for him (25:40, 45). Thus one may perform what amounts to ethical worship of Jesus by extending merciful care to those with whom he closely identifies himself.

The divine presence of Jesus as "God with us" resonates with the divine presence of God in the temple of Jerusalem as the central place for cultic worship. With Jesus and his disciples whom he allows to satisfy their hunger with work on the sabbath by exemplifying the mercy God desires as the ethical worship that complements cultic worship ("mercy I desire and not [simply] sacrifice" [12:7; cf. 9:13; Hos 6:6]), "something greater than the temple is here" (12:6). As "God with us," Jesus is not only worthy to be an object of divine worship, but establishes a new "place" for worship that surpasses the temple. The "place" he establishes, however, is not a building but the community of his followers with whom he is present when they are gathered for prayer (18:19–20), and who are to practice the ethical worship that complements their cultic worship (5:23–24). They are to be God's communal household of authentic prayer that the Jerusalem temple failed to be (21:13).[4]

The new form of communal worship that Jesus establishes takes place within a new realm of divine power known as the kingdom or rule of heaven/God in contrast to the kingdom or rule of the devil/Satan. After being worshiped as the newborn divine King of the Jews (2:2, 11), Jesus proved to be God's faithful royal Son when he was tempted by the devil (4:1–11). He began to actualize the kingdom of heaven as the realm for true worship when he resisted with the scriptural word of God the devil's temptation to worship him on a very high mountain (4:8–9): "Go, Satan, for it is written, 'the Lord your God shall you worship and him alone shall you serve' [Deut 6:13]" (4:10). In continuity with John the Baptist (3:2) Jesus went on to announce that the kingdom of heaven has come near (4:17). In contrast to the temptation to worship the devil on a mountain, on a mountain in Galilee the disciples worshiped the risen Jesus (28:16–17), who is "God with us" (1:23; 28:20). Worship in Matthew, then, is all about the true worship that is to take place within the new realm of the kingdom of heaven established by the divine King.

Methodological Presuppositions

I will treat the topic of worship in Matthew by means of a narrative-critical, audience-oriented exegetical methodology.[5] The focus will be on the responses expected by the implied or ideal audience members, the audience presupposed by the text, as they hear the narrative unfold and develop. With regard particularly to the topic of worship, the narrative presupposes an audience with knowledge of the OT scriptures and of such Jewish religious institutions as the synagogue, temple, Sabbath observance, ritual cleansings, meal fellowship, the Passover feast, prayer, fasting, almsgiving, etc.[6] In addition, it can be expected that, as believers, the members of the audience are familiar with such Christian sacramental worship as baptism (28:19) and the Eucharist (26:26–29). I understand the Gospel of Matthew to have been written sometime in the latter half of the first century for a specific

---

4. Perrin, *Jesus the Temple*, 59–61.
5. Powell, "Narrative-Critical," 341–46; Resseguie, *Narrative Criticism*.
6. Powell, "Readings of Matthew," 31–51.

community or communities of Christians located somewhere in the eastern Mediterranean region of the Roman empire, but with a general relevance for all Christian believers.[7]

The structure of the Gospel of Matthew is characterized by five major discourses delivered by Jesus during his ministry of teaching, preaching, and healing, each of which concludes with the same basic formula: "When Jesus finished these words" (7:28; 11:1; 13:53; 19:1; 26:1). The discourses include the sermon on the mount (5–7), the missionary discourse (9:36–11:1), the parables discourse (13:1–53), the community discourse (17:24–19:1), and the eschatological discourse (24–25). The narrative of the ministry of Jesus is preceded by an infancy narrative (1–2) and concludes with the passion, death, and resurrection narratives (26–28).

Accordingly, this book will trace the theme of worship in the Gospel of Matthew under the following headings, which also serve as the titles for the chapters to follow: worshiping the infant King (1–2); foundation for worship in the kingdom of heaven (3–4); teaching about worship in the kingdom of heaven (5–7); inviting people to worship in the kingdom of heaven (8–10); failures to repent and parables for worship in the kingdom of heaven (11–13); worshiping in the kingdom of heaven (14–18); worship and the coming kingdom of heaven (19–25); worshiping the risen King (26–28).

---

7. For detailed discussions regarding introductory issues for the Gospel of Matthew, see Morris, *Matthew*, 1–17; Nolland, *Matthew*, 1–43; France, *Matthew*, 1–22; Turner, *Matthew*, 1–51; Osborne, *Matthew*, 21–47; Boxall, *Matthew*, 1–13.

2

Worshiping the Infant King (Matthew 1–2)

The Genealogy and Birth of Jesus Christ (Matthew 1)

THE INTRODUCTORY DESIGNATION OF Jesus "Christ" as "the son of David" (1:1) indicates that Jesus is the royal "Christ" or "Messiah" (literally, "anointed one") God promised to send as a descendant of King David (2 Sam 7:12; Isa 11:1–9; Jer 23:5; Ezek 34:23). As God's royal messianic Son of David, Jesus possesses the status of a divine agent, which begins to indicate to the audience of Matthew that he is worthy to be an object of worship. This prepares the audience for Jesus to be addressed later as "Son of David" in acts of supplicatory worship (Matt 9:27; 15:22; 20:30–31) as well as of reverential worship (21:9, 15).

In addition, being the Son of David places Jesus in an ancestral line concerned with building a house/temple for the true worship of God. King David wanted to build it, but God promised that David's son Solomon (1:6) would build it (2 Sam 7:1–17). Jesus' status as the royal messianic Son of David thus prepares the audience for Jesus to surpass the building of the temple (Matt 12:6) by establishing a new communal household for true worship and prayer (21:13, 21–22).

But his genealogy also places Jesus in an ancestral line of sinful kings. The sinfulness of the Davidic royal line begins to be indicated with the notice that "Judah became the father of Perez and Zerah, whose mother was Tamar" (1:3). This recalls the sinfulness of Judah in not giving his daughter-in-law Tamar in marriage to his son Shelah (Gen 38:26), which led to Tamar's seduction of Judah (38:14–25).

David "the king" added to this sinfulness with his murder of Uriah with whose wife (Bathsheba) he had committed adultery (Matt 1:6; 2 Samuel 11). With the reference to David "the king" the genealogy reaches its first high point, but descends to its low point with the reference to the Babylonian exile (1:11), a consequence of the sinfulness of the Davidic kings. It reaches its climactic high point with the reference to the birth of Jesus, the royal Christ, from Mary whose husband was Joseph (1:16–17), with an implicit hope for the reversal of the sinfulness of the previous Davidic kings. This hope becomes explicit with the notice that Jesus, divinely conceived through the Holy Spirit (1:18, 20), will be given the name Jesus by Joseph, son of David (1:20), because he will save his people from their sins (1:21), including those of their kings, underlining his worthiness to be worshiped as Emmanuel, "God with us" (1:23).[1]

The designation of Jesus as "the son of Abraham" indicates to the audience that he is a member of the Jewish people (1:1; cf. 3:9). But it also places him within an ancestral line of Gentiles who acknowledged the God of Israel as worthy of true worship. Before he became the father of the Jewish people and thus while still a Gentile, Abraham, to whom God had promised that all the tribes of the earth will be blessed in him (Gen 12:3), built an altar and invoked the name of the Lord God in worship (12:8; 13:4; 21:33), as did also the patriarchs Isaac and Jacob (26:25; 33:20), who followed him in the genealogy (Matt 1:2).[2]

Two Gentile women, the Canaanite Rahab and the Moabite Ruth, both of whom acknowledged the God of Israel as worthy of worship (Josh 2:11; Ruth 1:16), are also included within the genealogy of Jesus (Matt 1:5).[3] These Gentile ancestors of Jesus were closely associated with the worship of the God of Israel. They prefigure and prepare the audience for Jesus' fulfillment of the Abrahamic promise of a universal divine blessing by bringing Gentiles and all peoples to true and authentic worship of God (2:1–12; 8:5–13; 15:22–28; 28:19–20).

---

1. "In the New Testament era 'Son of David' was the basic title for the Messiah, the longed-for ruler of David's line who, it was hoped, would free Israel from its current captivity and rule in peace and justice over a renewed people" (Byrne, *Lifting the Burden*, 19).

2. "Besides being 'father' of the Jewish people Abraham was also known in the tradition as the first 'proselyte' or convert from the nations of the world (Gentiles) to the worship of the one true God" (Byrne, *Lifting the Burden*, 20).

3. Heil, "Women in Matthew's Genealogy," 538–45. See also Clements, *Mothers on the Margin*.

Worship of the Infant King and Divine Son of God (Matthew 2)

Continuing the theme of Gentiles associated with true worship (1:5), a group of magi, experts in astrology/astronomy, arrived "from the east," and thus as Gentile foreigners, in Jerusalem after the birth of Jesus in Bethlehem of Judea (2:1).[4] Having observed the rising of a new star corresponding to the birth of a new messianic ruler (Num 24:17), the magi came to worship the newborn King of the Jews (2:2), the royal Davidic Christ (2:4). Jesus' birth in Bethlehem in the land of Judah, an ancestor of David (1:2–3), fulfills the prophetic word of God from the Jewish scriptures that "from you will come a ruler, who will shepherd my people Israel [2 Sam 5:2; Mic 5:1]" (2:6). The Gentile magi then have come to worship the newborn Davidic King of the Jews who will truly shepherd God's people (Ezek 34:23) in contrast to King Herod and all other earthly Jewish kings, who have failed to be true shepherds of God's people (34:1–22).[5]

Whereas King Herod and all Jerusalem were frightened at the news of a newborn King of the Jews (Matt 2:3), the Gentile magi rejoiced with very great joy (2:10) when they saw the heavenly star that led them to the place where the child was (2:9). Falling down, they worshiped him and, opening their treasures, they offered him very precious gifts, gold and frankincense and myrrh (2:11), offerings acceptable for divine worship (Isa 60:6–7).[6] The Gentile magi thus provide the Matthean audience with a stellar model for their own worship of Jesus not only as the newborn King of the Jews (2:2), the royal Christ (2:4) who will truly shepherd God's people (2:6), but as the Jesus who will save his people from their sins (1:21), the one whose name they will call Emmanuel, "God with us" (1:23).

Although King Herod told the magi that he also wanted to worship the child Jesus as the newborn King of the Jews (2:2, 8), an angel of the

---

4. "The Greek word *magos* denotes people possessed of special and superior knowledge, experts in some field, especially—as would appear to be the case here—astronomy/astrology. Though we do know of Jewish magi (cf. Acts 8:9), it seems clear that here we have to do with representatives from the non-Jewish (Gentile) world" (Byrne, *Lifting the Burden*, 28). On the magi as Gentiles, see also France, *Matthew*, 67n36. Contrary to some popular notions, the magi are neither kings nor wise men. Indeed, as those given divine revelation through the heavenly star, the magi stand in contrast not only to sinful human kings, such as Herod "the king" (Matt 2:1, 3, 9), but to the humanly "wise" from whom God has hidden divine revelation (11:25). Powell, "Magi as Kings," 459–80; Powell, "Magi as Wise Men," 1–20; Powell, "Neither Wise Nor Powerful," 19–31.

5. Heil, "Ezekiel 34," 698–708.

6. That the magi offer three gifts is probably the reason for the popular notion that there were three of them, but the text does not number them.

Lord informed Joseph that actually Herod is going to search for the child to destroy him (2:13). As directed by the angel, Joseph took the child and his mother to Egypt (2:14), thus enabling Jesus to relive the exodus experience of the people of Israel. He stayed there until the death of Herod, so that what was spoken by the Lord through the prophet might be fulfilled, "Out of Egypt I called my Son [Hos 11:1]" (2:15).

Originally, "my Son" in the scriptural quotation referred to the people of Israel as the corporate son of God (Exod 4:22), whom God called out of Egypt to "serve" him with true worship (4:23).[7] But now "my Son" refers to Jesus as the Son of God representative of his people (Matt 2:15), just as the Davidic king was also considered God's son as the representative leader of the people (2 Sam 7:14; Ps 2:7; 89:27). Whereas Israel as God's son engaged in idolatrous rather than true worship (Hos 11:2), and whereas King Solomon as son of David and son of God practiced and led Israel into idolatrous worship (1 Kings 11), Jesus is called to be the Son of God who not only practices true worship, but leads others to true worship as the ruler who will truly shepherd God's people Israel (Matt 2:6). Indeed, as not only Son of David and Son of Abraham (1:1) but Son of God (2:15), Jesus is called by God not only to practice and lead others to true worship, but to be an object of true worship as the Son of God (14:33; 16:13; 27:54), who is "God with us" (1:23).

In accord with his notorious reputation for ruthlessness, and as a further indication of the sinfulness of the Jewish kings, who failed to be true shepherds of their people, Herod had all of the male children two years old and under in Bethlehem and its vicinity murdered (2:16).[8] Then was fulfilled what was spoken through Jeremiah the prophet during the Babylonian exile of the people of Israel caused by the sinfulness of their kings (2:17; 1:11). The quotation (Jer 31:15 in Matt 2:18) portrays Rachel, wife of Jacob/Israel and thus matriarch of the people of Israel, inconsolably weeping, originally for her exiled children but now for the children murdered by Herod. Her weeping and loud lamentation caused by the sinfulness of King Herod present a stark contrast to the very great joy with which the magi rejoiced when they worshiped the child Jesus (2:10–11) as the newborn King of the Jews

---

7. It is continually repeated that once the people of Israel leave Egypt they are to "serve" God, with the connotation of "serving" by means of both ethical and cultic worship: Exod 3:12; 4:23; 7:16, 26; 8:16; 9:1, 13; 10:3, 7, 8, 11, 24, 26; 12:31.

8. Herod "was driven by innate distrust and constant fear of a rival claimant" (Kellermann, "Ἡρῴδης," 123). He murdered several of his rivals, including members of his own family.

(2:2), the ruler from Bethlehem who will truly shepherd God's people Israel (2:6) and save them from their sins (1:21).[9]

After the death of Herod an angel of the Lord directed Joseph to take the child Jesus and his mother from Egypt to the land of Israel (2:19–21). This enables Jesus to continue to relive the salvation history of his people, who eventually entered the promised land of Israel after their exodus from Egypt. Instead of returning to Judea, now ominous since a son of Herod was ruling there, Joseph departed for the region of Galilee (2:22), a region associated with Gentiles (Isa 8:23; Matt 4:15), and thus appropriate for a Jesus with Gentile ancestors (1:5).[10]

Joseph went with the child Jesus and his mother and dwelt in the town of Nazareth, so that what was spoken through the prophets might be fulfilled, "He will be called a Nazorean" (2:23). That the quotation was spoken through the "prophets" (plural) suggests an allusion to more than one OT prophetic text. On the one hand, "Nazorean," through a wordplay on the Hebrew *nezer* ("branch"), alludes to the Davidic messianic royal "branch" (Isa 11:1), and thus accords with Jesus as the Christ who is the Son of David (Matt 1:1). But on the other hand, "Nazorean," through a wordplay on the Hebrew *nazîr* ("nazirite"), alludes to one who is set apart and specially consecrated to God (Judg 13:5, 7) by an act of worship, a ritual vow (Num 6:2–8). "Will be called a Nazorean" in turn resonates with "will be called holy" (Isa 4:3), as nazirites are holy to the Lord (Num 6:8).[11] Unlike the previous sinful Davidic kings, Jesus will be called by God (divine passive) to be a "Nazorean," the Davidic royal Christ dedicated to God for the true and proper worship of God.

An angel of the Lord directed Joseph to "call" the name of the child conceived by the Holy Spirit (1:18, 20) Jesus, because he will save his people from their sins (1:21, 25). In turn his people "will call" his name Emmanuel, "God with us" (1:23). God "called" Jesus out of Egypt to be the divine Son of God (2:15). And Jesus "will be called" by God to be a Nazorean (2:23), one not only dedicated to the worship of God but one worthy to be an object of worship as a Nazorean who is also the divine Son of God, "God with us," the divinely conceived Jesus who will save his people from their sins.

---

9. "Nothing could portray more poignantly the need for the coming of a ruler who would 'shepherd' rather than ravage the flock of Israel" (Byrne, *Lifting the Burden*, 32). On Herod's sinfulness, see also Park, "Rachel's Cry," 473–85.

10. BDAG, 187.

11. Byrne, *Lifting the Burden*, 33 n31.

Summary on Matthew 1–2

As the Christ who is the Son of David (1:1), Jesus will not only be concerned with providing for the proper worship of God, but will himself be a worthy object of divine worship (9:27; 15:22; 20:30-31; 21:9, 15). As the royal Son of David, Jesus will reverse the sinfulness of the previous Davidic kings. Divinely conceived through the Holy Spirit (1:18, 20), he is to be given the name Jesus by Joseph, son of David (1:20), because he will save his people from their sins (1:21), including those of their kings, underlining his worthiness to be worshiped as Emmanuel, "God with us" (1:23).

The designation of Jesus as "the son of Abraham" indicates that he is a member of the Jewish people (1:1; cf. 3:9). But it also places him within an ancestral line of Gentiles who acknowledged the God of Israel as worthy of true worship. The Gentile ancestors of Jesus (1:5) were closely associated with the worship of the God of Israel. They prefigure and prepare the audience for Jesus' fulfillment of the Abrahamic promise of a universal divine blessing by bringing Gentiles and all peoples to true worship (2:1-12; 8:5-13; 15:22-28; 28:19-20).

The Gentile magi came to worship the newborn Davidic King of the Jews (2:1-2) who will truly shepherd God's people (2:6) in contrast to King Herod and all other earthly Jewish kings, who have failed to be true shepherds of God's people. Falling down, the magi worshiped the infant King and, opening their treasures, they offered him very precious gifts, gold and frankincense and myrrh (2:11), offerings acceptable for divine worship (Isa 60:6-7). The Gentile magi thus provide the Matthean audience with a stellar model for their own worship of Jesus not only as the newborn King of the Jews (2:2), the royal Christ (2:4) who will truly shepherd God's people, but as the Jesus who will save his people from their sins (1:21), the one whose name they will call Emmanuel, "God with us" (1:23).

Originally, "Out of Egypt I called my Son [Hos 11:1]" (Matt 2:15) referred to the people of Israel as the corporate son of God (Exod 4:22), whom God called out of Egypt to "serve" him with true worship (4:23). But now "my Son" refers to Jesus as the Son of God representative of his people, just as the Davidic king was also considered God's son as the representative leader of the people (2 Sam 7:14; Ps 2:7; 89:27). Israel as God's son engaged in idolatrous rather than true worship (Hos 11:2), and King Solomon as son of David and son of God practiced and led Israel into idolatrous worship (1 Kings 11). But Jesus is called to be the Son of God not only to practice and lead others to true worship, but to be an object of true worship as the Son of God (Matt 14:33; 16:13; 27:54), who is "God with us" (1:23).

The quotation of Jer 31:15 in Matt 2:18 portrays Rachel, wife of Jacob/Israel and thus matriarch of the people of Israel, inconsolably weeping. She mourned originally for her exiled children but now for the children murdered by Herod (2:16). Her weeping and loud lamentation caused by the sinfulness of King Herod present a stark contrast to the very great joy with which the magi rejoiced when they worshiped the child Jesus (2:10–11) as the newborn King of the Jews (2:2), the ruler from Bethlehem who will truly shepherd God's people Israel (2:6) and save them from their sins (1:21).

An angel of the Lord directed Joseph to "call" the name of the child conceived by the Holy Spirit (1:18, 20) Jesus, because he will save his people from their sins (1:21, 25). In turn his people "will call" his name Emmanuel, "God with us" (1:23). God "called" Jesus out of Egypt to be the divine Son of God (2:15). And Jesus "will be called" by God to be a Nazorean (2:23), one not only dedicated to the worship of God but one worthy to be an object of worship as a Nazorean who is also the divine Son of God, "God with us," the divinely conceived Jesus who will save his people from their sins.

3

Foundation for Worship in the Kingdom of Heaven (Matthew 3–4)

The Baptism of Jesus by John (Matthew 3)

JOHN "THE BAPTIST," THE one who performs acts of ritual worship by baptizing or cleansing with water for purification, arrived preaching in the wilderness of Judea (3:1), and saying, "Repent, for the kingdom of heaven has come near!" (3:2). The implication is that the "kingdom" of heaven, God's end-time reign or rule over the forces of evil and sinfulness, has come near in the person of Jesus, the newborn divine "King" of the Jews (2:2), "God with us" (1:23), the Jesus who will save his people from their sins (1:21). John is the one spoken about through Isaiah the prophet: "A voice of one shouting in the wilderness, 'Prepare the way for the Lord, make straight his paths [Isa 40:3]'" (3:3). Thus, by repenting, turning around and changing their lives, people may prepare the way for the Lord (God/Jesus) to allow them to experience the kingdom, reign, or rule of heaven/God in their lives.

Jerusalem, all Judea, and all the region around the Jordan were going out to John (3:5), who had an austere desert diet and clothing (3:4) reminiscent of Elijah (1 Kgs 1:8), the prophet expected to return to prepare Israel for the final manifestation of God's kingdom (Mal 3:23–24). They were engaging in an act of ritual worship by being baptized by John in the Jordan River while confessing their sins (Matt 3:6), thus indicating their willingness to repent and turn away from their past sinfulness in preparation for experiencing the kingdom of heaven. However, John warned the Pharisees and Sadducees, Jewish religious leaders, coming to his baptism (3:7) not simply to rely upon their descent from Abraham (3:9) to escape condemnation at the coming final judgment (3:7, 10), but to "produce fruit," that is, to perform good works, corresponding to their repentance (3:8). In other words, they demonstrate for the audience the need for the ethical behavior that God desires to complement their baptism as an act of ritual worship.

John baptizes with water for repentance, but the stronger one coming after him will baptize with the Holy Spirit and fire (3:11). John means that this stronger one (Jesus) will baptize metaphorically as an expression of his role in judging. In accord with harvesting imagery the stronger one will clean out his threshing floor and gather his "wheat," those who produce the good fruit of good works (3:10), into the barn (3:12a). This is the positive side of judgment and corresponds to "baptizing" with the Holy Spirit. But the "chaff," those who do not produce the good fruit of good works so that they are thrown into fire (3:10), he will burn with inextinguishable fire (3:12b). This is the negative side of judgment and corresponds to "baptizing" with fire. But the Matthean Christian audience can appreciate how John's baptism with water and Jesus' baptism with the Holy Spirit point to and have significance for their own sacramental baptism with water in the Holy Spirit (28:19).

Jesus arrived from Galilee at the Jordan before John to be baptized by him (3:13) to show his solidarity with those who are repenting and confessing their sins (3:2, 6).[1] Aware of Jesus' superior status and his need to be baptized by him as the stronger one (3:11), John was reluctant to baptize Jesus (3:14). But he did so, after Jesus assured him that it was proper for them to fulfill all righteousness (3:15), that is, to do what is right and pleasing to God within the divine plan of salvation. After Jesus was baptized, he had a vision of "the Spirit of God descending like a dove and coming upon him" (3:16). The voice of God from heaven interpreted the vision for the audience with the words, "This is my beloved Son, with whom I am well pleased [Gen 22:12, 16; Ps 2:7; Isa 41:8; 42:1; Jer 38:20]" (Matt 3:17).[2] This reaffirms for the audience the status of Jesus to be a worthy object of worship as the divine Son of God (2:15), not only conceived by the Holy Spirit (1:18, 20), but now equipped with the Holy Spirit of God, empowering him to save his people from their sins (1:21), as "God with us" (1:23).

---

1. The only three occurrences in Matthew of the verb "arrive" (παραγίνομαι) each precede an act of worship. The magi "arrived" in Jerusalem (2:1) before they worshiped Jesus in Bethlehem (2:11). John the Baptist "arrived" in the wilderness of Judea (3:1) before performing the ritual worship of baptizing in the Jordan River (3:6). And Jesus "arrived" from Galilee at the Jordan to receive John's baptism as a ritual act of worship (3:13).

2. Lentzen-Deis, *Taufe Jesu*; Gibbs, "Baptism of Jesus," 511–26.

The baptism of Jesus by John provides the members of the audience with a foundational model for their own Christian sacramental baptism. At his baptism Jesus was empowered with the Holy Spirit of God and declared God's beloved Son by the Father (3:16–17). The members of the audience have been baptized "into the name of the Father and of the Son and of the Holy Spirit" (28:19). The baptism of Jesus reminds them how their own baptism was in the Holy Spirit, which enables them to practice the ethical behavior, to "produce the fruit" (3:8) of good works and to fulfill all the righteousness (3:15) that God desires, thus complementing their sacramental baptism as an act of ritual worship.[3]

The Temptations of Jesus (Matt 4:1–11)

Equipped with the Spirit of God (3:16), Jesus, God's beloved Son (3:17), was led by that same Spirit into the wilderness to be tempted or tested by the devil (4:1). The people of Israel were similarly tempted in the wilderness to demonstrate whether they were really a faithful covenantal son of God (Deut 8:1–6; Exod 4:22; Hos 11:1).[4] Jesus was hungry after fasting for forty days and forty nights (4:2), thus practicing a form of ascetic worship.[5] The tempter enticed him to demonstrate his status as the Son of God by commanding stones to become bread (4:3). Whereas Israel failed the test of going hungry (Num 21:5–6; Deut 8:3a), the hungry Jesus overcame the devil's temptation by appealing to a scriptural word of God: "A person will not live by bread alone, but by every word coming forth through the mouth of God [Deut 8:3b]" (4:4). Jesus thus models for the audience how fasting from food or, more generally, detaching oneself from material things, facilitates obedience to the word of God heard in liturgical worship, in order to "live" both ethically and eternally by complementing liturgical worship with ethical worship.

---

3. "[W]hat Jesus experiences here following his baptism is something that all the baptized can claim. Each one, before any good work of which they may subsequently be capable and simply because of their union with Jesus, can take to themselves that same assurance: 'This is my beloved son/daughter, with whom I am well pleased'" (Byrne, *Lifting the Burden*, 41).

4. Gerhardsson, *Testing of God's Son*.

5. Fasting in the NT almost always has a "special religious (ritual or ascetic) sense" and it is closely associated with prayer as "signs of the worship of God" (Zmijewski, "νηστεύω," 465–66). "Fasting is particularly associated . . . with seeking the guidance of God, and with imploring God for his help in a particularly intense fashion or, more generally, with an intensity of focus on God" (Nolland, *Matthew*, 163n32). See also Wimmer, *Fasting in the New Testament*.

Then the devil took Jesus to the holy city of Jerusalem and stood him on the pinnacle of the temple (4:5), a place associated with both worship and protective refuge. The devil again enticed Jesus to demonstrate his status as the Son of God by throwing himself down (4:6a). He cleverly quoted from a psalm used in temple worship to celebrate God's promise of protection particularly for the Davidic Christ: "He will command his angels concerning you and on their hands they will lift you up, lest you strike your foot against a stone [Ps 91:11–12]" (4:6b).[6] But Jesus demonstrated how he is indeed truly God's faithful Son by not throwing himself down to test God, in contrast to Israel who failed to be a faithful son by continually testing God to sustain them (Exod 17:2, 7; Num 14:22; Ps 78:18; 106:14). Jesus again overcame the devil's temptation by appealing to another scriptural word of God: "You shall not test the Lord your God [Deut 6:16]" (4:7). With this second temptation Jesus models for the audience how authentic worship and prayer refrains from trying to manipulate God for one's personal benefit.

Again, the devil took Jesus to a very high mountain and showed him all the kingdoms of the world and their glory (4:8). He tempted him with the diabolical promise, "All these things I will give you, if you fall down and worship me" (4:9). In contrast to Israel, who failed to be a faithful son of God by worshiping false gods (Num 25:1–3; Deut 29:24–25), Jesus demonstrated his faithful divine Sonship by forcefully commanding Satan to go away, and he overcame this third temptation by again appealing to a scriptural word of God: "The Lord your God shall you worship and him alone shall you serve [Deut 6:13]" (4:10). With this third final and climactic temptation Jesus models for the audience how authentic worship must be centered totally on God alone and thus excludes giving oneself over to and making life's priority the pursuit of worldly power, prestige, and wealth, which amounts to the worship of false gods and/or the devil.

In ironic contrast to the devil's temptation for Jesus to throw himself down from the top of the temple, so that God's angels may rescue and protect him (4:6), once the defeated devil left Jesus, God's angels came and were ministering to him (4:11). This reaffirms for the audience that Jesus indeed is the Spirit-equipped beloved Son of God, with whom God is well pleased (3:16–17). By definitively overcoming the devil, the source of all evil and sinfulness, in this triplet of unique and fundamental temptations, each of which concerns authentic worship, Jesus has established the basic and firm foundation that will enable him to save his people from their sins (1:21), the diabolical sins that detract from and prevent a true worship of God. The

6. "Since the Psalms were traditionally attributed to David, they were considered to be first and foremost the 'book' of the Messiah, Son of David; they scripted the role he had to play" (Byrne, *Lifting the Burden*, 42n12).

defeat of the devil by Jesus as the divine royal Christ (2:2, 4, 15) signals that the reign and rule of the devil/Satan is coming to an end and that the reign and rule of heaven/God has indeed come near (3:2) in the person of Jesus, the King, whose heavenly kingdom will serve as the realm for the true and authentic worship of God.

The Beginning of the Ministry of Jesus (Matt 4:12–25)

When Jesus heard that John had been arrested, he withdrew from the ominous Judea and returned to Galilee (4:12). He left Nazareth and went to dwell in Capernaum by the Sea of Galilee in the region of Zebulun and Naphtali (4:13). This was to fulfill what had been spoken through Isaiah the prophet (4:14): "Land of Zebulun and land of Naphtali, way of the sea, beyond the Jordan, Galilee of the Gentiles, the people sitting in darkness have seen a great light, and on those sitting in a land overshadowed by death light has arisen for them [Isa 8:23–9:1]" (4:15–16). Jesus' residence in "Galilee of the Gentiles" indicates the significance of his ministry for both Jews and Gentiles. It recalls his association with Gentiles engaged in the true worship of the God of Israel (1:5; 2:11).[7] As the messianic King who will truly shepherd God's "people" Israel (2:6), the Jesus who will save his "people" from their sins (1:21), Jesus, who overcame the devil responsible for sin and death (4:1–11), represents the great light of life for the "people" sitting in the darkness of sin and death.

From the time that he dwelt in Capernaum (4:13), Jesus indicated how he represents a great light of life for those sitting in the darkness of death (4:16), as he began to preach and to say, "Repent, for the kingdom of heaven has come near" (4:17). After the arrest of John (4:12) Jesus took up and continued to preach the same message as John (3:2), but Jesus is the one, as the King (2:2) and "God with us" (1:23), through whom the kingdom of heaven has come near. Having overcome the temptations of the devil (4:1–11), which signals that the reign and rule of the devil responsible for sin and death is coming to an end, Jesus calls for people to repent and thus turn away from the darkness of sin and death and toward the light of a new life under the reign and rule of heaven. As the temptations of Jesus have indicated, life in the kingdom of heaven includes living by the word

---

7. "Though basically Jewish, Galilee had a mixed population at the time of Jesus" (Byrne, *Lifting the Burden*, 48). "While Jesus did not mingle much with Gentiles, the salvation he came to bring was just as much for them as for the Jews. It was important accordingly that he lived in an area greatly influenced by Gentiles" (Morris, *Matthew*, 82).

of God that is heard in worship (4:1–4), praying in a way that does not try to manipulate God (4:5–7), and worshiping God alone rather than power, prestige, or wealth (4:8–10).

Jesus' call of his first four disciples provides the audience with a preeminent illustration of the kind of repentance for which he appealed (4:17). He called two pairs of brothers—Simon Peter and his brother Andrew, James and his brother John—to repent by turning away from their occupation of catching fish and coming after Jesus in order to catch people to live in the kingdom of heaven. Compelled by such an intriguing offer, they indicated the authoritative and charismatic attraction of Jesus, as they immediately left their fishing occupation and followed Jesus (4:18–22). They left to follow Jesus in drawing people away from the darkness of sin and death (4:16) and into the light of a new life in the kingdom of heaven, a life characterized by the true and authentic worship of God make possible by Jesus (4:1–11).[8]

With his first disciples Jesus went around all of Galilee, teaching in their synagogues, preaching the gospel, the good news, of the kingdom, and healing every disease and every sickness among the people (4:23). That Jesus was teaching in their synagogues, places for prayer and worship, implies that he was teaching about true and authentic worship in the kingdom of heaven, the good news of the arrival of which he was preaching. And that he was healing every disease and every sickness among the "people" confirms how he represents a great light for the "people" living in the darkness of sickness, sin, and death (4:16). Jesus was thus beginning to truly shepherd God's "people" Israel (2:6) and to save his "people" from their sins (1:21), which were closely connected with their sickness, both of which are tied to the devil.

The news about Jesus spread to all of Syria, and they brought to him all who were sick with various diseases and oppressed with pains, those possessed by demons, those who were epileptics and paralytics, and he healed them (4:24). Because Jesus overcame the temptations of the devil (4:1–11), the prince of demons and the source of all evil and sickness, he was able to heal all of these severely sick people. Exceeding the number of people attracted by John (3:5), large crowds from Galilee, the Decapolis, Jerusalem, Judea, and beyond the Jordan followed Jesus (4:25).[9] With his first disciples Jesus was thus catching people (4:19) by calling them to repentance in order to live within the kingdom of heaven (4:17), a life he can make possible for them by saving them from the sins (1:21) and healing them from the sicknesses that detract from and prevent the true and authentic worship of God.

---

8. Carter, "Matthew 4:18–22," 58–75.
9. Carter, "Crowds in Matthew's Gospel," 54–67.

Summary on Matthew 3-4

Jerusalem, all of Judea, and the region around the Jordan were going out to John the Baptist (3:5). They were engaging in an act of ritual worship by being baptized by John in the Jordan River while confessing their sins (3:6), thus indicating their willingness to repent and turn away from their past sinfulness in preparation for experiencing the kingdom of heaven (3:2). However, John warned the Pharisees and Sadducees, Jewish religious leaders, coming to his baptism (3:7) not simply to rely upon their descent from Abraham (3:9) to escape condemnation at the coming final judgment (3:7, 10), but to "produce fruit," that is, to perform good works, corresponding to their repentance (3:8). In other words, they demonstrate for the audience the need for the ethical behavior that God desires to complement their baptism as an act of ritual worship.

John baptizes with water for repentance, but the stronger one coming after him will baptize with the Holy Spirit and fire (3:11). John means that this stronger one (Jesus) will baptize metaphorically as an expression of his role in judging. In accord with harvesting imagery the stronger one will clean out his threshing floor and gather his "wheat," those who produce the good fruit of good works (3:10), into the barn (3:12a). This is the positive side of judgment and corresponds to "baptizing" with the Holy Spirit. But the "chaff," those who do not produce the good fruit of good works so that they are thrown into fire (3:10), he will burn with inextinguishable fire (3:12b). This is the negative side of judgment and corresponds to "baptizing" with fire. But the Matthean Christian audience can appreciate how John's baptism with water and Jesus' baptism with the Holy Spirit point to and have significance for their own sacramental baptism with water in the Holy Spirit (28:19).

The baptism of Jesus by John provides the members of the audience with a foundational model for their own Christian sacramental baptism. At his baptism Jesus was empowered with the Holy Spirit of God and declared God's beloved Son by the Father (3:16-17). The members of the audience have been baptized "into the name of the Father and of the Son and of the Holy Spirit" (28:19). The baptism of Jesus reminds them how their own baptism was in the Holy Spirit, which enables them to practice the ethical behavior, to "produce the fruit" (3:8) of good works and to fulfill all the righteousness (3:15) that God desires, thus complementing their sacramental baptism as an act of ritual worship.

Whereas the people of Israel, as God's son (Deut 8:1-6; Exod 4:22; Hos 11:1), failed the test of going hungry (Num 21:5-6; Deut 8:3a), the hungry Jesus overcame the devil's temptation by appealing to a scriptural word of

God: "A person will not live by bread alone, but by every word coming forth through the mouth of God [Deut 8:3b]" (Matt 4:4). Jesus thus models for the audience how fasting from food (4:2) or, more generally, detaching oneself from material things, facilitates obedience to the word of God heard in liturgical worship, in order to "live" both ethically and eternally by complementing liturgical worship with ethical worship.

Jesus demonstrated how he is indeed truly God's faithful Son by not throwing himself down to test God (4:6), in contrast to Israel who failed to be a faithful son by continually testing God to sustain them (Exod 17:2, 7; Num 14:22; Ps 78:18; 106:14). Jesus again overcame the devil's temptation by appealing to another scriptural word of God: "You shall not test the Lord your God [Deut 6:16]" (4:7). With this second temptation Jesus models for the audience how authentic worship and prayer refrains from trying to manipulate God for one's personal benefit.

In contrast to Israel, who failed to be a faithful son of God by worshiping false gods (Num 25:1–3; Deut 29:24–25), Jesus demonstrated his faithful divine Sonship by forcefully commanding Satan to go away, and he overcame this third temptation by again appealing to a scriptural word of God: "The Lord your God shall you worship and him alone shall you serve [Deut 6:13]" (Matt 4:10). With this third final and climactic temptation Jesus models for the audience how authentic worship must be centered totally on God alone and thus excludes giving oneself over to and making life's priority the pursuit of worldly power, prestige, and wealth, which amounts to the worship of false gods and/or the devil (4:8–9).

By definitively overcoming the devil, the source of all evil and sinfulness, in the triplet of unique and fundamental temptations (4:1–11), each of which concerns authentic worship, Jesus has established the basic and firm foundation that will enable him to save his people from their sins (1:21), the diabolical sins that detract from and prevent a true worship of God. The defeat of the devil by Jesus as the divine royal Christ (2:2, 4, 15) signals that the reign and rule of the devil/Satan is coming to an end and that the reign and rule of heaven/God has indeed come near (3:2) in the person of Jesus, the King, whose heavenly kingdom will serve as the realm for the true and authentic worship of God.

With his first disciples (4:18–22) Jesus went around all of Galilee, teaching in their synagogues, preaching the gospel, the good news, of the kingdom, and healing every disease and every sickness among the people (4:23). That Jesus was teaching in their synagogues, places for prayer and worship, implies that he was teaching about true and authentic worship in the kingdom of heaven, the good news of the arrival of which he was preaching. Because Jesus overcame the temptations of the devil (4:1–11), the ruler of demons and the source of all evil and sickness, he was able to heal all of the severely sick people brought to him (4:24). Large crowds from Galilee, the Decapolis, Jerusalem, Judea, and beyond the Jordan followed Jesus (4:25). Jesus was thus catching people (4:19) by calling them to repentance in order to live within the kingdom of heaven (4:17), a life he can make possible for them by saving them from the sins (1:21) and healing them from the sicknesses that detract from and prevent the true and authentic worship of God.

4

Teaching about Worship in the Kingdom of Heaven (Matthew 5–7)

The Beatitudes, Salt, and Light (Matt 5:1–16)

SEEING THE CROWDS, THE large crowds who have followed him (4:25), attracted by his preaching of repentance in preparation for living in the kingdom of heaven (4:17), Jesus "went up the mountain" (5:1a), a place close to the heavenly realm and associated with the giving of divine revelation. After the exodus event of the people of Israel God invited Moses to "come up to the mountain," so that God could give him the law and commandments for how the people are to live (Exod 24:12, 13, 15). After Jesus "sat down," the posture for authoritative teaching, his disciples came to him (5:1b), presumably including his first followers (4:18–22) as well as others who have become his disciples.

Jesus was teaching his disciples with the crowds listening, after "opening his mouth" (5:2). This otherwise redundant expression signals and sets the stage for a significant pronouncement to follow. It recalls how Jesus overcame the devil's first temptation with the scriptural quotation (Deut 8:3) that a person will live by every word coming forth through the "mouth of God" (Matt 4:4). It prepares the audience to hear what will come through the mouth of Jesus as the word of "God with us" (1:23), teaching more fully and precisely what it means to repent in order to live in the kingdom of heaven, which includes how to properly and exclusively worship the Lord God (4:10) in response to the word of God.[1]

---

1. "The portrayal of Jesus as seated with 'disciples' gathered around him casts him in the role of a rabbinic teacher; sitting was the posture for authoritative teaching (cf.

In the first set of four beatitudes (5:3-6) Jesus pronounced God's blessing upon the unfortunate, and promised God's reversal of their situation. Blessed are the "poor in spirit" (cf. Isa 61:1), those dispirited from their poverty as victims of social injustice, humbled before the world and God. Although lacking in earthly riches, to them belongs the kingdom of heaven (5:3). Blessed are they who mourn (cf. Isa 61:2-3) the death of loved ones due to injustice by humans (e.g., Matt 2:16-18), for they will be comforted (5:4) by God (divine passive). Blessed are the meek, those dispossessed of the earth's resources, leaving them dependent upon God, for they will inherit the (heavenly) land (5:5; cf. Ps 37:11). Blessed are they who hunger and thirst for righteousness, the doing for the unfortunate of what is right and just in God's salvific plan and thus amounts to ethical worship pleasing to God. Although they are not satisfied by humans, they will be satisfied by God (5:6).

In the second set of four beatitudes (5:7-10) Jesus pronounced God's blessing upon those who help the unfortunate, especially the unfortunate exemplified in the first set of four beatitudes (5:3-6), and promised them God's heavenly reward. Blessed are the merciful, those who exhibit compassion for the unfortunate as the ethical worship God desires (Hos 6:6), for they will be shown mercy by God (Matt 5:7). Blessed are "the clean of heart," those who help the unfortunate with the honesty, sincerity, and integrity required to truly worship God (Ps 15; 24:3-6), for they will see God (Matt 5:8) as the goal of their worship (Ps 42:3). Blessed are the peacemakers, those who work for peace, an overall well-being with God and others, by working for justice for the unfortunate, for they will be called sons of God (Matt 5:9), with Jesus, the Son of God (2:15; 3:17), as their brother. Blessed are they who are persecuted for the sake of righteousness, for what is right and just for the unfortunate, for to them, as to the poor in spirit whom they may ironically become in being persecuted (5:3), belongs the kingdom of heaven (5:10).

13:2; 24:3; 26:55), as also in the synagogue (23:2; Luke 4:20). . . . while 'opened his mouth' is a familiar OT idiom to introduce a significant pronouncement (Job 3:1; 33:2; Ps 78:2; Dan 10:16; cf. Matt 13:35; Acts 8:35; 10:34). Matthew thus sets up a model of the authoritative teacher with which the discourse will conclude (7:28-29)" (France, *Matthew*, 157-58). "Against the background of the widespread sacralization of mountains among ancient peoples, including the Jews, the mountain setting undoubtedly underlines the importance of the event taking place there. The mountain here is often taken more specifically as providing an allusion to the giving of the law at Mount Sinai (cf. 5:17). . . . The content of the coming address is appropriately identified as teaching rather than proclamation, but what Jesus is to say is to be thought of as grounded in his proclamation of the near approach of the kingdom of God and as clarifying what, for the disciple, lies beyond the repentance called for in 4:17" (Nolland, *Matthew*, 192-93).

After the third-person address of the first eight beatitudes (5:3–10) Jesus addressed the ninth directly to his audience: "Blessed are you when they insult you and persecute and speak every kind of evil against you for the sake of me" (5:11). Jesus thus identified himself with the righteousness "for the sake of" which those persecuted for helping the unfortunate are blessed (5:10). "You" are to rejoice and be glad, resonating with the joyful worship exemplified by the magi (2:10–11), "for your reward is great in heaven" (5:12a), indicating that their being persecuted for the sake of righteousness/Jesus amounts to the ethical worship God desires. That "thus they persecuted the prophets who were before you" (5:12b) places the disciples in the line of the prophets sent by God to speak the word of God, especially upholding righteous behavior and the true worship of the one and only God (cf. 2 Chr 36:11–16).[2]

As those willing to be persecuted for living in accord with the beatitudes, the disciples are the metaphorical "salt," with a connotation of "wisdom," for the earth, but if the salt/wisdom "loses its taste/becomes foolish [μωρανθῇ]," with what will it be seasoned? (Matt 5:13a). If the disciples fail to exhibit the righteousness indicated in the beatitudes, they will not demonstrate divine wisdom for the benefit of the people of the world (5:13b).[3] As Jesus was identified with the light of the star (2:10–11) and represented a great "light" for those in the darkness of death (4:16), so the disciples are to be the "light" for the world (5:14a). They are to let their "light," their good deeds done in accord with the beatitudes, shine before people (5:14b–16a), so that they may see the good deeds of their ethical worship and be inspired to doxological worship, and thus "they may glorify your Father, the one in heaven" (5:16b).[4]

Jesus' New Teaching on the Mosaic Law (Matt 5:17–48)

Jesus assured his audience of followers that he has come not to abolish the scriptural Mosaic Law or the Prophets, but to bring them to their divinely

---

2. "The persecution of the prophets was an established feature of Jewish folk-memory, stated in general terms in 2 Chr 36:16 and Neh 9:26 and amply illustrated within the OT itself, notably in the case of Jeremiah (Jer 20:10; 26:10–19; 36–38, etc.) and his contemporaries" (France, *Matthew*, 173).

3. "Salt is thus a metaphor for one's exercising a beneficial influence on the world" (Turner, *Matthew*, 155). "The verb [μωρανθῇ] which I translated 'becomes tasteless' more literally means 'becomes foolish.' The apparently inappropriate verb points to the metaphorical role of the salt here, to symbolize the wholesome flavor of wisdom which disciples are to contribute" (France, *Matthew*, 175).

4. On Matt 5:3–16, see Powell, *God With Us*, 119–44.

intended fulfillment (5:17). The Law to be brought to fulfillment by Jesus has an enduring value within God's plan (5:18). Doing and teaching the commandments of the Law as taught by Jesus makes one great in the kingdom of heaven (5:19). But unless the righteousness of the disciples abounds beyond that of the scribes and Pharisees, those who were experts in teaching and zealous in doing the commandments of the Law, they will not even enter into the kingdom of heaven (5:20). This sets the stage for Jesus to teach his followers how their more abundant righteousness, their doing and teaching of what is right and just in accord with God's Law, which thus pleases God as ethical worship, will enable them to enter into and become great in the kingdom of heaven.

Jesus came to bring to its fulfillment (5:17), deepening and extending, the commandment not to murder (5:21; cf. Exod 20:13; Deut 5:17) by teaching the avoidance of anger (5:22), which can often lead to murder. Jesus went on to teach the need not just to avoid anger, but, more positively, to reconcile oneself with one's fellow human being. If someone comes to offer in cultic worship a sacrificial gift at the altar, and then remembers that someone has something against him (5:23), he is to leave the gift at the altar, go first to reconcile himself with the person, and then return to offer the gift (5:24).[5] Jesus indicated here the fundamental need for the ethical behavior, in this case, reconciliation, that is a precondition for and thus complements cultic worship. For cultic or liturgical worship to please God, it must be accompanied by the ethical behavior God desires ("I desire mercy and not [simply] sacrifice" [Hos 6:6; cf. Matt 9:13; 12:7]), so that the ethical behavior God desires amounts to what can be considered ethical worship.[6]

Continuing to bring the scriptural Law and Prophets to fulfillment (5:17), Jesus provided further examples of the ethical behavior that complements cultic worship: Avoid not only adultery (Exod 20:14, 17; Deut 5:18, 21) but thoughts desirous of adultery (Matt 5:27–30); avoid divorce (Deut 24:1–5), since it amounts to adultery (Matt 5:31–32); instead of taking oaths (Exod 20:7; Lev 19:12), which result in offending God, to verify what one does or says, be truthful in all relationships (Matt 5:33–37); go beyond merely limiting the vicious cycle of retaliation (Lev 24:20) by having the generosity to eliminate it altogether (Matt 5:38–42); love not only your neighbors and friends (Lev 19:18) but even your enemies (Matt 5:43–48) and include in your worship prayers for those who persecute you (5:44).

---

5. "It is not simply a matter of dealing with one's own feelings of anger, but of positively going out to recognize those of the aggrieved party and seeking to defuse them" (Byrne, *Lifting the Burden*, 59).

6. "Worship that is acceptable to God cannot take place against the background of a damaged human relationship which is being ignored" (Nolland, *Matthew*, 233).

If you love only those loving you, what reward or recompense will you have (5:46; cf. 5:12) with God in heaven?[7] In other words, love of one's enemies is what God desires and rewards as ethical worship. Loving one's enemies exemplifies the righteousness that goes beyond that of the scribes and Pharisees (5:20, 47). It amounts to ethical worship pleasing to God, since it makes one "perfect" as the heavenly Father is "perfect" (5:48), in the sense of being complete or inclusive by extending love to all, just as the heavenly Father, as the Creator of all, extends loving care to all people (5:45).[8]

Almsgiving, Prayer, and Fasting (Matt 6:1–18)

Jesus taught his followers to beware not to do their righteousness, acts that are right and just according to God, before people in order to be seen by them. Otherwise, they will have no reward with their Father, the one in heaven (6:1), and thus such acts will not count as ethical worship pleasing to God.[9] When they do almsgiving, giving to the poor as an act of ethical worship sometimes equated with sacrificial worship in the biblical tradition, they are not to draw attention to themselves, in order that "they may be glorified" (δοξασθῶσιν) by people (6:2), thus making themselves an object of false doxological worship.[10] Indeed, this would contradict Jesus' previous teaching for his followers to let people see their good deeds, so that "they may glorify" (δοξάσωσιν) the heavenly Father (5:16) as an act of true doxological worship. If they perform their almsgiving privately and in a way that does not draw attention to themselves, it will amount to ethical worship pleasing to God, who will reward them accordingly (6:3–4).

---

7. "Reward" or "recompense" (μισθός) often means "recognition (mostly by God) for the moral quality of an action" (BDAG, 653).

8. "'Perfect' (τέλειος) [is] . . . used often of a 'perfect' sacrifice ('without blemish,' often in Leviticus) and of the ethical uprightness or 'blamelessness' of God's people (Gen 6:9, 17:1; Deut 18:13; 2 Sam 22:24, 26), an absolute commitment and allegiance to God (Ps 15:2; 84:11)" (Osborne, *Matthew*, 214). "And this, finally (v. 48) is the true 'definition' of 'perfection': being perfect *as* one's heavenly Father is perfect, that is, acting toward others, including one's enemies, as the Creator acts toward all" (Byrne, *Lifting the Burden*, 62; emphasis original).

9. Eubank, "Storing Up Treasure with God," 77–92.

10. "Almsgiving was considered meritorious in the OT and Jewish theology; it was thought to result in the forgiveness of sins (Prov 11:4; Dan 4:24, etc.), was regarded as a condition of salvation (Isa 58:6–12), and was equated with sacrifice (Tob 11:4; Sir 32:5)" (Staudinger, "ἐλεημοσύνη," 429). "By the time of Jesus righteousness and almsgiving were virtually synonymous, and almsgiving was an important part of temple and synagogue services" (Osborne, *Matthew*, 219).

When the followers of Jesus pray, they are not to be like hypocritical Jews who love to pray while standing in synagogues and on street corners, so that they may be seen by people (6:5). Rather, when any one of them prays individually, he is to pray in private without drawing attention to himself, and his Father, who sees in private, will reward him (6:6). Neither are they to pray like pagans who think they will be heard by repeating a multitude of words (6:7), since their heavenly Father knows what they need before they ask him (6:8).

Jesus then provides the Matthean audience with a model prayer for their communal worship (6:9–13), a prayer that accents a disposition of humble submission to God, praying for the accomplishment of God's will, as the essence of authentic prayer.[11] After addressing God as "our Father," they are to pray that his name may be made holy (6:9), his kingdom may come, and his heavenly will may be done on earth (6:10). Having thus humbly submitted their own wills to God's will, they may then pray that God, who knows what they need (6:8), provide it for them (6:11), forgive their sins as they forgive those who sin against them (6:12), and deliver them from the evil one, the devil, so as not to be led into temptation (6:13; cf. 4:1–11). Finally, Jesus emphatically reaffirmed that they must forgive others in order to be forgiven by God (6:14–15).[12]

When the followers of Jesus fast as an act of ascetic worship (cf. 4:2), they are not to look gloomy like hypocritical Jews who neglect their appearance so that they may appear to people to be fasting. They have thus already received their reward on a human level (6:16). They have drawn attention to themselves rather than to God as the object of true worship. When disciples fast, they are to attend to their appearance (6:17), so that they do not appear to people to be fasting. Their heavenly Father, who sees what they are doing in private, will reward them (6:18), as then their fasting will be pleasing to him as an act of authentic worship.[13]

---

11. "It quickly became a liturgical prayer, prayed three time a day by mid-second century (*Did.* 8:3) . . . it is also intended more as a model for prayer as well as a statement of Christian priorities and a guide to a philosophy for living the Christian life (i.e., it is meant to be lived as well as prayed)" (Osborne, *Matthew*, 227). On the poetic devices in the prayer, see Martin, "Poetry of the Lord's Prayer," 347–72.

12. Mbabazi, *Significance of Interpersonal Forgiveness*, 117–47.

13. "Fasting, like almsgiving and prayer, must always be done not for the admiration of others but for the worship of God alone. Whenever fasting becomes a performance, it ceases to be righteous activity. Private communion with the Father is the true goal of fasting. Reward from God is predicated on the right attitude and motivation" (Osborne, *Matthew*, 237).

Worship Not Earthly Things But the Heavenly Father Alone (Matt 6:19-34)

Jesus warned his followers not to store up for themselves treasures on earth, which are transitory and susceptible to being lost (6:19). They should rather store up for themselves treasures in heaven, which are permanent and secure (6:20). Then one's focus will properly be on the priority of the heavenly treasure (6:21). And if one's focus is on heavenly treasure, then one will be filled with light (6:22), and thus enabled to be a light for the world (5:14) as one whose proper focus and good deeds inspire people to the doxological worship of glorifying the heavenly Father (5:16). But if one's focus is on earthly treasure, then one will be in great darkness, not having the proper priority for one's own life and unable to be light for others (6:23). No one can serve, love, or be completely devoted to two different masters simultaneously; you cannot totally serve and thus authentically worship God as well as earthly wealth (6:24). Jesus has thus reaffirmed for the audience his command to Satan: "The Lord your God shall you worship and him alone shall you serve" (4:10).[14]

Followers of Jesus are not to make the procurement of food and clothing for themselves the priority of their lives (6:25). Just as the heavenly Father feeds the birds, so he will assuredly feed human beings, who are much more important than animals (6:26). Worrying about what one needs will not extend the length of one's life (6:27). The God who splendidly clothes the flowers of the field (6:28-29) will most certainly clothe his human creatures, who have a much greater value, even if they are of little faith (6:30). Rather than worrying about the food and clothing (6:31) God knows they need (6:32), they are to have the great faith to seek first the kingdom of God and its righteousness, the doing of what is right and just as ethical worship pleasing to God, and then they will have all they need (6:33). They are thus to live for the present with the kingdom and worship of God as their priority and have the faith in the God they worship not to be overly concerned with the future, which is firmly in God's hands (6:34).[15]

---

14. "God is the only being one can 'serve' in the fullest sense and have freedom enhanced rather than restricted" (Byrne, *Lifting the Burden*, 67).

15. "We have already seen 'righteousness' used several times for living in the way God requires. In 5:10, 20 it represents the distinctive life-style of disciples. . . . The disciple's deepest wish and resolve must be to live in God's way" (France, *Matthew*, 271).

Pray for the Prudent Discernment Needed To Correct Faults (Matt 7:1–12)

Disciples of Jesus should not judge others, since they will ultimately be judged by God in the same way that they would judge others (7:1–2). One should first correct one's often greater own faults before trying to correct the faults of others (7:3–5). Prudent discernment is needed in offering to correct the faults of others to make sure such an offer will be received favorably. Otherwise, it will be like giving what is holy to wild dogs, who may turn and tear you to pieces, or like throwing your valuable pearls to indifferent swine, who may merely trample them underfoot (7:6). If disciples ask for such discernment in prayer, it will be given them by God, for everyone who asks will receive, just as one who seeks finds, and to one who knocks it will be opened (7:7–8). Just as parents do not give bad things to their children, so even more your heavenly Father will surely give good things to those who ask for them in prayer (7:9–11).[16] Pray to correct the faults of others, just as you would want them to correct your faults; such love for one another in essence sums up the meaning of the Law and the Prophets (7:12; cf. 5:20).[17]

The Worship Needed To Enter into Life in the Kingdom of Heaven (Matt 7:13–29)

Jesus had exhorted his followers that unless their righteousness, their doing of what is right and just according to God so that it pleases God as ethical worship, abounds beyond that of the scribes and Pharisees, "you will not enter" into the kingdom of heaven (5:20). Having taught how they are to do this more abundant righteousness (5:21–7:12), Jesus urged them to "enter" through the "narrow gate" of doing this more abundant righteousness, for the gate is wide and the way broad that leads to destruction, the loss of life in the kingdom, and many are entering through it (7:13). How narrow the gate and constricted the way that leads to "the life" in the kingdom of heaven and few are "finding" it (7:14). That few are "finding" the way indicates the need for prayer to be able to do the more abundant righteousness and enter

---

16. "Matthew 7:7–11 is a sort of postscript to the model prayer in 6:9–13. The prayer teaches the right way to pray, and this passage inspires confidence that prayer will be answered" (Turner, *Matthew*, 210).

17. "The appeal to 'the law and the prophets' in fact echoes Jesus' insistence, at the beginning of his interpretation (5:20), that he had not come to abolish but to fulfill them. The 'inclusion' thus formed implies that treating others as one would have them treat oneself goes to the heart of the interpretation of the Torah in the light of 'the prophets' (Hos 6:6) that Jesus has come to promote" (Byrne, *Lifting the Burden*, 69).

through the narrow gate into the kingdom, as it recalls Jesus' previous directive to pray (7:7), for everyone who asks in prayer receives, and the one who seeks "finds," and to the one who knocks it will be opened (7:8) by God (divine passive).

Disciples can discern who are the false prophets, the leaders who will mislead them, by their "fruits," the external deeds that are a product of their inner being (7:15–16). Every good tree/person produces good fruit, but a bad tree/person cannot produce good fruit (7:17–18). Repeating and thus reaffirming the warning of John the Baptist (3:10), Jesus warned that every tree/person that does not produce good fruit, the repentance needed to enter into the kingdom of heaven by doing the more abundant righteousness that pleases God as ethical worship, will be cut down and thrown into the fire at the final judgment (7:19). Disciples will know who are the false prophets to avoid by their fruits, their bad deeds (7:20). Disciples and thus the Matthean audience are thus implicitly called to be true prophets (cf. 5:12) by producing the good fruit of doing the more abundant righteousness that pleases God as ethical worship, in order to enter and to lead others to enter into the life of the kingdom of heaven.

Not everyone who cries out to Jesus as "Lord, Lord," an act of supplicatory worship, will enter into the kingdom of heaven at the final judgment, but only the one who does the will of his heavenly Father (7:21), as Jesus has revealed it in this discourse (5–7).[18] Supplicatory worship alone will not suffice; it must be complemented by ethical worship. Despite the prophecies, exorcisms, and great deeds many may have done in the name of Jesus (7:22), he will confess to them that he never knew them and they will be dismissed as workers of lawlessness, those who failed to do God's will (7:23), the ethical worship pleasing to God. For disciples and thus the Matthean audience to make sure that they will be known by Jesus at the final judgment they must do the will of his heavenly Father by doing the more abundant righteousness (5:20) Jesus has revealed to them, doing what is right and just in accord with the will of God, which pleases God as ethical worship.[19]

It is absolutely necessary for the Matthean audience to be wise rather than foolish by basing their lives on doing the more abundant righteousness that amounts to ethical worship and that Jesus has taught in this sermon on the mount, in order for them to have the firm foundation they need to

---

18. "The message here is that mere confession is useless unless accompanied by action. One can make a profession, but without a changed life, such an affirmation is without merit" (Osborne, *Matthew*, 273).

19. "'Enter the kingdom of heaven' echoes the language of 5:20 and thus guides the reader to equate the abundant righteousness of 5:20 with 'the will of my Father' here" (Nolland, *Matthew*, 340).

withstand all of life's difficulties and live in the kingdom of heaven (7:24–27). When Jesus finished the words of the sermon, the crowds (cf. 5:1) were astonished at his teaching (7:28). For he was teaching them as one having divine authority and not as their scribes, who taught merely human tradition (7:29).[20] This thus reaffirms for the audience Jesus' warning that unless their righteousness, their doing of what is right and just as ethical worship that pleases God, abounds beyond that of the scribes and Pharisees, they will not enter into the kingdom of heaven (5:20).

Summary on Matthew 5–7

In the second set of four beatitudes (5:7–10) Jesus pronounced God's blessing upon those who help the unfortunate, especially the unfortunate exemplified in the first set of four beatitudes (5:3–6), and promised them God's heavenly reward. Blessed are the merciful, those who exhibit compassion for the unfortunate as the ethical worship God desires (Hos 6:6), for they will be shown mercy by God (Matt 5:7). Blessed are "the clean of heart," those who help the unfortunate with the honesty, sincerity, and integrity required to truly worship God (Psalm 15; 24:3–6), for they will see God (Matt 5:8) as the goal of their worship (Ps 42:3). Blessed are the peacemakers, those who work for peace, an overall well-being with God and others, by working for justice for the unfortunate, for they will be called sons of God (Matt 5:9), with Jesus, the Son of God (2:15; 3:17), as their brother. Blessed are they who are persecuted for the sake of righteousness, for what is right and just for the unfortunate, for to them, as to the poor in spirit whom they may ironically become in being persecuted (5:3), belongs the kingdom of heaven (5:10).

After the third person address of the first eight beatitudes (5:3–10) Jesus addressed the ninth directly to his audience: "Blessed are you when they insult you and persecute and speak every kind of evil against you for the sake of me" (5:11). Jesus thus identified himself with the righteousness "for the sake of" which those persecuted for helping the unfortunate are blessed (5:10). "You" are to rejoice and be glad, resonating with the joyful worship exemplified by the magi (2:10–11), "for your reward is great in heaven" (5:12a), indicating that their being persecuted for the sake of righteousness/Jesus amounts to the ethical worship God desires. That "thus they

---

20. "Unlike the scribes who had to rely upon their own tradition, appealing to Moses, Jesus has spoken as the authoritative interpreter of the Torah, able to challenge that tradition in the name of an interpretation valid for the time of the kingdom" (Byrne, *Lifting the Burden*, 72).

persecuted the prophets who were before you" (5:12b) places the disciples in the line of the prophets sent by God to speak the word of God, especially upholding righteous behavior and the true worship of the one and only God (cf. 2 Chr 36:11–16).

As those willing to be persecuted for living in accord with the beatitudes, the disciples are the metaphorical "salt," with a connotation of "wisdom," for the earth, but if the salt/wisdom "loses its taste/becomes foolish," with what will it be seasoned? (Matt 5:13a). If the disciples fail to exhibit the righteousness indicated in the beatitudes, they will not demonstrate divine wisdom for the benefit of the people of the world (5:13b). As Jesus was identified with the light of the star (2:10–11) and represented a great "light" for those in the darkness of death (4:16), so the disciples are to be the "light" for the world (5:14a). They are to let their "light," their good deeds done in accord with the beatitudes, shine before people (5:14b-16a), so that they may see the good deeds of their ethical worship and be inspired to doxological worship, and thus "they may glorify your Father, the one in heaven" (5:16b).

Jesus came to bring to its fulfillment (5:17), deepening and extending, the commandment not to murder (5:21; cf. Exod 20:13; Deut 5:17) by teaching the avoidance of anger (5:22), which can often lead to murder. Jesus goes on to teach the need not just to avoid anger, but, more positively, to reconcile oneself with one's fellow human being. If someone comes to offer in cultic worship a sacrificial gift at the altar, and then remembers that someone has something against him (5:23), he is to leave the gift at the altar, go first to reconcile himself with the person, and then return to offer the gift (5:24). Jesus indicated here the fundamental need for the ethical behavior, in this case, reconciliation, that is a precondition for and thus complements cultic worship. For cultic or liturgical worship to please God, it must be accompanied by the ethical behavior God desires ("I desire mercy and not [simply] sacrifice" [Hos 6:6; cf. Matt 9:13; 12:7]), so that the ethical behavior God desires amounts to what can be considered ethical worship.

If you love only those loving you, what reward or recompense will you have (5:46; cf. 5:12) with God in heaven? In other words, love of one's enemies is what God desires and rewards as ethical worship. Loving one's enemies exemplifies the righteousness that goes beyond that of the scribes and Pharisees (5:20, 47). It amounts to ethical worship pleasing to God, since it makes one "perfect" as the heavenly Father is "perfect" (5:48), in the sense of being complete or inclusive by extending love to all, just as the heavenly Father, as the Creator of all, extends loving care to all people (5:45).

When Jesus' followers do almsgiving, giving to the poor as an act of ethical worship sometimes equated with sacrificial worship in the biblical tradition, they are not to draw attention to themselves, in order that "they may be glorified" by people (6:2), thus making themselves an object of false doxological worship. Indeed, this would contradict Jesus' previous teaching for his followers to let people see their good deeds, so that "they may glorify" the heavenly Father (5:16) as an act of true doxological worship. If they perform their almsgiving privately and in a way that does not draw attention to themselves, it will amount to ethical worship pleasing to God, who will reward them accordingly (6:3-4).

Jesus provides the Matthean audience with a model prayer for their communal worship (6:9-13), a prayer that accents a disposition of humble submission to God as the essence of authentic prayer. After addressing God as "our Father," they are to pray that his name be made holy (6:9), his kingdom come, and his heavenly will be done on earth (6:10). Having thus humbly submitted their own wills to God's will, they may then pray that God, who knows what they need (6:8), provide it for them (6:11), forgive their sins as they forgive those who sin against them (6:12), and deliver them from the evil one, the devil, so as not to be led into temptation (6:13; cf. 4:1-11). Finally, Jesus emphatically reaffirmed that they must forgive others in order to be forgiven by God (6:14-15).

When disciples fast, an act of ascetic worship, they are to attend to their appearance (6:17). They are not to appear to people to be fasting. Their heavenly Father, who sees what they are doing in private, will then reward them (6:18). Their fasting will be pleasing to him as an act of authentic worship.

Disciples should store up for themselves treasures in heaven, which are permanent and secure (6:20). Then one's focus will properly be on the priority of the heavenly treasure (6:21). And if one's focus is on heavenly treasure, then one will be filled with light (6:22), and thus enabled to be a light for the world (5:14) as one whose proper focus and good deeds inspire people to the doxological worship of glorifying the heavenly Father (5:16). No one can serve, love, or be completely devoted to two different masters simultaneously; you cannot totally serve and thus authentically worship God as well as earthly wealth (6:24). Jesus has thus reaffirmed for the audience his command to Satan: "The Lord your God shall you worship and him alone shall you serve" (4:10).

Rather than worrying about the food and clothing (6:31) God knows they need (6:32), the followers of Jesus are to have the great faith to seek first the kingdom of God and its righteousness, the doing of what is right and just as ethical worship pleasing to God. Then they will have all they need (6:33). They are thus to live for the present with the kingdom and worship of God as their priority and have the faith in the God they worship not to be overly concerned with the future, which is firmly in God's hands (6:34).

One should first correct one's often greater own faults before trying to correct the faults of others (7:3–5). Prudent discernment is needed in offering to correct the faults of others to make sure such an offer will be received favorably (7:6). If they ask for such discernment in prayer, it will be given them by God, for everyone who asks will receive, just as one who seeks finds, and to one who knocks it will be opened (7:7–8). Just as parents do not give bad things to their children, so even more your heavenly Father will surely give good things to those who ask for them in prayer (7:9–11). Pray to correct the faults of others, just as you would want them to correct your faults; such love for one another in essence sums up the meaning of the Law and the Prophets (7:12; cf. 5:20).

Not everyone who cries out to Jesus as "Lord, Lord," an act of supplicatory worship, will enter into the kingdom of heaven at the final judgment, but only the one who does the will of his heavenly Father (7:21), as Jesus has revealed it in this sermon on the mount (5–7). Supplicatory worship alone will not suffice; it must be complemented by ethical worship. For disciples, and thus the Matthean audience, to make sure that they will be known by Jesus at the final judgment (7:22) they must do the will of his heavenly Father by doing the more abundant righteousness (5:20) Jesus has revealed to them, doing what is right and just in accord with the will of God, which pleases God as ethical worship.

5

Inviting People to Worship in the Kingdom of Heaven (Matthew 8–10)

Healings, Controversies, and Worship (Matt 8:1—9:34)

WHEN JESUS CAME DOWN from the mountain after his discourse (Matthew 5–7), large crowds continued to follow him (8:1; cf. 4:25). And then a leper, a man with a contagious skin disease which was not only personally painful, but rendered him ritually unclean and thus excluded him from the worshiping community, approached and "worshiped" (προσεκύνει) Jesus, expressing the faith that Jesus can heal him: "Lord, if you will, you can make me clean" (8:2).[1] Whereas the Gentile magi "worshiped" (προσεκύνησαν) the infant Jesus (2:11) as an act of homage honoring his status as the new-born King of the Jews (2:2), this Jewish leper performed an act of supplicatory worship, praying to Jesus with faith that he has the divine power to heal him.[2] In the biblical tradition curing leprosy was considered equivalent to the divine power of raising from the dead. A king of Israel once responded to a request for him to cure a leper with the dismissive question, "Am I a

---

1. "In the New Testament the description 'leper' covers a variety of skin diseases rather than being restricted to the affliction known clinically today as Hansen's disease. Besides physical distress, all such conditions involved ritual uncleanness and the stigma of social exclusion prescribed by biblical law (Leviticus 13–14), not to mention the belief that disfiguring diseases of this kind were a divine punishment for sin (cf. Num 12:10–15; 2 Kings 5:25–27)" (Byrne, *Lifting the Burden*, 76).

2. "[A]ll such responses to Jesus are on the way towards the Christian recognition of Jesus as worthy of divine worship. With the leper we begin to be nudged in the direction of religious worship. The address, 'Lord,' is not significant by itself, but in light of what follows we perhaps hear echoes of the use of 'Lord' in the worship of God as exalted Lord" (Nolland, *Matthew*, 349).

god, to put to death and to make alive, that this one sends to me to recover a man from his leprosy?" (2 Kgs 5:7).

Ostensibly risking uncleanness as well as contraction of the contagious skin disease, Jesus compassionately stretched out his hand and touched the desperate leper, declaring, in a directly concise answer to his act of prayerful worship, "I will; be clean" (Matt 8:3a). And immediately his leprosy was cleansed as a result of the dramatic touch of Jesus' divine healing power (8:3b). Jesus thus gave this leper a personal experience of salvation in the kingdom of heaven by not only healing his painful disease, but fully restoring him to the worshiping community.[3] He directed him to go, show himself to the priest to be certified as cleansed to enter the worshiping community, and offer the gift Moses prescribed as an act of sacrificial worship (8:4; cf. Lev 14:1–9). Jesus' healing of the leper presents the audience with a model for their own supplicatory worship. They are called to imitate the remarkable faith of the leper in their own praying to Jesus. His answer to the prayer indicates his divine will and power to eliminate whatever personal difficulties may prevent one from a full participation in communal worship.[4]

Then a centurion, a Roman military officer in charge of a hundred men, performed an act of supplicatory worship, praying to Jesus (8:5) on behalf of his paralyzed servant (8:6). When Jesus offered to come and heal him (8:7), the centurion, respectful of Jewish avoidance of Gentile dwellings, expressed the faith that Jesus need only say the word and his servant will be healed (8:8). He compared his military authority to Jesus' implicit divine authority over the army of demons responsible for sickness (8:9). Jesus marveled at his faith as greater than any he has found in Israel (8:10), qualifying him to participate in the future banquet of the kingdom of heaven (8:11–12). He answered the intercessory prayer of the centurion in accord with his great faith, as at the mere word of Jesus his servant was healed (8:13). Jesus' healing of the centurion's servant presents the audience with a model for their own intercessory prayer. They are called to pray for others in need with the great faith of the centurion. The answer to his prayer indicates that Jesus has the divine power, as "God with us" (1:23), to help those for whom we pray.

---

3. Heil, "Healing Miracles in Matthew," 274–87.

4. "In its combination of words and actions, this sequence of events outlines the same basic procedure according to which ancient supplicants would have worshipped at cultic centers, including cultic centers of healing. From a structural perspective, then, it seems that Jesus functions for the man very much like a temple" (Wilson, *Healing in Matthew*, 43).

Jesus then entered the house of Peter and saw his mother-in-law lying down sick with a fever (8:14). He compassionately touched her hand and the demonic fever left her, enabling her to rise and "serve" (διηκόνει) him (8:15), as the one whom angels similarly "served [διηκόνουν]" (4:11) after he refused to worship the devil (4:8-10). Her service of Jesus reaffirms his status as a worthy object of supplicatory worship, having gained divine healing power over the devil responsible for the evil of sickness.[5] That evening, as a gesture of intercessory supplicatory worship, they brought to him many possessed by demons, and in compassionate response to their implicit intercessory prayer he powerfully drove out the spirits with a word (cf. 8:8) and healed all who were sick (8:16; cf. 4:24). This fulfilled what was spoken through Isaiah the prophet, which invites the audience to participate in and make their own the exuberant communal act of worship celebrating the divinely compassionate healing power of Jesus: "He himself took on *our* infirmities and bore *our* diseases [Isa 53:4]" (8:17).

To a scribe willing to obey Jesus' order to cross the sea (8:18-19) Jesus warned of the difficulty involved in following him (8:20). And to a disciple who would first bury his father (8:21) Jesus indicated the urgency of following him now (8:22). After his disciples then followed him into a boat (8:23), suddenly there was a great storm on the sea, but he was sleeping (8:24). They woke him with an act of supplicatory worship, praying, "Lord, save, we are perishing!" (8:25). After chastising their little faith, Jesus answered their prayer as he "rebuked" the wind and the sea as personified demons, and there was great calm (8:26). The men were amazed at this epiphany of Jesus' divine power to still a stormy sea (Ps 65:8; 89:10), and raised the question of his more profound identity as one whom not only the demons responsible for sickness but the demonic winds and sea obey (8:27). For the audience, knowing that Jesus is Son of God (2:15; 3:17) and "God with us" (1:23), this scene calls them to great faith in Jesus' divine power to answer their prayers to be saved from all the demonic evils symbolized by a stormy sea.[6]

---

5. "In the context the natural reference of διηκόνει is to activities associated with domestic hospitality; the restoration is so complete that she can immediately resume such activities. But since service to Jesus emerges in 25:44 as important and privileged activity and is identified in 27:55 as having played a significant role (by women) in supporting his ministry, the domestic service here gains in significance as the story unfolds" (Nolland, *Matthew*, 359-60).

6. "Like the disciples in the boat, members of the Church may well feel that their Lord is 'asleep,' unheeding of their peril. When they echo the cry, "Lord, save us! We are perishing' (v. 25), they can take comfort from the majestic authority with which he instantly brings about calm" (Byrne, *Lifting the Burden*, 78). See also Heil, *Jesus Walking on the Sea*, 86-87.

The demons possessing two demoniacs (8:28) ironically answered the disciples' question of Jesus' profound identity (8:27), addressing him as "Son of God," who has come before the end-time to torment them (8:29). This recalls that Jesus revealed himself as the faithful Son of God, who overcame the devil, the ruler of demons, in anticipation of the end-time demise of demonic power (4:1–11). The demons performed an act of pseudo-worship, as they "beseeched/prayed" (παρεκάλουν) for Jesus to send them into a herd of swine (8:30–31). Jesus answered their "prayer," but instead of remaining in the region, the demons along with the swine were drowned in the abyss of the sea (8:32), as Jesus powerfully rid this Gentile region of both the demons and animals unclean from the Jewish perspective. After the reporting of it by the swineherds (8:33), in contrast to the Gentile centurion "beseeching/praying" (παρακαλῶν) for Jesus to heal his servant (8:5), the whole Gentile town "beseeched/prayed" (παρεκάλεσαν) for Jesus to leave their region (8:34).[7]

Jesus' dramatic exorcism of the Gadarene demoniacs (8:28–34) presents the audience with counter examples for their own worship of Jesus. In contrast to the demons who "prayed" to Jesus as the Son of God not to destroy them (8:29–31), the members of the audience are to have the faith to pray to Jesus as the Son of God who has the divine power to rid their lives of demonic evils. And in contrast to the whole town who "prayed" for Jesus to leave their region (8:34), the members of the audience are to pray to Jesus as the Son of God to remain with them, the one who has divine saving power (1:21; 8:25) as "God with us" (1:23).

After Jesus returned to Capernaum (9:1), they brought to him a paralytic lying on a stretcher (9:2a), thus performing a gesture of intercessory supplicatory worship. Seeing their faith, Jesus began to answer their implicit prayer for his healing, as he pronounced to the paralytic that his sins are forgiven (9:2b) by God (divine passive) through the agency of Jesus, the one who will save his people from their sins (1:21). Some scribes thought Jesus was blaspheming (9:3) by usurping a divine prerogative for himself. In response to them (9:4) Jesus indicated that both forgiveness of sins and healing the sick involve divine authority (9:5). He then pronounced that he, as the Son of Man, a heavenly figure with divine authority (cf. Dan 7:13–14), now has the divine authority *on earth* to forgive sins, and demonstrated this by exercising the divine authority to heal, as he enabled the paralytic to rise, take up his stretcher, and return home (9:6–7). This overawed the crowds

---

7. "It might only be fortuitous, but the verb used to speak of the plea [παρεκάλεσαν] of the townspeople is the same as that [παρεκάλουν] used in relation to the demons. Is an unflattering commonality between the demons and the townspeople being hinted at?" (Nolland, *Matthew*, 378). See also Morris, *Matthew*, 212.

and inspired them to perform an act of doxological worship, as they glorified the God who gave such authority to human beings (9:8).

Jesus' healing and forgiveness of a paralytic (9:1-8) reinforces for the audience his teaching that their praying is to include their forgiveness of those who wrong them (6:12). Indeed, forgiveness of others is a precondition for, and goes hand in hand with, divine forgiveness (6:14-15), as God has now given the authority and power to forgive to human beings (9:8).[8] That the healing and forgiveness of the paralytic by Jesus, as the Son of Man with divine authority on earth to forgive sins (9:2, 6), inspired the crowds to the doxological worship of "glorifying" God (9:8) exemplifies for the audience how their own good deeds can similarly inspire people to the worship of "glorifying" God (5:16).[9]

Similar to his call of the first four disciples, who were fishermen (4:18-22), Jesus called a man named Matthew to follow him as a disciple, but unlike the first disciples Matthew was considered a public sinner due to his collecting taxes from his own people on behalf of the Roman Gentile government (9:9). When Jesus and his disciples then shared table fellowship with Matthew and many other tax collectors and sinners (9:10), the Pharisees objected (9:11), since such people were considered ritually unclean for failing to observe the cultic food regulations, which gave meals a worship dimension.[10] Jesus replied that those who are sick, rather than those who are well, need a physician (9:12).[11] He then directed the Pharisees to go and learn the meaning of the divine scriptural pronouncement, "Mercy I desire and not [simply] sacrifice" (Hos 6:6), for Jesus did not come to call the righteous but sinners to repentance (Matt 9:13; cf. 4:17). Jesus thus extended to sinners, as those who are "sick," the healing mercy God desires as the ethical worship that complements cultic worship.[12]

---

8. "God has been pleased not to keep the power in heaven, but to give it to people here on earth in and through Jesus" (Morris, *Matthew*, 218).

9. "There may be an echo here of the pattern in 5:16 according to which God is to be glorified for the works of his people (cf. 15:31)" (Nolland, *Matthew*, 383).

10. "The term 'sinners' may designate those whose behavior was egregiously ungodly, but from the Pharisaic viewpoint, it would also include those who did not observe the traditional interpretations of the Hebrew Bible (15:2) on such matters as ritual purity, food laws, and Sabbath observance.... Fellowship around a table was taken seriously in Jesus's time as implying a deeper unity" (Turner, *Matthew*, 252).

11. Whereas Jesus forgave the sins and healed the literal sickness of the paralytic (9:1-8), he now forgives the sins and heals those who are metaphorically sick.

12. "The phrase, 'mercy, not sacrifice,' does not imply the complete exclusion of sacrifice. Operative in the text, both in its original location in Hosea and as quoted by Jesus, is a Hebrew idiom lending the sense 'mercy *before* sacrifice'; cf. 5:23" (Byrne, *Lifting the Burden*, 81n11; emphasis original). On the quotation of Hos 6:6 in both

Jesus' call of the tax collector Matthew to follow him (9:9–13) presents the audience with a two-fold model. First, they are to identify with Matthew by repenting of their sinfulness, accepting divine mercy, and following Jesus (9:9). And secondly, they are to imitate Jesus in calling others to repent of their sinfulness by extending to them the mercy God desires as the ethical worship that complements their cultic, liturgical, and ritualistic worship (9:13).

The disciples of John questioned Jesus as to why they and the Pharisees practice the ascetic worship of fasting but his disciples do not (9:14). Alluding to the biblical tradition comparing God to a bridegroom (Isa 54:5–6; 62:4–5), Jesus responded by pointing out to them the inappropriateness for the wedding guests/his disciples to mourn/fast as long as the bridegroom/Jesus is with them (9:15a). With a reference to his being put to death, Jesus went on to declare that the days will come when he as the bridegroom will be taken away from them, and then they will fast (9:15b). Jesus assured them, however, that both the "new wineskins" associated with the celebratory worship at the arrival of the bridegroom and the "old wineskins" associated with the ascetic worship of fasting are to be preserved (9:16–17). This calls for the audience to celebrate in their liturgical worship the arrival of Jesus ("God with us") as the bridegroom of the messianic wedding feast of the kingdom of heaven, but also to practice the ascetic worship of fasting, as exemplified (4:2–4) and taught (6:16–18) by Jesus.

A ruler then came to Jesus and, like the leper (8:2), "worshiped" (προσεκύνει) him with an intercessory prayer: "My daughter has just died, but come, lay your hand on her, and she will live" (9:18).[13] As Jesus and his disciples followed him (9:19), a woman bleeding from a hemorrhage for twelve years, thus rendering her ritually unclean and disqualified from communal worship (Lev 15:25–30), came up behind him and touched the tassel of his cloak (9:20), thinking that she will thus be "saved" (9:21).[14] That she touched Jesus' "tassel," which served as a reminder to do all the commandments and worship God alone (Num 15:37–41), seems to imply her desire to be restored to communal worship. Jesus assured her that her faith has "saved" her, and the woman was "saved" from that hour (9:22).[15]

Matt 9:9–13 and 12:1–14 as an important hermeneutical key for Matthew, see Viljoen, "Hosea 6:6," 214–37. See also Ottenheijm, "Shared Meal," 1–21.

13. The verb προσκυνέω can "indicate the worship of a deity (as in 4:10), and it is probable that this is why Matthew uses it so often of Jesus" (Morris, *Matthew*, 228n59).

14. "She could not join in worship, and her contact with other people would have been restricted because even a touch from her would make people unclean (Lev. 15:27). It was probably this that made her take the approach she did" (Morris, *Matthew*, 229).

15. "His declaration that her faith has made her well (literally 'has saved' her) works

Jesus' miraculous "saving" of the hemorrhaging woman calls the audience to have the faith that Jesus can "save" them from the sins (1:21) and all other death-threatening evils (8:25) that prevent their participation in communal worship.

When Jesus came to the house of the ruler who had prayed for him to raise to life his daughter who had died (9:18), he told the crowd of mourners who had gathered (9:23) to go away, for the little girl was not dead only sleeping, but they ridiculed him (9:24). When the crowd was put outside, Jesus went in, grasped her hand, and the little girl was raised from death/sleep to life (9:25), and this news went out to all the land (9:26). Jesus' raising of the dead daughter, as if she were only sleeping, to life in answer to the intercessory supplicatory worship of the ruler calls the audience to likewise engage in intercessory prayer for those who have died with the faith that Jesus will raise them from the "sleep" of death to life eternal.[16]

As Jesus passed on from there, two blind men performed an act of supplicatory worship, crying out to Jesus, "Have mercy on us, Son of David!" (9:27), addressing Jesus as the messianic Son of David (cf. 1:1) who can fulfill the messianic promise that the eyes of the blind will be opened (Isa 35:5).[17] This would enable them to worship in the temple from which the blind were traditionally excluded (2 Sam 5:8; cf. Matt 21:14).[18] In the private space of the house, after they assured Jesus of their faith in his power to heal them (9:28), in accord with that faith (9:29) their eyes were opened (9:30a).[19] Although Jesus sternly warned them not to make it known (9:30b), it was too great a miracle for them to remain silent and in celebration they spread the news in all that land (9:31).[20]

---

the healing and makes public her fitness to be restored to the community" (Byrne, *Lifting the Burden*, 82).

16. "By so echoing the language of resurrection Matthew has made the story of this particular raising symbolic of a wider hope. Jesus' own experience of death has not abolished death, but his resurrection means death does not have the last word. Relationship with God—and within that, all other relationships—transcends the barrier of physical death and lives on in eternal life" (Byrne, *Lifting the Burden*, 83).

17. The Son of David title "is affirming Jesus as the true Messiah of Israel who heals the nation's sick. . . . They [the two blind men] believe the messianic promises of Isa 35:5, 'Then will the eyes of the blind be opened.' The healing of the blind was viewed as the messianic miracle par excellence, and these two men view Jesus as the Messiah, heir of David" (Osborne, *Matthew*, 354–55).

18. Avalos, "Blindness," 193.

19. "Matthew departs from Mark by having the exchange take place in the private space of 'the house' (Matt. 9:28; cf. Mark 10:46), a reference that for his readers would have brought to mind the experience of gathering in the house-*church*, that is, in the place of Christian worship" (Wilson, *Healing in Matthew*, 239; emphasis original).

20. "The men are so overwhelmed with the incredible miracle they have experienced

Then, in a gesture of supplicatory worship they brought to Jesus a mute demoniac (9:32; cf. 4:24; 8:16; 9:2). When the demon was cast out and the mute man spoke, the amazed crowds excitedly celebrated this unique display of divine healing power, declaring that "nothing like this has ever been seen in Israel" (9:33).[21] But the Pharisees accused him of casting out demons by the ruler of demons (9:34), Satan/the devil, thus contradicting his refusal to worship the devil, whereby he gained the divine power to cast out the demons that prevent the worship of the only true God (4:10).

Jesus' miraculous healing of the two blind men (9:27–31) and his exorcism of the mute demoniac (9:32–34) present the audience with further models for their own supplicatory worship. The members of the audience are called to pray to Jesus with the faith (9:28–29) that he can eliminate from their lives the evils, including their spiritual "blindness," that hinder their participation in worship. They may then celebrate (9:31, 33) his divine power over the devil, the ruler of demons (9:34), the power that can enable them to fulfill the scriptural pronouncement by which he refused to worship the devil/Satan: "The Lord your God shall you worship and him alone shall you serve [Deut 6:13]" (Matt 4:10).

The Missionary Discourse and Worship (Matt 9:35—10:42)

Jesus went around to all the towns and villages, and, as Matthew reiterates and thus reinforces for the audience, he was teaching in their synagogues, preaching the gospel, the good news, of the kingdom, and healing every disease and every sickness (9:35; cf. 4:23). That Jesus was teaching in their synagogues, places especially devoted to prayer and worship, reminds the audience that he was teaching about true and authentic worship in the kingdom of heaven, the good news of the arrival of which he was preaching. And that he was healing every disease and every sickness recalls how he was eliminating the demonic evils that hinder people from participating in communal worship.

Seeing the crowds, Jesus had compassion for them, "for they were distressed and dejected, like sheep not having a shepherd" (9:36). That Jesus "had compassion" for the crowds suggests that he is concerned to extend

---

that no amount of warning can keep them silent, so they disobey Jesus. Yet it is doubtful that Matthew is emphasizing their disobedience. The emphasis is on Jesus' desire to avoid publicity and the impossibility of remaining silent when touched by Jesus. So as in 9:26, the news spreads throughout Galilee" (Osborne, *Matthew*, 356).

21. In Mark 2:12, after Jesus healed a paralytic, those who saw it performed an act of doxological worship and glorified God with a similar declaration: "We have never seen anything like this!"

to them the "mercy" God desires as the ethical worship that complements cultic worship (9:13).²² And that the crowds were "like sheep not having a shepherd" (cf. Num 27:17; 1 Kgs 22:17; Ezek 34:5-6) not only laments the failure of their rulers and leaders to truly guide and care for them like shepherds, but it recalls and reaffirms that Jesus is the divinely promised messianic shepherd-king who will truly shepherd God's people (2:6). Jesus has been leading the people like a shepherd by not only teaching them with divine authority about authentic worship in his sermon on the mount (5-7), in contrast to their scribal leaders (7:29), but healing them of the demonic infirmities and diseases (8:17) that hinder their communal worship of the only true God (4:10).

However, as Jesus told his disciples, although the "harvest" of people needing to be shepherded is large, the "workers" to help shepherd them are few (9:37). He then urged them to perform an act of supplicatory worship and ask the Lord of the "harvest" to send out "workers" to help shepherd his "harvest" of people (9:38). Jesus then provided a preliminary answer to their prayer, as he summoned his twelve disciples and gave them a share in his own divine authority over unclean spirits to cast them out and "heal every disease and every sickness" (10:1; cf. 4:23; 9:35).²³ His twelve disciples thus serve as the first "workers" needed to help shepherd the large "harvest" of distressed and dejected people (9:36-38).²⁴ By giving them a share in his divine authority to heal every disease and every sickness, Jesus has enabled them to perform the ethical worship of extending to the people the compassionate mercy God desires (9:13, 35), and to eliminate the demonic evils that hinder the people from full participation in their communal worship.

Jesus sent out the group of twelve disciples (10:2-4), instructing them not to go to Gentile territory or enter a Samaritan town (10:5). They are rather to respect the salvation-historical preeminence of the Jews as God's chosen people and go "to the lost sheep of the house of Israel" (10:6). They are thus to share in Jesus' messianic mission to be the true shepherd of God's

---

22. "What we are to see here is not purely human pity, but divine compassion for troubled people" (Morris, *Matthew*, 239).

23. "The selection of twelve disciples to be the nucleus of a new leadership will signal a reconstitution of Israel, a fresh start for the people originally founded upon the twelve sons of Jacob. The people may now be harassed and helpless, but they are potentially a 'rich harvest' (9:37-38) that awaits gathering in for the kingdom" (Byrne, *Lifting the Burden*, 85).

24. "In 4:19 Jesus promised the disciples he would 'make [them] fish for people,' but up to this time he has performed the mission by himself. He now begins to fulfill the promise of 4:19 and involves the disciples in his mission in two stages: first by having them pray for workers and second by commissioning them to become the very workers they have been praying for (10:1-4)" (Osborne, *Matthew*, 366).

people (2:6) who are like sheep not having a shepherd (9:36). They are to proclaim the same message that John (3:2) and Jesus (4:17) proclaimed: "The kingdom of heaven has come near!" (10:7). Like Jesus, they are to give people a personal experience of the kingdom of heaven and enable them to fully participate in communal worship by healing the sick (cf. 8:16), raising the dead (cf. 9:18–26), and driving out demons (cf. 8:28–34; 9:33), thus feely giving what they have freely received from Jesus (10:8).

During their mission the disciples are to practice the teaching of Jesus that you cannot serve and thus worship both God and money (6:24). They are not to take gold or silver or copper in their belts (10:9); no bag for the journey, or a second tunic, or sandals, or a walking stick, for the "worker" (ἐργάτης) is deserving of his "food [τροφῆς]" (10:10). As "workers" (ἐργάτας) whom Jesus has sent out to help bring the harvest of people into the kingdom of heaven (9:38), the disciples are to follow the teaching of Jesus and not worry about their "food" (τροφῆς) or clothing (6:25). They are to be devoted first to the kingdom of God and his righteousness—doing what is right according to God's will as the ethical worship God desires—and they can be assured that they will have all they need (6:33).

Whatever town or village the disciples enter on their mission, they are to look for someone "worthy" (ἄξιός) to receive their message and to give to the disciple, as a worker, the food of which he is "deserving" or "worthy [ἄξιος]" (10:10), and they are to stay there until they leave (10:11). As they enter into a household, they are to greet it (10:12), presumably with a greeting, a wish-prayer, that includes or is followed by the proclamation that the kingdom of heaven has come near (10:7). If the household demonstrates that it is worthy by receiving their message, then they are to let their peace come upon it, otherwise they are to let their peace return to them (10:13). They are to shake the dust off their feet in judgment against those who fail to receive them or listen to their words (10:14–15). Their "peace" refers to the gift of God's peace as the overall well-being resulting from their proclamation of the arrival of the kingdom of heaven and from their exercise of the divine healing power (10:8) that enables people to properly participate in the communal worship of God.[25]

The disciples of Jesus can expect to be persecuted like their teacher (10:16–24). Indeed, if they have called Jesus, as the "master of the house," Beelzebul, how much more his disciples, as the "members of his household" (10:25). This recalls that the Pharisees accused Jesus of driving out demons by the ruler of demons (9:34), the devil/Beelzebul. But associating Jesus and

---

25. For the Jewish people greetings "were also 'wish-prayers' of well-being for others. Jesus takes the greeting to the next level, where the wish-prayer becomes an offer of salvation, of attaining the true 'peace of God'" (Osborne, *Matthew*, 380).

his disciples with the devil contradicts Jesus' refusal to worship the devil (4:8-10a), whom he drove out and defeated with the scriptural word of God: "The Lord your God shall you worship and him alone shall you serve [Deut 6:13]" (4:10b). Rather than associates of Beelzebul, Jesus and his disciples, to whom he gave a share in his power to drive out demons (10:8), free people from the demonic evils that prevent them from worshiping the only true God. Like the disciples, the members of the audience are not to be afraid of those who kill the body but cannot kill the soul; rather they are to "fear," in the sense of reverently worship, the God who can destroy both soul and body (10:28), but who cares for them even more than for sparrows (10:29-31).[26]

Like the disciples, the members of the audience are to publicly confess Jesus before people, including in their communal worship, so that Jesus will confess them before his Father in heaven in the final judgment (10:32-33).[27] They must endure opposition to Jesus even in their families, and be more devoted to Jesus than to their family members (10:34-37). They are to follow Jesus to the point of performing the ethical self-sacrificial worship of taking up their cross and losing their lives for his sake in order to find them (10:38-39). Those who receive and extend merciful care ("a cup of cold water," 10:42) for them as disciples, who are to be like prophets and righteous people, are actually receiving Jesus and the God who sent him. This adds another dimension to the way that Jesus is present and an object of worship as "God with us" (1:23). Those who extend merciful care to disciples of Jesus are thus performing ethical worship ("I desire mercy, not [simply] sacrifice" [9:13; cf. Hos 6:6]) for which they will receive a heavenly reward (10:40-42).[28]

Summary on Matthew 8-10

Jesus' healing of the leper (8:1-4) presents the audience with a model for their own supplicatory worship. They are called to imitate the remarkable faith of the leper in their own praying to Jesus. His answer to the prayer indicates his divine will and power to eliminate whatever personal difficulties may prevent one from a full participation in communal worship.

---

26. "While 'fear of the Lord' can mean outright fear of God's presence, it also means to revere God" (Jolley, "Fear," 457. See also BDAG, 1061).

27. "The term 'confesses' . . . here has the idea of public proclamation of allegiance to Jesus" (Osborne, *Matthew*, 403).

28. "The cup of cold water is an essential though inexpensive provision in a hot climate, an act of expected hospitality as well as of kindness" (France, *Matthew*, 416).

Jesus' healing of the centurion's servant (8:5–13) presents the audience with a model for their own intercessory prayer. They are called to pray for others in need with the great faith of the centurion. The answer to his prayer indicates that Jesus has the divine power, as "God with us" (1:23), to help those for whom we pray.

The service of Jesus by Peter's mother-in-law after he healed her (8:14–15) reaffirms his status as a worthy object of supplicatory worship, having gained divine healing power over the devil responsible for the evil of sickness (4:8–10). That evening, as a gesture of intercessory supplicatory worship, they brought to him many possessed by demons, and in compassionate response to their implicit intercessory prayer he powerfully drove out the spirits with a word (cf. 8:8) and healed all who were sick (8:16; cf. 4:24). This fulfilled what was spoken through Isaiah the prophet, which invites the audience to participate in and make their own the exuberant communal act of worship celebrating the divinely compassionate healing power of Jesus: "He himself took on *our* infirmities and bore *our* diseases [Isa 53:4]" (8:17).

During a great storm on the sea (8:23–24) the disciples woke the sleeping Jesus with an act of supplicatory worship, praying, "Lord, save, we are perishing!" (8:25). After chastising their little faith, Jesus answered their prayer as he "rebuked" the wind and the sea as personified demons, and there was great calm (8:26). The men were amazed at this epiphany of Jesus' divine power to still a stormy sea (Ps 65:8; 89:10), and raised the question of his more profound identity as one whom not only the demons responsible for sickness but the demonic winds and sea obey (8:27). For the audience, knowing that Jesus is Son of God (2:15; 3:17) and "God with us" (1:23), this scene calls them to great faith in Jesus' divine power to answer their prayers to be saved from all the demonic evils symbolized by a stormy sea.

Jesus' dramatic exorcism of the Gadarene demoniacs (8:28–34) presents the audience with counter examples for their own worship of Jesus. In contrast to the demons who "prayed" to Jesus as the Son of God not to destroy them (8:29–31), the members of the audience are to have the faith to pray to Jesus as the Son of God who has the divine power to rid their lives of demonic evils. And in contrast to the whole town who "prayed" for Jesus to leave their region (8:34), the members of the audience are to pray to Jesus as the Son of God to remain with them, the one who has divine saving power (1:21; 8:25) as "God with us" (1:23).

Jesus' healing and forgiveness of a paralytic (9:1–8) reinforces for the audience his teaching that their praying is to include their forgiveness of those who wrong them (6:12). Indeed, forgiveness of others is a precondition for, and goes hand in hand with, divine forgiveness (6:14–15), as God has now given the authority and power to forgive to human beings (9:8). That the healing and forgiveness of the paralytic by Jesus, as the Son of Man with divine authority on earth to forgive sins (9:2, 6), inspired the crowds to the doxological worship of "glorifying" God (9:8) exemplifies for the audience how their own good deeds can similarly inspire people to the worship of "glorifying" God (5:16).

Jesus' call of the tax collector Matthew to follow him (9:9-13) presents the audience with a two-fold model. First, they are to identify with Matthew by repenting of their sinfulness, accepting divine mercy, and following Jesus (9:9). And secondly, they are to imitate Jesus in calling others to repent of their sinfulness by extending to them the mercy God desires as the ethical worship that complements their cultic, liturgical, and ritualistic worship (9:13).

The disciples of John questioned Jesus as to why they and the Pharisees practice the ascetic worship of fasting but his disciples do not (9:14). Alluding to the biblical tradition comparing God to a bridegroom (Isa 54:5-6; 62:4-5), Jesus responded by pointing out to them the inappropriateness for the wedding guests/his disciples to mourn/fast as long as the bridegroom/Jesus is with them (9:15a). With a reference to his being put to death, Jesus went on to declare that the days will come when he as the bridegroom will be taken away from them, and then they will fast (9:15b). Jesus assured them, however, that both the "new wine"/celebratory worship at the arrival of the bridegroom and the "old wineskins"/ascetic worship of fasting are to be preserved (9:16-17). This calls for the audience to celebrate in their liturgical worship the arrival of Jesus ("God with us") as the bridegroom of the messianic wedding feast of the kingdom of heaven, but also to practice the ascetic worship of fasting, as exemplified (4:2-4) and taught (6:16-18) by Jesus.

When Jesus came to the house of the ruler who had prayed for him to raise to life his daughter who had died (9:18), he told the crowd of mourners who had gathered (9:23) to go away, for the little girl was not dead only sleeping, but they ridiculed him (9:24). When the crowd was put outside, Jesus went in, grasped her hand, and the little girl was raised from death/sleep to life (9:25), and this news went out to all the land (9:26). Jesus' raising of the dead daughter, as if she were only sleeping, to life in answer to the intercessory supplicatory worship of the ruler calls the audience to likewise engage in intercessory prayer for those who have died with the faith that Jesus will raise them from the "sleep" of death to life eternal.

Jesus' miraculous healing of the two blind men (9:27-31) and his exorcism of the mute demoniac (9:32-34) present the audience with further models for their own supplicatory worship. The members of the audience are called to pray to Jesus with the faith (9:28-29) that he can eliminate from their lives the evils, including their spiritual "blindness," that hinder their participation in worship. They may then celebrate (9:31, 33) his divine power over the devil, the ruler of demons (9:34), the power that can enable them to fulfill the scriptural pronouncement by which he refused to worship the devil/Satan: "The Lord your God shall you worship and him alone shall you serve [Deut 6:13]" (Matt 4:10).

As Jesus told his disciples, although the "harvest" of people needing to be shepherded is large, the "workers" to help shepherd them are few (9:37). He then urged them to perform an act of supplicatory worship and ask the Lord of the "harvest" to send out "workers" to help shepherd his "harvest" of people (9:38). Jesus then provided a preliminary answer to their prayer, as he summoned his twelve disciples and gave them a share in his own divine authority over unclean spirits to cast them out and "heal every disease and every sickness" (10:1; cf. 4:23; 9:35). His twelve disciples thus serve as the first "workers" needed to help shepherd the large "harvest" of distressed and dejected people (9:36-38). By giving them a share in his divine authority to heal every disease and every sickness, Jesus has enabled them to perform the ethical worship of extending to the people the compassionate mercy God desires (9:13, 35), and to eliminate the demonic evils that hinder the people from full participation in their communal worship.

Like the disciples, the members of the audience are to publicly confess Jesus before people, including in their communal worship, so that Jesus will confess them before his Father in heaven in the final judgment (10:32-33). They must endure opposition to Jesus even in their families, and be more devoted to Jesus than to their family members (10:34-37). They are to follow Jesus to the point of performing the ethical self-sacrificial worship of taking up their cross and losing their lives for his sake in order to find them (10:38-39). Those who receive and extend merciful care ("a cup of cold water," 10:42) for them as disciples, who are to be like prophets and righteous people, are actually receiving Jesus and the God who sent him. This adds another dimension to the way that Jesus is present and an object of worship as "God with us" (1:23). Those who extend merciful care to disciples of Jesus are thus performing ethical worship ("I desire mercy, not [simply] sacrifice" [9:13; cf. Hos 6:6]) for which they will receive a heavenly reward (10:40-42).

6

Failures to Repent and Parables for Worship in the Kingdom of Heaven (Matthew 11–13)

Worship Regarding John and Jesus and the Failure To Repent (Matt 11:1–24)

WHEN JOHN THE BAPTIST heard in prison of the deeds of the Christ, he sent his disciples (11:2) to ask Jesus, "Are you the one who is to come, or should we look for another?" (11:3). This question arose since John expected "the one to come" (3:11) to immediately execute judgment (3:12). Jesus told them to go and report to John what they hear and see (11:4), namely that he has come to perform the miraculous deeds promised for the messianic age: "The blind see again [9:27–30] and the lame walk [9:5], lepers are cleansed [8:2–3] and the deaf hear [9:32–33], the dead are raised [9:25] and the poor have good news proclaimed to them [4:23; 9:35]" (11:5).[1] Jesus' challenging exhortation, "blessed is the one who takes no offense at me" (11:6), calls for John and the audience to appreciate that Jesus has come as the Christ not first of all to execute judgment. Rather he has come as the Christ who not only compassionately answers supplicatory prayers and gestures for healing (8:2, 5–6, 16; 9:2, 18, 27, 32), but by his healings enables and inspires people to worship God (8:4, 17; 9:8, 33).[2]

---

1. "The list (v. 5) covers all the works of compassion reported in chapters 8–9. It draws together a number of statements in the prophet Isaiah traditionally related to the blessings of the messianic age (Isa 29:18–19; 35:5–6; 61:1)" (Byrne, *Lifting the Burden*, 92).

2. "The beatitude has been expressed in a generic third person form, and we have no account of John's reaction. It is the Christian community that is to relate itself to the challenge of Jesus' words" (Nolland, *Matthew*, 452).

Jesus then pointed out to the crowds that they went out into the desert to see John as the great prophet, the final prophet of the old age (11:13), the Elijah figure to come as the forerunner of the new messianic age (11:14), whom God sent to prepare the way for Jesus (11:7–10).³ But even one who is the least in the kingdom of heaven is greater than John (11:11). Each member of the audience, then, is to pay very close attention to what Jesus is saying about being in the kingdom of heaven (11:15), and not allow the violent to take it away from any of them (11:12). The members of the audience are to be motivated to obey both John's and Jesus' appeals to repent for the kingdom of heaven has come near (3:2; 4:17). And they may enter into the kingdom of heaven by a repentance that includes doing the greater righteousness (5:20), that which is right according to God and thus pleases God as the ethical worship that complements cultic worship (5:21–7:29; see especially 5:23–24).

"This generation" of unbelievers, who rejected the appeals to repent by both John and Jesus (11:16–17) present the audience with a negative example. They accused John, who practiced an ascetic worship of fasting, of having a demon (11:18). This recalls the similar charge by the Pharisees that Jesus casts out demons by the ruler of demons (9:34), whereas Jesus, who also fasted (4:2), refused to worship the ruler of demons, appealing rather to the worship of the one true God (4:10).⁴ But "this generation" also accused Jesus of being a friend of tax collectors and sinners (11:19a), whereas he ate and drank with them in order to call them as sinners to repentance, extending to them the compassionate mercy God desires as the ethical worship that complements cultic worship (9:13).⁵ In contrast to "this generation," then, the members of the audience are to repent by following the positive examples of both John and Jesus. In the kingdom of heaven they may practice both the ascetic worship of fasting (9:15) and the ethical worship of performing the compassionate mercy that complements cultic worship.

Despite the failure of "this generation" to repent, Jesus declared that divine wisdom will be vindicated, shown to be right, by her "deeds [ἔργων]" (11:19b). These include not only the deeds done by John, but most especially the "deeds [ἔργα] of the Christ" (11:2), namely, Jesus' miraculous healings and preaching (11:5).⁶ These are the "mighty deeds [δυνάμεις]" (11:20, 21,

---

3. "John is indeed the expected Elijah, the forerunner to the Messiah" (Osborne, *Matthew*, 422).

4. "To accuse John of being demon-possessed is of a piece with accusing Jesus of casting out demons by the ruler of demons (9:34)" (Nolland, *Matthew*, 464).

5. "The accusation, despite itself, aptly testifies to Jesus' ministry: the celebration of the compassionate mercy of God (9:10–13)" (Byrne, *Lifting the Burden*, 93).

6. "It seems clear that Jesus identifies himself with the work of Wisdom, so that

23) that failed to move such Galilean towns as Chorazin, Bethsaida, and Capernaum to repent (11:20–24). In contrast to these failures, the members of the audience are to repent, change their lives, by allowing the mighty deeds of Jesus' miraculous healings to inspire them to the supplicatory worship of praying to Jesus for healing (8:2, 5–6; 9:18, 27) and to the doxological worship of glorifying God for the good deeds of Jesus as the Christ (9:8; cf. 5:16).

Jesus' Mercy as Ethical Worship and the Failure To Repent (Matt 11:25—12:50)

Jesus taught his disciples and thus the audience to pray that the will of their heavenly Father may be done on earth (6:9–10). He later performed an act of laudatory worship, praising his heavenly Father for the accomplishment of his gracious will: "I praise you, Father, Lord of heaven and earth, that you have hidden these things from the wise and intelligent, but have revealed them to the childlike. Yes, Father, such has been your good pleasure" (11:25–26). The divine Father has hidden the significance of Jesus' words and deeds as signs of the arrival of the kingdom of heaven from the humanly wise and intelligent, exemplified by the Galilean towns (11:20–24) and "this generation" of unbelievers (11:16–19), including especially the scribes and Pharisees, as indicated by their failure to repent. But those in the audience who have repented are to see themselves as the "childlike," disciples who as "little ones" (10:42) are humble recipients of divine revelation.[7] They are invited to join Jesus in praising his Father, whose true character Jesus, to whom his Father has handed over everything, has revealed to them (11:27).[8]

Jesus gained his first disciples with his invitation to "come [δεῦτε] *after me*" (4:19). But then all who are weary and burdened from the teaching about God's will by the humanly "wise and intelligent" (11:25)—primarily

---

Wisdom's deeds are Jesus' deeds (and those of his followers)" (Osborne, *Matthew*, 428). "It is true that 'her deeds' takes us back to the 'deeds of the Christ' in v. 2, but the journey in between now encourages us to see the activity of John as also to be included within the scope of the deeds of wisdom" (Nolland, *Matthew*, 464).

7. "'Little ones' seems to have been a cherished self-description of the Matthean community, while 'wise and intelligent' would refer, in the first instance, to the scribes and Pharisees, who laid claim to superior wisdom based upon knowledge of Scripture and their own tradition" (Byrne, *Lifting the Burden*, 95).

8. For what Jesus has already revealed to the audience about his heavenly Father at this point, see 5:48; 6:4, 6, 8, 14–16, 18, 26, 32; 7:11; 10:20, 29; 11:25. "All the teaching and healing activity in which Jesus has been engaged ('these things' [v. 25]) is ultimately a revelation on his part of God and God's compassionate saving will for humankind" (Byrne, *Lifting the Burden*, 95).

the scribes and Pharisees, he invited to "come [δεῦτε] *to* me," and he will give them rest (11:28).⁹ They are to take his "yoke" (ζυγόν), his teaching about God's will as the unique revealer of the Father (11:27b), upon themselves and learn from him, for he is meek and humble of heart as the Son to whom the Father has graciously handed over all things (11:27a), and they will find rest for themselves (11:29).¹⁰ That they are to "learn [μάθετε] from me" recalls his exhortation to "learn [μάθετε] what this means: 'Mercy I desire and not [simply] sacrifice' [Hos 6:6]" (9:13). By learning from Jesus to practice the loving mercy God desires as the ethical worship that complements cultic worship, the members of the audience will find that doing the greater righteousness (5:20) and entering the "narrow gate" (7:13) by following Jesus' challenging teaching will be an easy "yoke" and a light "burden" (11:30).¹¹

"At that time," the same time that Jesus praised his Father (11:25) and promised rest to the weary and burdened (11:28-29), Jesus went on the Sabbath through grain fields.¹² His disciples "were hungry" and began to pick heads of grain and "eat" them to satisfy their hunger, thus performing work not permitted on the Sabbath (12:1; cf. Exod 34:21). The Pharisees objected that Jesus' disciples were doing what was not permitted in accord with God's

---

9. "The call to come to Jesus partly echoes the call of the disciples of 4:19; cf. 9:9, but it is a coming *to* rather than a coming *after*" (Nolland, *Matthew*, 475).

10. "'My yoke' (Matt 11:29f.) as a positive metaphor for being taken into service by wisdom itself, which gives rest (Sir 51:26f.), appears in Jesus' 'call of the Savior.' There it specifies the Matthean content of the revelatory statement in vv. 25-27 . . . ζυγός belongs to the terminology of the Matthean understanding of discipleship, in which one follows Jesus' interpretation of the law rather than that of the Pharisees" (Schenk, "ζυγός," 104). This "is the eschatological rest promised for the kingdom age (4 *Ezra* 7:36; 8:52) and is closely aligned with the 'rest' theme of Heb 3:7—4:16, especially the 'Sabbath-rest' of 4:3-11. In the Hebrews passage as here, the rest is both present and future, both the present relationship with God and the eternal rest in heaven. In coming to Jesus, the disciple enters the rest of God" (Osborne, *Matthew*, 442).

11. "The quality of 'ease' and the 'lightness' cannot consist in a lesser level of virtue or ethical demand. It must have something to do with the sense that all fulfillment in practice is preceded and facilitated by an intense relationship with Jesus and a sense of being grasped by his love. His claim to be 'gentle and humble of heart' is ultimately a claim to personal attractiveness and an invitation to enter into an exchange of love. Such love, which is ultimately an extension of the love of the Father (v. 27), is what can make even the most difficult requirements 'easy' and 'light'" (Byrne, *Lifting the Burden*, 95).

12. "'At that time' links these stories [12:1-14] with 11:25-30, as the same phrase linked those verses with 11:16-24. Both the theme of 'rest' and that of Jesus' 'kind yoke' in contrast with the burdens of scribal demands (23:4) will be illustrated as Jesus' understanding of the sabbath is contrasted with that of the Pharisees—note especially the 'mercy' of v. 7" (France, *Matthew*, 457).

will/law on the Sabbath (12:2), a day for rest from work and for worship.[13] Jesus referred them to the scriptural account (1 Sam 21:2–7) of what David did when he and those with him "were hungry" (12:3), how he went into the house of God and they "ate" the sacred bread of the presentation, which was not permitted for him to eat or those with him but for the priests alone (12:4) as a liturgical observance on the Sabbath (Lev 24:5–9). Thus, just as David and those with him, so also Jesus, the messianic Son of David (1:1; 9:27), and his disciples, were permitted to eat and satisfy their hunger as an act of priestly worship appropriate for the Sabbath.[14]

Jesus then referred the Pharisees to the stipulation in the law that on the Sabbath the priests in the temple violate the Sabbath by doing the work necessary for sacrificial worship (Num 28:9–10), yet they are "innocent" (12:5), since priestly sacrificial worship overrides the work regulation. But "something greater" than the temple is here (12:6), namely, the "mercy" embodied by Jesus, meek and humble of heart (11:29), in permitting his disciples to do the work necessary to satisfy their hunger, and that God desires as the ethical worship that complements sacrificial worship (12:7a; cf. Hos 6:6).[15] If the Pharisees understood this, they would not have condemned the "innocent" (12:7b)—Jesus and his disciples, who, like the priests in the temple, are "innocent," since they are engaged in worship appropriate for the Sabbath. For Jesus, the Son of Man, is "Lord" of the Sabbath (12:8) in the sense that not only does he have divine authority over it (11:27), but, as demonstrated in compassionately extending to his disciples the "mercy" to "rest" from their hunger, gives the "rest" (11:28–29) that the Sabbath anticipates.[16]

---

13. "The sabbath serves as a day of rest (excessively interpreted both at the time of the NT and subsequently) and of worship (in the temple and synagogue)" (Beilner, "σάββατον," 220).

14. The sacred bread of the presentation "belonged to the priests alone, the priests of Aaron's line. They alone prepared the loaves, set them out in the sanctuary, and consumed them when the time came for removal and replacement. Eating the holy loaves was a priestly prerogative—laymen were not allowed to do it. But the Scripture, the very Scripture on which the Pharisees professed to rely, did not condemn David or his men. David was not breaking the Sabbath; the relevance of what he did was that the need to satisfy hunger overrode a liturgical provision" (Morris, *Matthew*, 302).

15. Both "something greater [μεῖζόν]" (12:6) and "mercy [ἔλεος]" (12:7) are neuter forms, but the "something greater" includes the person of Jesus, who embodies and actualizes "mercy" for his disciples. "The neuter is sometimes used with reference to persons if it is not the individuals but a general quality that is emphasized" (BDF, 76§138).

16. The Sabbath was viewed "as a specific day on which God acts to bestow his blessing on Israel. This begins with Gen 2:1–3, where God rests from his work of creation and blesses the seventh day. It becomes a paradigmatic day when the creation can imitate the creator and enter the blessing of rest ordained from the creation of the

The controversy between Jesus and the Pharisees over proper worship on the Sabbath (12:1-8) provides the audience with a model for their own worship. In compassionately allowing his disciples to satisfy their hunger as an act of priestly worship appropriate on the Sabbath (12:1-4), Jesus demonstrated that he is "Lord" of the Sabbath (12:8). He gave them the rest and refreshment that the Sabbath anticipates by extending to them the mercy God desires as the ethical worship that complements cultic worship (12:7a). The sacrificial worship performed by the priests in the temple rendered them innocent with regard to doing work on the Sabbath (12:5). As something greater than the sacrificial worship of the temple (12:6), the mercy embodied and actualized by Jesus for his disciples rendered them as innocent as the priests in the temple (12:7b). All of this reinforces Jesus' invitation for the audience to come to him to experience the divine mercy he offers as rest for them (11:28-29), and to learn from him to extend to others the mercy God desires as their ethical worship (12:7; 9:13).[17]

On that same Sabbath Jesus went into "their," the Pharisees' (12:2, 14), synagogue (12:9), a place for worship.[18] To accuse him of violating proper worship on the Sabbath, they questioned whether it is permitted in accord with God's will/law to do the work of healing a man there who had a withered hand (12:10). He pointed out that surely anyone of them would do the work of taking hold of and lifting out his sheep who fell into a pit on the Sabbath (12:11). Since a human being is much more valuable to God than an animal (cf. 6:26; 10:31), it is permitted to do good on the Sabbath (12:12) by healing the man and thus extending to him the mercy God desires as ethical worship (12:7).[19] But after he healed the man (12:13), further demonstrating how he is Lord of the Sabbath (12:8), the Pharisees plotted to destroy Jesus (12:14). This further reinforces Jesus' invitation for the audience to come to him to experience the divine mercy he offers as rest for

---

world. . . . Primarily, it is meant to bring rest and refreshment to the people of God" (Burer, *Divine Sabbath Work*, 111).

17. "'Something greater than the temple is here' (v. 6): Jesus liberates people to do works of mercy (v. 7; cf. Hos 6:6). Matthew is probably orienting the pericope toward the theme of rest effected by Jesus (11:28-30)" (Beilner, "σάββατον," 221).

18. "Jesus went into the local *synagogue*. It was the center of community life, but here it is its function as the place of worship that is in mind" (Morris, *Matthew*, 305; emphasis original).

19. "'Much more valuable' has the overtone 'much more valuable in the sight of God' (cf. 6:30; 10:31). God, who wants 'mercy' to be the criterion of interpretation of the Torah (9:13; 12:7; 23:23), because of the supreme value of human beings will surely want to see 'good,' rather than nothing, done to an afflicted human being on the Sabbath (v. 12b)" (Byrne, *Lifting the Burden*, 100). "Doing good on the Sabbath is equivalent to prioritizing compassion over sacrifice (12:7)" (Turner, *Matthew*, 313).

them (11:28-29), as those more valuable to God than animals, and to learn from him to extend to others, despite opposition, the mercy God desires as their ethical worship.[20]

Despite the Pharisees' decision to kill him (12:14), Jesus continued to heal the many crowds who followed him (12:15). But he warned them not to make him publicly known (12:16). This was to fulfill God's scriptural plan as spoken through Isaiah the prophet (12:17). According to the quotation (Isa 42:1-4 in Matt 12:18-21), Jesus is God's servant whom God has chosen, "my beloved," in whom God is "well pleased" and upon whom God will place his Spirit, and he will proclaim God's merciful "justice" (κρίσιν) to the Gentiles (12:18; cf. 23:23), but in a less public way (12:19).[21] This recalls that the Spirit of God descended upon Jesus at his baptism (3:16), and God declared him to be "my beloved" Son, with whom I am "well pleased" (3:17). The quotation from Isaiah affirms that Jesus has been equipped with God's Spirit for the salvation not only of his own Jewish people (1:21; 10:6) but of all peoples.

In accord with the quotation from Isaiah, Jesus, in a less public way (12:16, 19), will continue to compassionately extend God's mercy (12:7) to those in need of healing (12:10-13, 15), characterized by the quotation as a "bruised reed" that he will not break and a "smoldering wick" that he will not extinguish, until he brings to victory God's merciful justice (12:20).[22] In his name, that is, the name "Jesus" as the one who will save his people from their sins (1:21), and the name "Emmanuel" as the one who is "God with us" (1:23), the Gentiles will hope (12:21). The scriptural quotation (Isa

---

20. "Since the man's condition was hardly life-threatening, Jesus could have avoided the problem by putting off dealing with it till the following day. But, presented with the situation, Jesus confronts the issue head on: for him the Sabbath is not primarily about avoiding things one should not do but for doing more intensely what God wants: the enhancement of human life through the exercise of mercy" (Byrne, *Lifting the Burden*, 101).

21. "The Greek word κρίσις is more normally translated 'judgment.' But this does not seem appropriate here—especially in view of the later appearance of κρίσις, along with 'mercy' and 'faith,' in the triad Jesus dubs the 'weightier matters of the Torah' (23:23)" (Byrne, *Lifting the Burden*, 102n20).

22. "The central part (vv. 19-20) provides scriptural ratification not just for the present 'withdrawal' of the Son, but for the way in which he has been fulfilling his messianic role from the start: not through force and violence but as one who, personally 'gentle and humble of heart' (11:29), has made the afflicted crowds ('the bruised reeds'; 'the smoldering wicks') his principal object of concern" (Byrne, *Lifting the Burden*, 101-2). "Who are the 'bruised reed' and the 'smoldering wick' (both stand first for emphasis)? There is general agreement that the two are metaphors for the weak and helpless, the 'harassed and helpless' of 9:36, the 'weary and burdened' of 11:28" (Osborne, *Matthew*, 467).

42:1-4) thus reaffirms for the audience that Jesus is worthy to be an object of worship as God's beloved Son/Servant, equipped with God's Spirit (Matt 3:16-17; 12:18). In accord with his name of "Jesus" and of "Emmanuel/God with us" he will save from their sins not only his own Jewish people (10:6) but the Gentiles and thus all peoples (cf. 2:1-12; 4:15-16; 8:5-13; 12:18, 21), by extending to them the merciful justice God desires as ethical worship (9:13; 12:7; 23:23).[23]

In a gesture implicit of supplicatory worship, a demoniac who was blind and mute was brought to Jesus (12:22a). In answer to the implicit intercessory prayer for him, Jesus healed him, so that he could speak and see (12:22b). All the crowds were amazed and said, "Surely this one is not the Son of David, is he?" (12:23). They thus reaffirm for the members of the audience, as those who know that Jesus is indeed the Son of David (1:1), the worthiness for Jesus to be an object of supplicatory worship as the messianic Son of David (9:27).

After Jesus healed a mute demoniac (9:32-33), the Pharisees claimed, "By the ruler of demons he drives out demons" (9:34). After he healed a mute and blind demoniac (12:22-23), the Pharisees even more emphatically insisted, "This man drives out demons only by Beelzebul, the ruler of demons" (12:24). If that were true, then, as Jesus pointed out, they would be absurdly claiming that Satan/Beelzebul is destroying his own kingdom through Jesus and others who exorcize (12:25-27). But the kingdom of God has now come upon them and the kingdom of Satan is being destroyed not by Satan himself but by the Spirit of God through which Jesus drives out demons (12:28). As the "stronger one" (3:11), Jesus metaphorically tied up the "strong one"/Satan and plundered his house (12:29), when by the Spirit of God (3:16; 4:1) he overcame Satan's temptations (4:2-11).[24] That Jesus drives out demons by the Spirit of God reaffirms for the audience that he frees people from the demonic grip of Satan, so that they may worship not Satan but the Lord their God and serve God alone (4:10).

Jesus taught his followers to pray for God's forgiveness, just as they forgive others (6:12). Indeed, unless they forgive others, they will not be

---

23. "Matthew may well intend his readers to link hope in the servant's name here with the significance of the names Jesus and Emmanuel in 1:21, 23" (Nolland, *Matthew*, 495).

24. "The tying up represents not an exorcistic technique, but the comprehensive superiority of Jesus' authority over that of Satan, and so the coming into force of the kingship of God. It is that 'tying up' that distinguishes Jesus' all-out assault on Satan's kingdom from the little local forays of other exorcists of the time" (France, *Matthew*, 481). "If we are to locate the 'binding' of Satan in any precise way, then it must be seen as taking place in Jesus' success in resisting the temptations of Satan in 4:1-11" (Nolland, *Matthew*, 502).

forgiven by God (6:14-15). People will also not be forgiven by God for blasphemy against the Spirit (12:31-32), if they fail to appreciate that it is not by Satan/Beelzebul but by the holy Spirit of God that Jesus drives out demons (12:24-28). By driving demons out of people, Jesus indicates to the members of the audience that he can also free them from the demonic powers of the devil, so that they may seek and obtain God's forgiveness through their worship of the Lord their God (4:10).[25]

Jesus also taught his followers to pray to their heavenly Father that his "will" be done on earth as it is in heaven (6:10). He warned that not everyone who says to him, "Lord, Lord," will enter the kingdom of heaven, but only the one who does the "will" of his Father in heaven (7:21). He then redefined the members of his family (12:46-48) as his disciples (12:49) who do what God desires. For whoever does the "will" of his Father in heaven is his brother and sister and mother (12:50). Jesus has repeatedly indicated the hallmark of God's will by quoting the scriptural words of God himself: "Mercy I desire and not [simply] sacrifice [Hos 6:6]" (9:13; 12:7). The members of the audience are thus called to become disciples who are members of Jesus' family because they do God's will especially by extending to others the mercy God desires as the ethical worship that complements their cultic and liturgical worship (cf. 5:24).[26]

Parables for Worship in the Kingdom of Heaven (Matt 13:1-58)

In the parable of the sower (13:3-9), the sower who "went out" to sow (13:3b) portrays Jesus who just "went out" of the house (13:1) and addressed

---

25. "Presumably what makes the blasphemy . . . unforgivable is that it excludes people from participating in what God is doing in Jesus, and thus from the 'forgiveness project'. No doubt such blasphemy remains unforgivable only as long as it is sustained. It too may be repented of" (Nolland, *Matthew*, 505). "It is not that God refuses to forgive; it is that the person who sees good as evil and evil as good is quite unable to repent and thus to come humbly to God for forgiveness. And there is no way to forgiveness other than by the path of repentance and faith" (Morris, *Matthew*, 318-19).

26. "The ethical mandate is to 'do the will of the Father,' i.e., to obey his commands and live according to his precepts, which renews another element of the Lord's Prayer, 'may your will be done on earth as it is in heaven' (6:10). This, in fact, is the definition of the key theme of 'righteousness' in Matthew, and God's will is stressed also in 6:10; 7:21; 21:31; 26:42" (Osborne, *Matthew*, 494). "Old Israel may be fragmenting and dividing, but anyone prepared to do the will of the Father in heaven, practicing righteousness in the sense of 'what God wants' (Hos 6:6; Matt 9:13; 12:7), belongs to a renewed Israel that here and now enjoys a familial relationship with God" (Byrne, *Lifting the Burden*, 104).

the crowds in parables (13:3a).[27] Just as the sower sowed the seed, symbolic of the effective word of God (Isa 55:10–11), upon the soil, so Jesus spoke/sowed the word/seed of God included in "the many things he spoke in parables" (13:3a) to the crowds standing upon the soil of the seashore (13:2). The crowds epitomize the continued failures to repent that Jesus as the sower has already experienced (9:3–4, 11, 33–34; 11:1–24; 12:14, 23–24, 38–45) and can expect to experience in the future (13:4–7). But the implicitly present disciples (13:10) represent the surprising success of the seed that falls on good soil and produces abundant "fruit" (13:8). They produced the "fruit" worthy of repentance (3:8) by doing the will of God as members of Jesus' family (12:49–50). The parable invites the audience to be part of the great success that will far exceed failures, by repenting and doing the will of God, especially practicing the mercy God desires as ethical worship (9:13; 12:7).

The sower also portrays the disciples Jesus empowered to join him in his ministry to the many crowds as shepherds (10:6), harvesters (9:37; 10:10), and fishers of people (4:19). Jesus commissioned them to preach/sow the same word/seed of God calling for repentance that he and John preached (3:2; 4:17; 10:7). As Jesus "went out of the house" (13:1), away from the crowds who have not heard his appeal to do the will of God and become members of his true family (12:46–50), so his disciples may find themselves "going out of the house" that does not receive them and hear their words (10:14). Like Jesus the disciples can expect to experience the threefold failure of the sower (13:4–7) in their ministry (10:16–23). But they may take courage in the far greater success (13:8) they will also experience as disciples (10:40–42). The parable encourages the audience to preach the word of God's kingdom despite the many failures they will experience, because the success of gaining those who repent and do the will of God that includes the mercy God desires as ethical worship will eventually and inevitably far outstrip the failures.

In contrast to the crowds, who do not see, hear, and understand (Isa 6:9–10 in Matt 13:13–15), and in accord with Jesus' appeal, "Let whoever has ears hear!" (13:9), the disciples' ears hear and understand the sower parable and the mysteries of the kingdom of heaven (13:11) that it and the other parables Jesus speaks (13:3) contain. The privilege of the disciples contrasts not only with the crowds but also with the prophets and righteous ones of the past who longed to see and hear what the disciples now see and hear (13:16–17). The knowledge of the mysteries of the kingdom of heaven contained in the parables empower the disciples to fulfill their ministry as

---

27. A parable "is a literary device drawing an analogy or comparison from everyday experience to deepen one's understanding of a concept" (Osborne, *Matthew*, 506).

the prophets and righteous ones (10:40–42) now sent to the unrepentant crowds with the hope that they will open their hearts to see, hear, understand, repent, and be healed (13:15).[28] The parables equip the disciples, as well as the audience, to endure persecution for preaching the kingdom of heaven (10:7) as prophets and doing the righteousness, the will of God, as righteous ones and thus practice the ethical worship that pleases God in the kingdom of heaven (5:10–12, 20).[29]

In his allegorical interpretation of the sower parable (13:18–23) Jesus further explained, exclusively to his divinely privileged disciples (13:11, 16–18) and thus also to the audience, why the crowds, although they "hear," do not really "hear" nor "understand" (13:13–14). When anyone "hears" the word of the kingdom and does not "understand," the evil one/Satan/devil comes and snatches what was sown in his "heart" (13:19a), so that he does not "understand" with his "heart" (13:15). "This one" is what was sown along the way (13:19b; cf. 13:4).[30] The seed sown by the sower thus represents not only the word of the kingdom but the person who hears the word.[31] Although Jesus has overcome the temptation to worship the evil one instead of the "Lord your God" (4:8–10), in their preaching of the word, the disciples and the audience must still reckon with the threat of the evil one to prevent people from understanding the word and thus participating in the true worship of God in the kingdom of heaven. This reinforces for the audience their need to pray for God to "deliver us from the evil one" (6:13; cf. 5:37).

Jesus' allegorical explanation of the sower parable then progressed to a different type of failure. The person sown upon the rocky ground is the one who hears the word and immediately receives it with joy (13:20). This person has no root in himself but endures only for a time; when tribulation or persecution arises on account of the word, he immediately falls away (13:21; cf. 13:5–6). Not only can the disciples and the audience expect this kind of failure in those to whom they preach, but they themselves are susceptible to it. Jesus warned the disciples he sent to preach the word of the kingdom

---

28. "The crowds are not so much condemned as pitied. In refusing to hear the good news with repentant hearts they isolate themselves from what above all Jesus longs to bring them: namely, healing" (Byrne, *Lifting the Burden*, 110).

29. On the role of the disciples as "prophets," proclaimers of the kingdom of heaven (10:7), and "righteous ones," those identified with the "righteousness" Jesus put forth as distinctive of the kingdom of heaven (3:15; 5:6, 10, 20; 6:33), in their mission to the crowds, see Weaver, *Missionary Discourse*, 119–23.

30. "Jesus uses the masculine 'this' (οὗτος) rather than the neuter, so it seems to refer not to the seed but the one who receives the seed" (Osborne, *Matthew*, 513).

31. On the seed as a double-duty metaphor representing not only the word but the people who hear the word, see Heil, "Mark 4:1–34," 278.

(10:7) about being persecuted (10:16–25). He exhorted them that whenever they are persecuted in one city, they are to persevere by going to others (10:23). Bolstered by Jesus' promise that whoever perseveres to the end will be saved (10:22), the members of the audience are to persevere through the persecution they will encounter for the sake of righteousness (5:10–12)—doing what is right in accord with God's will, especially practicing the mercy God desires as ethical worship (9:13; 12:7).

In his explanation of the sower parable Jesus then progressed to yet another type of discipleship failure. The person sown among thorns is the one who hears the word, but the worries of the world and the deceitful lure of wealth choke the word and it becomes unfruitful (13:22; cf. 13:7). Jesus encouraged his disciples not to worry about any of life's needs (6:25–34), but to seek first the kingdom of God and the doing of its righteousness, and God will provide them with everything they need (6:33). And he cautioned the disciples against storing up treasures on earth rather than in heaven, for where their treasure is there will their heart be (6:19–21). As he pointed out, no one can serve two "lords" (κυρίοις), for he will hate the one and love the other, or he will be devoted to one and despise the other, for no one can serve God and money (6:24). Indeed, as Jesus declared when he dismissed with the powerful word of God the temptation to worship the devil, who tried to seduce him with wealth (4:8–9), "The Lord [κύριον] your God shall you worship and him alone shall you serve [Deut 6:13]" (4:10).

In climactic contrast to the previous failures, the person sown upon good soil is the one who hears the word and understands, who indeed bears fruit abundantly (13:23; cf. 13:8). In contrast to the crowds who hear but do not understand (13:13, 14, 19), the disciples hear and understand (13:23). In contrast to those who fail by falling away in persecution (13:20–21) or because of worries and the lure of wealth become "unfruitful" (13:22), the disciples who succeed by hearing and understanding "bear fruit." This calls for the audience not only to produce the "fruit" of repentance needed for them to enter the kingdom of heaven (3:8), but to bring others into the kingdom by proclaiming the word that produces fruit, the harvest (9:37–38), of people to populate the kingdom in an abundance that far surpasses the failure of those who hear the word but do not understand (13:19). They are people who pray to be delivered from the evil one (6:13; 13:19), who endure persecution for practicing the mercy God desires as ethical worship (5:10–12, 24; 9:13; 12:7; 13:20–21), and who worship God rather than money (4:8–10; 6:24; 13:22).[32]

---

32. "The fruit is not specified but in Matthew must mean ethical living, conduct that reflects the kingdom obligations specified in Jesus' discourses of chs. 5–7, 10 thus far. While the first three soils reflect the conflict of chs. 10–12, this final soil is positive

The "evil one" who "comes" and snatches away what was "sown" in the heart of the one who hears the word of the kingdom but does not understand (13:19) progresses to the "enemy" who "came" and "sowed" weeds (those who do not understand) among the wheat (those who hear and understand) (13:25) in the parable of the weeds (13:24-30). The servants (disciples) of the householder (Jesus) (cf. 10:24-25) who sowed the wheat (13:24, 27) offered to uproot the weeds (13:28). But the householder declined lest they uproot the wheat as well (13:29).[33] They are to have the patience to allow the weeds to grow with the wheat until the harvest when the weeds will be burned but the wheat gathered into the barn (13:30). The eschatological harvest imagery that John used with emphasis on the burning to sternly warn (3:12), Jesus used with emphasis on the gathering of the wheat to encourage. The parable thus encourages the audience to have the patience to live with the weeds (those do not understand) and pray, as those among the wheat (those who hear and understand), to be ultimately delivered from the evil one (6:13).

Jesus then compared the kingdom of heaven to a mustard seed that a person sowed in his field (13:31). It symbolizes not only the word of the kingdom but those who hear and understand it (13:19-23). Although it is the smallest of seeds, when it has grown (by God, divine passive), it is the largest of plants and becomes a tree, so that the birds of the sky come and dwell in its branches (13:32). This parable encourages the audience to live with the present small number of those who hear and understand with the sure hope that the kingdom of heaven will ultimately embrace all peoples of the world, symbolized by the birds of the sky.[34] Similarly, the kingdom is like leaven that a woman "hid" in three measures of flour, an enormous quantity, until the whole was leavened (13:33).[35] This parable encourages the audience to live with the present hiddenness of those who hear and understand with the sure hope that the kingdom will inevitably, through the hidden, "leavening" activity of God, totally transform the whole world.[36] These two

---

paraenesis, calling the disciples to right living" (Osborne, *Matthew*, 515).

33. "The weed would seem to be darnel, a poisonous plant that affects crops in Palestine. In the early stages of growth the darnel shoots look very like the young shoots of wheat. By the time both plants have grown sufficiently to be distinguished, the roots are so entwined as to make tearing out the darnel destructive of the wheat" (Byrne, *Lifting the Burden*, 111n12).

34. LXX Ezek 17:23; 31:5-6; Dan 4:10-12, 20-21.

35. "The amount is highly unusual. Three measures equals 39.4 liters or 14.75 gallons, about fifty pounds of flour... that much would feed 100—150 people" (Osborne, *Matthew*, 526-27).

36. The "verb 'hid' to describe the mixing of the leaven into the dough in v. 33 draws attention to, and invites reflection on, the hiddenness of the kingdom of heaven,

parables reaffirm the need for the audience to pray: "May your kingdom come!" (6:10).

In the allegorical explanation of the parable of the weeds (13:36-43) the "field" where the one (Jesus as Son of Man) sowed good seed (those who belong to the kingdom) represents the "world" (13:37-38; cf. 13:24). At the end of the age (harvest) the Son of Man will send his angels (harvesters) (13:19) and they will collect not from the weeds (those who belong to the evil one, 13:38), as expected from the parable of the weeds (13:28-30; cf. 13:40). Rather, they will collect from his kingdom, from the good seed as those who belong to the kingdom (13:38), all causes of sin and those who do lawlessness (13:41).[37] This encourages the audience to have patience with evildoers not only in the world (13:38) but even in the kingdom, as they will be eliminated in the final judgment (13:42). But it also encourages the audience to be the righteous who will shine like the sun in the kingdom of their Father (13:43; cf. Dan 12:3) by doing not lawlessness (cf. Matt 7:23) but, as members of Jesus' true family, the will of his heavenly Father (7:21; 12:49-50).[38] This reinforces their need to pray: "May your will be done!" (6:10).

The parables of the hidden treasure (13:44) and of the valuable pearl (13:45-46) provide the audience with criteria for discerning whether they are the righteous who will shine in the kingdom of their Father, rather than the doers of lawlessness who will be excluded (13:41-43). Do they experience the kingdom of heaven as those finding a hidden treasure to which they joyfully give their hearts and all they have in a complete commitment? Do they experience the kingdom of heaven as those who have found and committed themselves completely to what is the most valuable thing (pearl) they can seek in their lives?[39] The parable of the "treasure" reaffirms the need for the audience to set their hearts on the heavenly rather than earthly

---

hidden from the wise and intelligent (11:25), and given to the disciples only as a 'secret' which is not available to others (13:11), the 'hidden things' of v. 35; note also the hidden treasure of v. 44" (France, *Matthew*, 527).

37. "The new feature here is that the collecting will be 'out of his kingdom.' . . . It is probably best to see the rooting out of evil as part of what the Son of Man does to establish his rule, in which case 'his kingdom' should be equated neither with the field nor with the church" (Nolland, *Matthew*, 560).

38. "The kingdom of the Son of man [13:41] becomes the Father's kingdom [13:43] not because of any essential or temporal difference between the kingdoms, but solely for a warning emphasis on the Son of man's judgmental authority and an assuring emphasis on the Father's care of the righteous" (Gundry, *Matthew*, 274).

39. These parables "are about enthusiastic and wholehearted commitment to the kingdom of heaven, with the secondary theme of costly renunciation for the sake of the greater good" (France, *Matthew*, 539).

"treasure" (6:19-21), and thus to worship God rather than money (6:24; cf. 4:8-10). The parable of the one who "seeks" and "finds" a pearl of great value reinforces Jesus' exhortation regarding the certainty of prayers being answered by the heavenly Father: "Seek and you will find . . . the one who seeks finds" (7:7-8).

The parable of the fish net (13:47-50) advances the imagery of Jesus and his disciples as "fishers" of people (4:19) in their shared ministry of proclaiming the word of the kingdom of heaven (4:17; 10:7).[40] At the end of the age the angels will separate the evil ones, the bad fish/people (13:48) that Jesus and his disciples will collect as "fishers" of people, from the midst of the righteous (13:49). This refers to the disciples, the righteous who will shine like the sun in the kingdom of their Father (13:43), as well as the righteous people, the good "fish" (13:48), they will gather in their ministry.[41] The parable encourages the audience to live patiently with the undesirable, evil people they may gather along with the righteous in their ministry of being "fishers" of people for the kingdom of heaven, leaving the separation of the bad from the good to God's final judgment (13:50).[42] In addition, it reaffirms for the audience Jesus' exhortation to pray to the "Lord of the harvest" to keep sending workers/fishers for the "harvest" of people/fish to be gathered into the kingdom of heaven (9:38).

The parabolic climax and conclusion of the parables discourse (13:51-53) enables the disciples and thus the audience to realize that their understanding and experience of the mysteries of the kingdom of heaven communicated by the parables of Jesus (13:11, 23, 51) makes them "scribes" who have been trained as disciples for the kingdom of heaven (13:52). Jesus has equipped them to be like him, a "householder" (10:25; 13:27, 52), who brings out of his "treasure" (cf. 12:35) "new and old" (13:52).[43] This recalls and reinforces for the audience how Jesus assured that both the "new wineskins"/celebratory worship at the arrival of him as the "bridegroom" and the "old wineskins"/ascetic worship of fasting are to be preserved (9:16-17).

40. "The metaphor of fishing may come immediately from Jesus' taking to a boat at the start of chap. 13, and ultimately from fishing for men as a figure of evangelism (4:19)" (Gundry, *Matthew*, 279).

41. "In Matthew the 'righteous' are those who persevere in right living according to God's will" (Osborne, *Matthew*, 543).

42. "The net does not discriminate as it gathers the fish, and neither should disciples of the kingdom as they fish for people" (Turner, *Matthew*, 354).

43. "The ideal is to become 'scribe(s) discipled for the kingdom of heaven,' an intriguing description, further elaborated (v. 52) with an image—almost an eighth parable—concerning a wise master of a household. Such a master has his 'treasure' store well stocked and knows when to bring out what is new and what is old" (Byrne, *Lifting the Burden*, 116).

The members of the audience may thus celebrate in their liturgical worship the "new," the arrival of Jesus ("God with us") as the bridegroom of the messianic wedding feast of the kingdom of heaven, but also continue to practice the "old," the ascetic worship of fasting, as exemplified (4:2-4) and taught (6:16-18) by Jesus.[44]

Immediately before the parables discourse (13:1-53) Jesus redefined the members of his family as his disciples who do the will of his heavenly Father (12:46-50). Immediately after the parables discourse those Jesus taught in the synagogue of his home town questioned where he got such wisdom and mighty deeds, since they knew the members of his earthly family (13:54-56).[45] They took offense at him (cf. 11:6) and did not even honor him as a prophet (13:57), so that he did not do many mighty deeds there because of their unbelief (13:58).[46] They ridiculed him as only the "son" of the carpenter and knew nothing of his other family of disciples (13:55-56). For the audience as those who know the divine origin of Jesus, this reaffirms the worthiness of Jesus to be worshiped not only as the messianic "Son" of David (1:1; 9:27) but as the "Son" of God (2:15; 3:17; 4:3, 6; 8:29; 11:27) who is "God with us" (1:23). They are called to appreciate his divine origin by becoming members of Jesus' family who do the will of his heavenly Father, epitomized by their extending mercy to others as the ethical worship desired by God (9:13; 12:7).

Summary on Matthew 11–13

Jesus' challenging exhortation, "blessed is the one who takes no offense at me" (11:6), calls for John the Baptist (11:2-3) and the audience to appreciate that Jesus has come as the Christ not first of all to execute judgment. Rather he has come as the Christ who not only compassionately answers supplicatory prayers and gestures for healing (8:2, 5-6, 16; 9:2, 18, 27, 32), but by his healings enables and inspires people to worship God (8:4, 17; 9:8, 33).

---

44. This connection is enhanced for the audience by the fact that the Greek terms "new [καινά]" and "old [παλαιά]" (13:52) occur previously in Matthew only in 9:16-17: "old [παλαιῷ] cloak" . . . "old [παλαιούς] wineskins" . . . "new [καινούς] wineskins." "The sense of the newness of what Jesus brings is pervasive in Matthew, but the language of newness likely takes us back to 9:17" (Nolland, *Matthew*, 571). For a detailed discussion of the parables in 13:1-53, see Carter and Heil, *Matthew's Parables*, 64-95.

45. "The question of origin was important for them: Did these things come from God? Or were they of human or even demonic origin?" (Morris, *Matthew*, 365).

46. "'And they took offense at him' provides a negative counterpoint to 11:6: these people cannot be declared fortunate" (Nolland, *Matthew*, 576).

Despite the failure of "this generation" of unbelievers to repent, Jesus declared that divine wisdom will be vindicated, shown to be right, by her "deeds" (11:19). These include not only the deeds done by John, but most especially the "deeds of the Christ" (11:2), namely, Jesus' miraculous healings and preaching (11:5). These are the "mighty deeds" (11:20, 21, 23) that failed to move such Galilean towns as Chorazin, Bethsaida, and Capernaum to repent (11:20-24). In contrast to these failures, the members of the audience are to repent, change their lives, by allowing the mighty deeds of Jesus' miraculous healings to inspire them to the supplicatory worship of praying to Jesus for healing (8:2, 5-6; 9:18, 27) and to the doxological worship of glorifying God for the good deeds of Jesus as the Christ (9:8; cf. 5:16).

Jesus taught his disciples and thus the audience to pray that the will of their heavenly Father may be done on earth (6:9-10). He later performed an act of laudatory worship, praising his heavenly Father for the accomplishment of his gracious will (11:25-26). The divine Father has hidden the significance of Jesus' words and deeds as signs of the arrival of the kingdom of heaven from the humanly wise and intelligent (11:25). But the audience who have repented are to see themselves as the "childlike" (11:25), disciples who as "little ones" (10:42) are humble recipients of divine revelation. They are invited to join Jesus in praising his Father, whose true character Jesus, to whom his Father has handed over everything, has revealed to them (11:27).

Jesus gained his first disciples with his invitation to "come *after* me" (4:19). But then all who are weary and burdened from the teaching about God's will by the humanly "wise and intelligent" (11:25), he invited to "come *to* me," and he will give them rest (11:28). They are to take his "yoke," his teaching about God's will as the unique revealer of the Father (11:27b), upon themselves and learn from him, for he is meek and humble of heart as the Son to whom the Father has graciously handed over all things (11:27a), and they will find rest for themselves (11:29). That they are to "learn from me" recalls his exhortation to "learn what this means: 'Mercy I desire and not [simply] sacrifice' [Hos 6:6]" (9:13). By learning from Jesus to practice the loving mercy God desires as the ethical worship that complements cultic worship, the members of the audience will find that doing the greater righteousness (5:20) and entering the "narrow gate" (7:13) by following Jesus' challenging teaching will be an easy "yoke" and a light "burden" (11:30).

The controversy between Jesus and the Pharisees over proper worship on the Sabbath (12:1-8) provides the audience with a model for their own worship. In compassionately allowing his disciples to satisfy their hunger as an act of priestly worship appropriate on the Sabbath (12:1-4), Jesus gave them the rest and refreshment that the Sabbath anticipates by extending to them the mercy God desires as the ethical worship that complements cultic worship (12:7a). The sacrificial worship performed by the priests in the temple rendered them innocent with regard to doing work on the Sabbath (12:5). As something greater than the sacrificial worship of the temple (12:6), the mercy embodied and actualized by Jesus for his disciples rendered them as innocent as the priests in the temple (12:7b). This reinforces Jesus' invitation for the audience to learn from him to extend to others the mercy God desires as their ethical worship (12:7; 9:13).

Jesus taught his followers to pray to their heavenly Father that his "will" be done on earth as it is in heaven (6:10). He warned that not everyone who says to him, "Lord, Lord," will enter the kingdom of heaven, but only the one who does the "will" of his Father in heaven (7:21). He then redefined the members of his family (12:46-48) as his disciples (12:49) who do what God desires. For whoever does the "will" of his Father in heaven is his brother and sister and mother (12:50). Jesus has repeatedly indicated the hallmark of God's will by quoting the scriptural words of God himself: "Mercy I desire and not [simply] sacrifice [Hos 6:6]" (9:13; 12:7). The members of the audience are thus called to become disciples who are members of Jesus' family because they do God's will especially by extending to others the mercy God desires as the ethical worship that complements their cultic and liturgical worship (cf. 5:24).

The parable of the sower (13:1-9) invites the audience to be part of the great success that will far exceed failures, by repenting and doing the will of God, especially practicing the mercy God desires as ethical worship (9:13; 12:7). And it encourages the audience to preach the word of God's kingdom despite the many failures they will experience, because the success of gaining those who repent and do the will of God that includes the mercy God desires as ethical worship will eventually and inevitably far outstrip the failures.

In climactic contrast to the previous failures, the person sown upon good soil is the one who hears the word and understands, who indeed bears fruit abundantly (13:23; cf. 13:8). In contrast to the crowds who hear but do not understand (13:13, 14, 19), the disciples hear and understand (13:23). In contrast to those who fail by falling away in persecution (13:20-21) or because of worries and the lure of wealth become "unfruitful" (13:22), the disciples who succeed by hearing and understanding "bear fruit." This calls for the audience not only to produce the "fruit" of repentance needed for them to enter the kingdom of heaven (3:8), but to bring others into the kingdom by proclaiming the word that produces fruit, the harvest (9:37-38), of people to populate the kingdom in an abundance that far surpasses the failure of those who hear the word but do not understand (13:19). They are people who pray to be delivered from the evil one (6:13; 13:19), who endure persecution for practicing the mercy God desires as ethical worship (5:10–12, 24; 9:13; 12:7; 13:20–21), and who worship God rather than money (4:8–10; 6:24; 13:22).

The parable of the weeds (13:24–30) encourages the audience to have the patience to live with the weeds (those do not understand) and pray, as those among the wheat (those who hear and understand), to be ultimately delivered from the evil one (6:13).

The parable of the mustard seed (13:31–32) encourages the audience to live with the present small number of those who hear and understand with the sure hope that the kingdom of heaven will ultimately embrace all peoples of the world, symbolized by the birds of the sky. Similarly, the kingdom of heaven is like leaven that a woman "hid" in three measures of flour, an enormous quantity, until the whole was leavened (13:33). This parable encourages the audience to live with the present hiddenness of those who hear and understand with the sure hope that the kingdom will inevitably, through the hidden, "leavening" activity of God, totally transform the whole world. These two parables reaffirm the need for the audience to pray: "May your kingdom come!" (6:10).

The allegorical explanation of the parable of the weeds (13:36–43) encourages the audience to have patience with evildoers and all who do lawlessness not only in the world (13:38) but even in the kingdom of heaven (13:41), as they will be eliminated in the final judgment (13:42). But it also encourages the audience to be the righteous who will shine like the sun in the kingdom of their Father (13:43; cf. Dan 12:3) by doing not lawlessness (cf. Matt 7:23; 13:41) but, as members of Jesus' true family, the will of his heavenly Father (7:21; 12:49–50). This reinforces their need to pray: "May your will be done!" (6:10).

The parable of the hidden "treasure" (13:44) reaffirms the need for the audience to set their hearts on the heavenly rather than earthly "treasure" (6:19–21), and thus to worship God rather than money (6:24; cf. 4:8–10). The parable of the one who "seeks" and "finds" a pearl of great value (13:45–46) reinforces Jesus' exhortation regarding the certainty of prayers being answered by the heavenly Father: "Seek and you will find . . . the one who seeks finds" (7:7–8).

The parable of the fish net (13:47–50) encourages the audience to live patiently with the undesirable, evil people they may gather along with the righteous in their ministry of being "fishers" of people for the kingdom of heaven (4:19), leaving the separation of the bad from the good to God's final judgment (13:50). In addition, it reaffirms for the audience Jesus' exhortation to pray to the "Lord of the harvest" to keep sending workers/fishers for the "harvest" of people/fish to be gathered into the kingdom of heaven (9:38).

The parabolic climax and conclusion of the parables discourse (13:51–53) enables the disciples and thus the audience to realize that their understanding and experience of the mysteries of the kingdom of heaven communicated by the parables of Jesus (13:11, 23, 51) makes them "scribes" who have been trained as disciples for the kingdom of heaven (13:52). Jesus has equipped them to be like him, a "householder" (10:25; 13:27, 52), who brings out of his "treasure" (cf. 12:35) "new and old" (13:52). This recalls and reinforces for the audience how Jesus assured that both the "new wineskins"/celebratory worship at the arrival of him as the "bridegroom" and the "old wineskins"/ascetic worship of fasting are to be preserved (9:16–17). The members of the audience may thus celebrate in their liturgical worship the "new," the arrival of Jesus ("God with us") as the bridegroom of the messianic wedding feast of the kingdom of heaven, but also continue to practice the "old," the ascetic worship of fasting, as exemplified (4:2–4) and taught (6:16–18) by Jesus.

7

Worshiping in the Kingdom of Heaven (Matthew 14–18)

The Worship of Jesus as the Divine Son of God (Matthew 14)

Herod the tetrarch had put John the Baptist in prison for confronting him on his adulterous marriage to Herodias, the wife of his brother Philip (14:3–4). At a birthday celebration for Herod the daughter of Herodias danced and pleased Herod (14:6) so much that he confessed with an oath, a practice Jesus had condemned as offensive to God (5:34–35) and from the evil one (5:37), to assure that he would "give" her whatever she "asked" (14:7).[1] When she asked for something evil, the killing of John, whom the crowd held as a prophet (14:5), he was forced to order that John's head be "given" to her because of his oaths (14:8–9). This instance of someone who is evil giving what is evil because of an evil oath serves as a negative counter-example in contrast to Jesus' positive teaching about authentic supplicatory worship: "If then you who are evil know how to give good gifts to your children, how much more will your Father in heaven give good things to those who ask him" (7:11).

Characterized as "the king" who was "distressed" (14:9), Herod the tetrarch (14:1) was manipulated by Herodias and her daughter (14:6–8) to kill John, whom the "crowd" held as a prophet (14:5). In contrast, Jesus "had compassion" on the large "crowd" who followed him and healed them (14:14). This recalls that when Jesus saw the "crowds," he "had compassion"

---

1. "The purpose of an oath is more often to provide assurance and confidence on the part of those for whose benefit the oath is made" (Thiselton, "Oath," 311).

on them, for "they were like sheep without a shepherd" (9:36), indicating that they were lacking a true shepherd-king, as confirmed by the failure of Herod "the king" to shepherd the "crowd." But Jesus' compassion for the "crowd" reaffirms for the audience that he is the true shepherd king, the one who "will shepherd" God's people (2:6), worthy to be worshiped as their true messianic King (2:2, 11).

Because of his oaths and those "reclining with" him at his birthday celebration (14:6) for an elite group rather than the crowd, Herod "ordered" that the head of John be "given" to the daughter of Herodias (14:9). In contrast, Jesus "ordered" the crowds to "recline" on the grass (14:19a), a posture anticipating those who "will recline" at the banquet in the kingdom of heaven (8:11).[2] He then performed an act of worship customary for a meal as, looking up to heaven, he blessed the loaves and fish as gifts from God and "gave" them to the disciples to give to the crowds (14:19b).[3] He thus empowered the disciples, who had wanted to dismiss the crowds (14:15), to feed them—"*You* give them something to eat" (14:16).[4] After John was beheaded by Herod, the disciples of John came and "took up" (ἦραν) John's dead body and buried it (14:12). In contrast, after all of the crowds ate and were satisfied by the food Jesus blessed, the disciples of Jesus "took up" (ἦραν) the life-giving overabundance of leftovers—twelve baskets full (14:20), after more than five thousand people had eaten (14:21).[5]

In contrast to the death-bringing meal celebrated by Herod the "king" (14:1–12), Jesus, the true shepherd-king, empowered his disciples to provide the crowds with a celebratory meal of life-giving overabundance (14:13–21). Jesus' act of worship in "taking" the five "loaves," looking up to heaven, "blessing" and "breaking" the "loaves" he "gave to the disciples" (14:19) reminds the audience of the eucharistic meals that are part of their communal worship (cf. 26:26: "taking" the "loaf" and "blessing" it, he "broke" it and "gave to the disciples"). Jesus' overabundant feeding of the crowds teaches the audience that in the Eucharist they have a life-giving spiritual overabundance available to them. It reminds them that their celebration

---

2. "The infinitive 'to sit down' (ἀνακλιθῆναι) is used for 'reclining' at banquets" (Osborne, *Matthew*, 566).

3. "His looking up to heaven indicates that the 'blessing' is an act of praise to God the provider" (France, *Matthew*, 562).

4. The "redundant 'you' [ὑμεῖς] puts the emphasis on the disciples' responsibility" (Osborne, *Matthew*, 566).

5. "The incident looks back to the biblical traditions telling of miraculous provision of food: the manna on which Israel fed in the wilderness (Exodus 16; Numbers 11); the prophet Elisha's feeding of a hundred (2 Kings 4:42–44). It looks forward to the Eucharist and, ultimately, to the final banquet in the kingdom of God, of which the Eucharist is both foretaste and prefigurement (cf. 26:29)" (Byrne, *Lifting the Burden*, 118).

of the Eucharist anticipates the overabundance awaiting them at the final banquet in the kingdom of heaven (cf. 8:11; 26:29). And it assures them that their celebration of the Eucharist can equip them to fulfill their responsibility to enable those who are hungry physically, as well as those who hunger and thirst for righteousness, to be "satisfied" (14:20; cf. 5:6).[6]

After Jesus forced the disciples to embark in the boat and precede him to the other side, while he dismissed the crowds (14:22) who had been miraculously fed (14:13-21), he went up the mountain by himself to pray (14:23), thus performing an act of worship placing him in communion with God. The only time Jesus had prayed previously the audience heard him praise his heavenly Father for his gracious will of revealing to the childlike the things he has hidden from the wise and learned (11:25-26). Jesus had previously taught his disciples to pray that the will of their heavenly Father be done on earth (6:9-10). And now, after praying, Jesus, to whom his Father has handed over all things, actualized his Father's gracious will by revealing to his "childlike" disciples his unique divine Sonship (11:27). He came to his disciples and revealed to them his unique divine power to walk on the sea (14:25), thus treading down the stormy waters of chaos (14:24) and making the sea crossable (Job 9:8; Ps 77:20; Isa 43:16) for his disciples, demonstrating that he has an absolute divine power to save from all dangers (Wis 14:1-4).[7]

After Jesus identified himself as the one with the unique divine power to walk on the sea (14:26-27), Peter wanted to participate in it, as he asked Jesus to command him to come to Jesus on the water (14:28). When Jesus issued the command for him to come, Peter got out of the boat, walked on the water, and came to Jesus (14:29). But, seeing the strong wind, and beginning to sink, he performed an act of supplicatory worship as he cried out, "Lord, save me!" (14:30; cf. Ps 69:2-4, 14-16). Peter received an immediate answer to his prayer as Jesus, stretching out his hand, took hold of him and saved him from sinking (cf. Ps 18:17; 144:7), as he said, "O you of little faith,

---

6. "The Evangelist expects that readers familiar with the eucharistic celebration will understand that when they participate in that rite they are enjoying the same divine hospitality the Galilean crowds experienced in this 'lonely place' from Jesus, and experiencing it in the same extravagant degree. . . . When the Church celebrates the Eucharist the same Lord is there present in the community, instructing its leaders as he instructed his disciples, 'Give them something to eat yourselves.' The Eucharist will never be complete so long as people still go hungry in our world" (Byrne, *Lifting the Burden*, 118-19).

7. Wisdom 14:1-4 is concerned with the providence of God as manifested in navigation. The author affirms that although people may plan and build ships through their technical skill (14:1-2), it is the providence of God which guides them through the sea, "showing that you can save from all" (14:3-4).

why did you doubt?" (14:31). This recalls that at a previous storm on the sea Jesus similarly addressed the disciples as those of "little faith," before he calmed the storm (8:26) and thus answered their prayer, "Lord, save, we are perishing!" (8:25). Jesus' answer to Peter's prayer provides a model for every individual in the audience, assuring them that Jesus has the divine power to likewise answer their prayers to be saved from any and all dangers.[8]

After Jesus miraculously empowered his disciples to feed the crowds with an overabundance, remarkably there was no response to this, either by the crowds or the disciples (14:13–21). But when Jesus and Peter got into the boat and the wind ceased (14:32), the disciples remaining in the boat "worshiped" Jesus, saying, "Truly you are the Son of God!" (14:33). This answers the disciples' previous question, "What sort of man is this, for even the winds and the sea obey him?" (8:27). Whereas others have "worshiped" Jesus (2:11; 8:2; 9:18), the disciples, in contrast to the demons (8:29), are the first humans to worship him with an acknowledgment of his unique divine Sonship.[9] Jesus has demonstrated that he is truly the Son of God, not by changing stones into bread to feed himself (4:3), or by throwing himself off of the parapet of the temple (4:5–6). Rather, in accord with his prayer (11:25–27; 14:23), he has revealed to his disciples his unique divine Sonship by first empowering them to miraculously feed the crowds and then by walking on the sea, demonstrating his absolute power to save.[10]

When the people of Gennesaret, where the boat landed (14:34), recognized Jesus, they and those from the surrounding region "brought to him all who were sick" (14:35), recalling that, when people previously "brought to him all who were sick," he healed them (4:24). All the sick who were brought to him now performed a noteworthy act of supplicatory worship, as they "beseeched/prayed [παρεκάλουν]" (cf. 8:5, 31, 34) that they might "only touch the tassel of his cloak," and as many as touched it were "healed/

---

8. "This scene assures the faithful that divine concern is never truly absent but is ever ready, even in the darkest moments, to save" (Byrne, *Lifting the Burden*, 120).

9. "The word προσκυνέω sometimes describes only a respectful bow to a superior, not the religious worship of deity (18:26), but in the overall and immediate contexts of Matthew, the translation 'worship' is warranted in most cases" (Turner, *Matthew*, 376).

10. "When the disciples 'worship' him, saying 'truly, you are the Son of God' (v. 33), they show that the whole traumatic experience has led to a new awareness of God's saving presence among them in the person of Jesus" (Byrne, *Lifting the Burden*, 121). "The rescued disciples' confession that Jesus is God's Son should be seen in the light of biblical texts that represent the stormy sea as a place of evil chaos from which only God can deliver" (Turner, *Matthew*, 373). "The worship of the disciples prefigures the worship of the church. There those who discover, in their experience of being rescued by Jesus, that in Jesus they encounter God, worship God, and Jesus as the Son of God" (Nolland, *Matthew*, 603). For a detailed exegesis of Matt 14:22–33, see Heil, *Jesus Walking on the Sea*, 31–67.

saved [διεσώθησαν]" (14:36), implying that they were not only healed of their sickness but saved from their sins. This recalls that when the hemorrhaging woman "touched the tassel of his cloak" (9:20), saying to herself, "If only I touch the tassel of his cloak, I will be saved [σωθήσομαι]" (9:21), Jesus affirmed that her faith had indeed "saved" (σέσωκέν) her (9:22). The members of the audience are thus encouraged to have the faith to pray to Jesus as the divine Son of God (14:33) who not only can heal their sicknesses but "will save" (σώσει) them from their sins (1:21; cf. 9:1-8).[11]

Examples of Inauthentic and Authentic Worship (Matthew 15)

Pharisees and scribes came to Jesus from Jerusalem (15:1) and accused his disciples of transgressing the tradition of the elders by not washing their hands when they eat a meal (15:2), implying that they are thereby ritually unclean and thus prevented from properly partaking in an act of worship.[12] Jesus countered by accusing them of transgressing the commandment of God on account of their merely human tradition (15:3). Their tradition allowed them to declare any financial support which would be due to their parents as a gift dedicated to God, and thus as an act of worship (15:5).[13] But this amounts to inauthentic worship as it nullifies the word of God (15:6) that calls for the authentic ethical worship of honoring parents, a very serious divine mandate (15:4; cf. Exod 20:12; 21:17; Lev 20:9; Deut 5:16). Isaiah aptly prophesied about their hypocritical worship (Matt 15:7), speaking on behalf of God: "This people honors me with their lips, but their heart is far away from me; in vain they worship [σέβονταί] me, teaching as doctrines precepts of human beings" (15:8-9; cf. Isa 29:13).[14]

11. "As in the use of 'save' (σῴζω) in 9:21-22, 'healed' (διεσώθησαν) here also stresses the combined physical and spiritual effects of the healing/salvation experience (σῴζω means spiritual salvation in 1:21; 10:22; 19:25)" (Osborne, *Matthew*, 581).

12. "This was not a matter of personal hygiene but of the removal of ceremonial defilement. In the law it was prescribed that the priests must wash their hands (and feet) when they were ministering (Exod 30:17-21), but the tradition extended this to all people and was concerned with removing ceremonial defilement incurred in daily life" (Morris, *Matthew*, 390-91). Both moral and ritual impurity or defilement "prevent worship" (Harrington, "Clean and Unclean," 681). On the washing of hands for Jewish ritual purity, see Nolland, *Matthew*, 611-15.

13. "This tradition allowed children to escape their biblical obligation of taking care of their parents by dedicating their money as a gift to God upon their death" (Osborne, *Matthew*, 586).

14. "Not only does this text distinguish merely human precepts from true worship of God. It also introduces the sense of 'the heart' as the true focus and source of what

Jesus further developed the importance of the heart for authentic worship, as he urged the crowd to hear and understand (15:10; cf. 13:23) that "not what enters into the mouth defiles a person, but what comes out of the mouth, this defiles a person" (15:11), thus preventing authentic worship. After warning the disciples not to be led into inauthentic worship by the "blind," hypocritical leadership of the Pharisees (15:12–14), he explained to them (15:15–17) that "the things that come out of the mouth come from the heart, and these things defile a person" (15:18; cf. 12:34).[15] For from the heart come the kinds of behavior that transgress the commandments of God—evil thoughts, murder, adultery, sexual immorality, theft, false witness, blasphemy (15:19; cf. Exod 20:13–16; Deut 5:17–20). Eating with unwashed hands does not defile a person (15:2), but the evil things that come from the heart are what defile a person (15:20), as they break the very commandments of God, the obedience of which God wants as authentic ethical/moral worship.[16]

Jesus' teaching about the centrality of the "heart" for authentic worship (15:1–20) reaffirms for the audience his exhortation for them to learn from him, who is meek and humble of "heart" (11:29), to practice the loving mercy God desires as the ethical worship that complements cultic worship (Hos 6:6 in Matt 9:13; 12:7). They are to keep their "heart" focused on heavenly treasure (6:21), the kingdom of heaven which is like a treasure (13:44), so as to authentically worship God rather than earthly wealth (6:24). They are to be those who are clean of "heart," those who help the unfortunate with the honesty, sincerity, and integrity required to truly worship God (Psalm 15; 24:3–6), for then they will see God (Matt 5:8) as the goal of their worship (Ps 42:3).

Jesus then withdrew to the Gentile region of Tyre and Sidon (Matt 15:21).[17] Previously two Jewish blind men engaged in an act of supplica-

---

God wants from human beings" (Byrne, *Lifting the Burden*, 122).

15. "As discussed at 5:8, the 'heart' locates the core identity of a person, that place from which one feels and thinks and determines one's actions" (Nolland, *Matthew*, 626).

16. "Jesus has totally redefined the notion of 'clean/unclean' in the direction of moral rather than ritual purity, with Scripture (Isa 29:13, quoted in v. 8) once again taken as indicating 'what God wants' . . . the struggle to live as God wants begins in the heart—in a right perception at the core of a person that the Torah's 'weightier' precepts (justice, mercy, and faith [23:23]) have priority over ritual commandments" (Byrne, *Lifting the Burden*, 122–23).

17. "The destination is significant. Having just challenged the 'clean/unclean' barrier in his dispute with the Pharisees, Jesus now *enacts* such boundary-crossing 'geographically' by moving to the Gentile region" (Byrne, *Lifting the Burden*, 123; emphasis original).

tory worship as they cried out to Jesus, "Have mercy on us, Son of David!" (9:27). Similarly, but with an address of Jesus not only as the Jewish Davidic messiah but as "Lord," a Gentile Canaanite woman cried out in an act of intercessory supplicatory worship: "Have mercy on me, Lord, Son of David! My daughter is badly demon-possessed!" (15:22). Jesus refused to answer her and his disciples asked him to "dismiss" (ἀπόλυσον) her (15:23), just as they wanted him to "dismiss" (ἀπόλυσον) the hungry crowds (14:15) upon whom Jesus had compassion and healed their sick (14:14), as those who were like sheep without a shepherd (9:36). Jesus then declared that he was sent only to the lost sheep of the house of Israel (15:24), recalling that he had directed his disciples, whom he sent out with authority to heal every disease and illness (10:2), not to go to Gentiles or Samaritans but rather to the lost sheep of the house of Israel (10:5–6).

The Canaanite woman then intensified her petition, as she came and "worshiped" (προσεκύνει) Jesus, saying, "Lord, help me!" (15:25; cf. 2:11; 8:2; 9:18; 14:33).[18] Jesus replied that it is not right to take "the bread of the children," recalling "the bread" with which he overabundantly fed the Jewish crowds (14:19), as "children" of Abraham (3:9), and throw it to the "little dogs" (15:26), that is, Gentiles, as represented by the Canaanite woman.[19] In a noteworthy contrast to the silence after Jesus overabundantly fed the Jewish crowds (14:13–21), the Gentile woman gave voice to the overabundance. She replied, "Yes, Lord, but even the little dogs eat from the crumbs that fall from the table of their masters" (15:27). Jesus acknowledged that "great" is the faith of this woman (15:28a), like the faith of the Gentile centurion (8:10) and of Rahab, the Canaanite ancestor of Jesus (1:5), but in contrast to the "little faith" of the Jewish disciples (6:30; 8:26; 14:31). Jesus then answered her prayer, as he did for the centurion, "Let it be done for you as you wish." And her daughter was healed from that hour (15:28b; cf. 8:13).

Jesus' healing of the daughter of the Canaanite woman (15:21–28) presents the audience with an outstanding model for their own supplicatory and intercessory worship. They are encouraged to have the great faith of the Canaanite woman that Jesus will provide for their own needs, as well as the needs of those for whom they pray to him, because of his divine compassion and power to provide an overabundance of salvific benefits. This unnamed Gentile woman reaffirms that "in his name the Gentiles will hope" (12:21),

---

18. "προσκυνέω is often used in the sense 'worship,' which may well be the meaning here; after all, the woman had spoken of Jesus as 'Lord' and as 'Son of David,' so she clearly had a high view of his person" (Morris, *Matthew*, 404n57).

19. "'The children's food/bread (ἄρτον)' embraces all the needs of Israel, but an echo of the feeding in 14:13–20 is likely, as well as an anticipation of that coming in 15:32–39" (Nolland, *Matthew*, 634).

as she demonstrates for the audience that, regardless of their ethnic origin or gender,[20] they may be confident that the compassionate Jesus will answer their prayers when they pray with faith for him to help them.[21]

Moving on from a Gentile region (15:21), Jesus walked along the Sea of Galilee (15:29a), still in a Gentile milieu in "Galilee of the Gentiles" (4:15).[22] He went up the mountain and sat down there (15:29b), the same authoritative position from which he had earlier taught the disciples and crowds (5:1). Many crowds, having a variety of sick people, performed a gesture suggestive of supplicatory worship, as they placed the sick at the feet of Jesus, who answered their implicit prayer by healing them (15:30).[23] The crowds were "amazed" and inspired to engage in an act of doxological worship, as they "glorified" the God of Israel (15:31).[24] These Gentile crowds complemented the Jewish crowds who "glorified" God for giving the authority to heal and forgive sins to human beings (9:8), and the crowds who, after Jesus healed a mute demoniac, were "amazed" that "nothing like this has ever been seen in Israel!" (9:33). This reaffirms Jesus' exhortation for the disciples as well as the audience to do the good deeds that inspire people to worship God, to "glorify" the heavenly Father (5:16).

Recalling that Jesus "had compassion" on the large Jewish crowd (14:14) before he empowered his disciples to overabundantly feed them (14:15–21), Jesus told his disciples that "I have compassion" on the Gentile crowd, who have been with him three days (15:29–31) with nothing to eat, and he did not want to send them away hungry (15:32).[25] Surprisingly, the disciples again questioned how they can feed such a large crowd (15:33), as

---

20. "This is the first time Matthew reports a woman as addressing Jesus" (Nolland, *Matthew*, 632).

21. "This unnamed woman, surely one of the great heroes of the gospel tradition, drags the Jewish Messiah from an understanding that his powers were solely for the benefit of his own people to one in which he uses them for a representative of the Gentile world" (Byrne, *Lifting the Burden*, 124). See also Gullotta, "Among Dogs and Disciples," 325–40; Lee, "Faith of the Canaanite Woman," 12–29.

22. "Jesus leaves the region of Tyre and apparently travels east toward Decapolis and climbs a hill 'beside' (παρά) the shore of the lake, meaning he is still in Gentile territory" (Osborne, *Matthew*, 601).

23. "Matthew's language suggests placing the afflicted in a posture of entreaty that they may not have been able to achieve unaided" (Nolland, *Matthew*, 640n232). "They put the sufferers *at his feet* (where they would have his full attention), and *he healed them*" (Morris, *Matthew*, 408; emphases original).

24. This "terminology suggests that the crowd are Gentiles, recognizing the special power of the Jewish Messiah" (France, *Matthew*, 597).

25. This time Jesus himself "takes the initiative and draws them into his own compassionate view of the crowd" (Byrne, *Lifting the Burden*, 125).

they have only seven loaves and a few fish (15:34; cf. 14:17).[26] After he instructed the crowd to recline for a meal (15:35), Jesus again performed an act of worship resonating with the eucharistic meals celebrated by the audience, as he "took the seven loaves" and the fish, and "giving thanks," he "broke" them and gave them to the disciples who gave them to the crowds (15:36; cf. 14:19; 26:26-27).[27] Four thousand ate and were satisfied with seven baskets of leftovers underscoring the overabundance (15:37-38; cf. 14:20-21).[28] But again there is no response to the miraculous feeding, as Jesus dismissed the crowds and came by boat to the region of Magadan (15:39).

Jesus' empowerment of his disciples to overabundantly feed a Gentile crowd of four thousand with seven loaves and seven baskets full of leftovers but no response (15:32-39) complements his similar empowerment of his disciples to overabundantly feed a Jewish crowd of five thousand with five loaves and twelve baskets full of leftovers but no response (14:13-21). With their eucharistic allusions these two overabundant meals reinforce for the audience that in the Eucharist they have a life-giving spiritual overabundance available to them, and that their celebration of the Eucharist anticipates the overabundance awaiting them at the final banquet in the kingdom of heaven (cf. 8:11; 26:29). These two complementary miraculous meals for both Jewish and Gentile crowds assure the audience that their celebration of the Eucharist can equip them to fulfill their responsibility to enable those who are hungry physically to be "satisfied" (14:20; 15:33, 37) regardless of their ethnic origins. They call for the audience to join the disciples in worshiping Jesus as the divine Son of God (14:33).[29]

---

26. "The disciples have forgotten all about the previous miracle" (Osborne, *Matthew*, 607).

27. "The 'eucharistic' wording of the miracle in v. 36 is as clear and detailed here as in 14:19, thus reinforcing the message of 8:11-12 that Gentiles are to share with Jews in the messianic banquet; and the Lord's Supper which anticipates that banquet is thus for people of all races and backgrounds who share the woman's faith that there is also bread for the dogs [15:21-28]" (France, *Matthew*, 601).

28. "Again, this is close to 14:20, except that now there are seven baskets of scraps left over. It is likely that like the 'twelve' in the earlier story, this number is symbolic of the perfect provision of God for his people" (Osborne, *Matthew*, 608).

29. "Resonant once more are the eucharistic echoes in the actions of Jesus and the distribution performed by the disciples (v. 36), while the sense of 'all being filled' (v. 37) foreshadows the hospitality of the kingdom" (Byrne, *Lifting the Burden*, 125). "Matthew's purpose in including a second miracle meal story is evidently to demonstrate Jesus's concern for the Gentiles and to underline the theme of Gentile world mission, with which this Gospel concludes" (Turner, *Matthew*, 392).

The Self-Sacrificial Worship of Jesus (Matt 16:1—17:23)

The Pharisees and Sadducees (cf. 3:7) then approached Jesus and, "testing," they asked him to show them a sign from heaven (16:1).[30] This recalls how Jesus was similarly "tested" (4:1) by the devil to demonstrate his divine sonship (4:3, 6). Jesus pointed out that, although they are able to discern the weather by looking at the sky, they are not able to discern the signs of the times (16:2–3), an allusion to his mighty deeds and teaching which authenticate his divine status. He then declared that "an evil and adulterous generation seeks a sign, but no sign will be given to it except the sign of Jonah" (16:4). This repeats what he had said (12:39) to the scribes and Pharisees who previously wanted to see a sign from him (12:38). He then added that just as Jonah was in the belly of the large fish three days and three nights (Jonah 2:1), so Jesus, the Son of Man, will be in the heart of the earth three days and three nights (12:40). This indicates to the audience that the ultimate sign of Jesus' divine sonship, his status as an object of worship, is his being raised by God after being dead for three days and nights (cf. 16:21; 17:23; 20:19).[31]

Jesus then warned the disciples, who had forgotten to take bread with them (16:5), to beware of the "leaven" of the Pharisees and Sadducees (16:6), a metaphorical allusion to the corrupting influence of their testing Jesus by asking for a sign from heaven (16:1).[32] When the disciples think he is referring to literal leaven because they took no bread (16:7), he chastised their "little faith" (16:8), their failure to have faith in his divine power to provide for them (6:30; 8:26; 14:31). He then asked if they do not yet comprehend or remember the overabundance of bread he provided when he empowered them to feed both the five and the four thousand (16:9–10). But they did not answer, intensifying the suspense of their silence after each feeding miracle (14:13–21; 15:32–39). When Jesus repeated his warning to beware of the

---

30. "This is not a test to discern the truth as to whether he is from God or is a false prophet, for these groups have already judged him and sought his life (12:14).... They are only looking for reasons to turn the crowds against him" (Osborne, *Matthew*, 612). The verb "testing" (πειράζοντες) "signifies that they were not sincere in their seeking a sign" (Morris, *Matthew*, 413).

31. "Jesus's resurrection will be the ultimate sign from heaven, yet this generation will still not believe Jesus's message as the Ninevites believed Jonah's message" (Turner, *Matthew*, 397).

32. "Leaven here, in contrast to 13:33, is clearly a symbol for the pervasiveness of something bad, as it is also in 1 Cor 5:6–8 (cf. Gal 5:9), where the imagery derives from the removal of leaven from the house to prepare for the Passover season" (France, *Matthew*, 609). "The link with 16:1 suggests that it is the approach shown by the Pharisees and Sadducees in vv. 1–4 which will point us towards the identity of the leaven in v. 6" (Nolland, *Matthew*, 652).

"leaven" of the Pharisees and Sadducees (16:11), they understood that he was referring to their teaching (16:12). This incident reinforces for the disciples as well as the audience the basis to worship Jesus as the Son of God (14:33) because of their faith in his divine power to provide overabundance.

In the region of Caesarea Philippi the disciples reported to Jesus that people have identified him with one of the notable prophetic figures of the past (16:13-14). As spokesman for the disciples (16:15), Peter performed what amounts to an act of confessional worship, as he declared to Jesus, "You are the Christ, the Son of the living God!" (16:16). This complements and develops the worship the other disciples performed when Peter was reentering the boat with Jesus (14:32), as they declared to him, "Truly you are the Son of God!" (14:33). Peter developed the identification of Jesus by the other disciples in their worship, and the identification of Jesus by others as a prophetic figure (16:14), when he became the first to explicitly worship Jesus as "the Christ" (cf. 2:4, 11).[33] And Peter went beyond the confession of the other disciples by worshiping Jesus as the Son of the "living" God, underlining the life-giving power of God, while subtly alluding to the previously implied resurrection of Jesus by the living God (cf. 12:40).[34]

Jesus then declared Peter blessed to perform this act of confessional worship, since it was due to divine rather than human revelation (16:17; cf. 11:27). Peter appropriately worshiped Jesus as "the Son of the living God" (16:16), since Jesus had saved his life as he was sinking down into the waters (14:28-31). Jesus then appropriately addressed Peter as "son of Jonah" (16:17), since Peter, like the prophet Jonah, was saved from sinking to his death in the sea after he prayed for deliverance (14:30-31; Jonah 2:2-11). That Jesus saved Peter from sinking to his death bolsters his promise that "the gates of Hades," the realm of death, will not prevail over the church built upon Peter, the rock (16:18).[35] Jesus also promised to give Peter the "keys of the kingdom of heaven," which include an authority to "bind" and "loose"

---

33. "Though Jesus' messianic identity has been recognized with the language 'Son of David' in 9:27; 15:22 (and questioningly in 12:23), this is the first and only confession of Jesus as 'the Christ' in the Gospel" (Nolland, *Matthew*, 661).

34. "Matthew 16:16 confirms the existence of an early Christian tradition which identifies Jesus as the Hosean 'son of the living God.' . . . For Paul and other early Christians, the living God's raising of Jesus has its roots in biblical tradition. The resurrection fulfills scriptural prophecy (Hos 2:1 LXX) and is an extension of the biblical and Jewish theme of the living God as giver of life. Jesus' resurrection is the means by which the living God is active in rescuing his people from death and destruction" (Goodwin, *Living God*, 133-34).

35. Heil, *Jesus Walking on the Sea*, 106-11. "'The gates of Hades' is a metaphor for death, which here contrasts strikingly with the phrase 'the living God' in v. 16" (France, *Matthew*, 624).

on earth as in heaven (16:19) that will enable him to actualize the prayer that "your kingdom come, your will be done, on earth as in heaven" (6:10).[36] But Jesus' order to tell no one that he was the Christ (16:20) suggests that there is more to be revealed with regard to worshiping him as the Christ (16:16).

Indeed, to worship Jesus as the Christ includes worshiping him as the Christ whom God will raise to life after his suffering and death (16:21). When Peter rebuked Jesus for announcing that he "must" (δεῖ), as a divine necessity, undergo suffering, death, and resurrection (16:22), Jesus in turn said to Peter, "Go [ὕπαγε] behind me, Satan! You are an obstacle to me, for you are not thinking the things of God but the things of human beings" (16:23).[37] This recalls the words, "Go [ὕπαγε], Satan!," with which Jesus overcame the temptation to worship the devil rather than the one true God (4:10). On the one hand, Jesus told Peter to go "behind me" (ὀπίσω μου) in the sense of "get out of my way." But at the same time he renewed his initial call for Peter to be his disciple, when he said, "Come behind me [ὀπίσω μου]" (4:19). Indeed, whoever does not take up his cross and follow "behind me" (ὀπίσω μου) is not worthy of being a disciple of Jesus (10:38).[38] In not thinking the things of God, Peter is contradicting what Jesus taught his disciples to pray, namely, that God's will, the things of God, be done on earth as in heaven (6:10).

Jesus then reiterated how being his disciple includes the ethical self-sacrificial worship involved in following him (10:38-39), as he said to his disciples, "If anyone wishes to come behind me [ὀπίσω μου], let him deny himself and take up his cross and follow me" (16:24).[39] To deny oneself includes submitting to the will of God in and through prayer (6:10), rather

---

36. "'Keys' (κλεῖδας) in the ancient world symbolized access to power and the ability to open the doors to the heavenly realms" (Osborne, *Matthew*, 628). "Peter has the keys in order to be able to let people into the kingdom of heaven.... At least in the Matthean context, binding and loosing are a subset of using the keys: they have to do with getting people into the kingdom of heaven" (Nolland, *Matthew*, 676, 681). "Keys may symbolize authority, and the authority includes forbidding and permitting (literally, 'binding' and 'loosing')" (Turner, *Matthew*, 405).

37. "δεῖ in the NT is normally an expression for the decree and esp. of the plan of God" (Popkes, "δεῖ," 279). "Peter seems to hear only that Jesus will be killed; the words about resurrection do not register" (Turner, *Matthew*, 411).

38. Jesus' rebuke of Peter (16:23) "is in effect a command to adopt the correct position of discipleship" (Byrne, *Lifting the Burden*, 133n18).

39. "It is not so much that believers would themselves suffer crucifixion as that each will have to confront a measure of suffering, possibly even loss of life, as the price of being followers of this kind of Messiah. Each will have his or her own 'cross' to bear" (Byrne, *Lifting the Burden*, 133). "It is likely that there is a twofold thrust: cross-bearing as a symbol of the total denial of self, and a willingness to die for Christ if necessary. Again Jesus is the supreme model who has done both" (Osborne, *Matthew*, 637).

than "thinking the things of human beings" (16:23). Whoever wishes to save his life, his transcendent life within the kingdom of heaven, by not denying himself will lose it, but whoever "loses his life" by spending it in ethical self-sacrificial worship for the sake of Jesus (cf. 5:11), will find his life in the kingdom (16:25).[40] For what will it profit a person if he gains the whole world, but forfeits his life in the kingdom? Or what can a person give in exchange for his life in the kingdom of heaven? (16:26). Therefore, to gain a transcendent life in the kingdom of heaven one must engage one's life in ethical self-sacrificial worship, inspired by the self-sacrificial worship Jesus demonstrated in undergoing suffering and death in accord with the will of God.[41]

As the Son of Man, Jesus will come a final time at the end of the world in the glory of his Father with his angels, and then at the final judgment he will reward each person according to his conduct (16:27), that is, according to his self-sacrificial service, his denying of self and taking up his cross, as a follower of Jesus (16:24-26).[42] That Jesus "will reward" (ἀποδώσει) each person according to his or her conduct of ethical self-sacrificial worship complements how the heavenly Father "will reward" (ἀποδώσει) each person who engages in the authentic ethical and ritual worship of giving alms, praying, and fasting not for human but for divine recognition (6:4, 6, 18). That there are some disciples who will not experience death until they see Jesus as the Son of Man coming in his kingdom (16:28) prepares the audience for the next scene in which some of his disciples will see an anticipation of Jesus' final coming in glory (16:27).

Among those disciples who will not experience death until they see Jesus coming in the glory of his heavenly kingdom (16:28) are Peter, James, and John his brother, three of the first four disciples Jesus called (4:18-22). He led these three from the group of twelve apostles (10:2-4) up a high

---

40. "Jesus was speaking about a death to a whole way of life; he was talking about the utmost in self-sacrifice, a very death to selfishness and all forms of self-seeking" (Morris, *Matthew*, 431).

41. "Within the eschatological perspective of the gospel, 'life' can be understood in two ways: (1) as referring simply to one's present span of life, which death will terminate; or (2) as referring to a personal existence that includes present life but also extends, through God's gift, to life 'in the kingdom,' transcending physical death.... The radical, transcendent sense of 'life' relativizes the value of the otherwise supreme good of being alive in this world" (Byrne, *Lifting the Burden*, 134).

42. "Though this may include punishment upon wrongdoers, the context, where encouragement is chiefly in view, places the accent upon the positive: those who have faithfully given up their 'lives' (either literally or ascetically) in the earthly sense will receive from the Son of Man the gift of eternal life that their following his self-emptying way has merited" (Byrne, *Lifting the Burden*, 134).

mountain, a place close to the heavenly realm, by themselves (17:1), where they were privileged to see a prefiguration of his coming in heavenly glory as he was transfigured and "his face shone as the sun, while his clothes became white as light" (17:2; cf. Dan 7:9; 10:6).[43] There also appeared to them two other heavenly figures, Moses and Elijah, and they were talking with Jesus (17:3). These prophets became heavenly figures without being killed by their own people, unlike most prophets (23:30–31). At the end of his life Elijah went up to heaven in a fiery chariot (2 Kgs 2:11). Moses died and was buried, but since no one knew the place of his burial (Deut 34:5–6), traditions arose about his assumption to heaven.[44] In contrast, as a prophetic figure (Matt 13:57), Jesus will enter heavenly glory only after being killed by his people (16:21).

Peter offered to make three "booths" or "tents" (σκηνάς): one for the transfigured Jesus, one for Moses, and one for Elijah (17:4). He apparently wanted to make these three "tents" as places for worship, analogous to the commemorative tents used for the Feast of Tabernacles, to celebrate and commemorate what God has done in providing this spectacular epiphany of three people in heavenly glory.[45] Peter's mistake, however, was to place Jesus in the same category as Moses and Elijah, prophets who entered into heavenly glory without being killed by their people. Consequently, God intervened from a bright cloud and declared emphatically that "this one," Jesus (not Moses or Elijah), "is my beloved Son, with whom I am well pleased; listen to him!" (17:5; cf. 3:17).[46] God thus directed the disciples as well as the audience to listen to how Jesus, in contrast to Moses and Elijah, will become a heavenly figure, namely, only after being killed and raised from the dead (16:21) to the heavenly glory prefigured by his transfiguration (17:2).

When the disciples heard the voice of God from the bright cloud (17:5), they "fell upon their face and were greatly frightened" (17:6), suggesting that they were in a posture for worship (cf. 2:11 and 4:9, where "falling down" precedes an act of worship). After Jesus was briefly transfigured

43. On the mountain of the transfiguration in Matthew, see Donaldson, *Jesus on the Mountain*, 136–56.

44. For these traditions, see Heil, *Transfiguration*, 101–13.

45. "Through these booths, analogous to the tabernacles, the heavenly glory will have a locus for appearance" (Bühner, "σκηνή," 251), and thus they may serve as places for cultic worship. On σκηνή as "a movable cultic tent," see BDAG, 928. See also Heil, *Transfiguration*, 120–22.

46. "A cloud regularly signals the presence of the unseen God in the biblical tradition (Exod 16:10; 19:9; 24:15–16; 33:9)" (Byrne, *Lifting the Burden*, 136n30). "The divine voice speaks the same words as at the baptism, then adds 'Listen to him' from Deut 18:15, where Moses prophesied of a coming 'prophet like me' and demanded that the people listen carefully to that messianic figure" (Osborne, *Matthew*, 648).

on a high mountain, giving the disciples a temporary view of his future coming in heavenly glory (17:1–2), he approached and touching them, said, "Arise and do not be afraid" (17:7; cf. 14:26–27). Raising their eyes, the disciples "saw no one but him, Jesus alone" (17:8). This underscores that Jesus alone, not Moses or Elijah (17:3) or anyone else, is worthy of having a "tent" (17:4) where he may be an object of worship as a human being who will attain heavenly glory. But the disciples as well as the audience must heed the voice of God and "listen" to Jesus (17:5), who has announced the divine necessity of his suffering, death, and resurrection (16:21) before his coming in the glory of his heavenly kingdom (16:28).[47] Only then will they be able to properly worship Jesus as "the Christ, the Son of the living God!" (16:16; cf. 16:20).[48]

As the disciples were coming down the mountain where they witnessed the temporary transfiguration of Jesus into a glorious heavenly figure (17:1–2), Jesus issued the first thing they should "listen" to in accord with God's voice from the bright cloud (17:5), as he commanded them not to tell what they had seen to anyone until he, as the Son of Man, has been raised from the dead (17:9). Then they will understand that he will enter into heavenly glory only after being killed and raised by God.[49] The disciples then asked why the scribes say that Elijah, whom they just saw with Jesus on the mountain (17:3), must come first (17:10).[50] Jesus acknowledged the expectation that Elijah will come and restore all things (17:11). But he pointed out that the Elijah figure has already come and suffered, just as Jesus, the Son of Man, will suffer (17:12). Although the disciples understood that he was referring to John the Baptist (17:13) as the Elijah figure who was to come (11:14), suspense remains whether they understood the divine necessity for Jesus to suffer, die, and be raised (16:21) before attaining to heavenly glory.[51]

47. "This is no generalized command, but a specific instruction to attend carefully to what he has been saying and will continue to insist upon in the days ahead: namely, that he is destined to suffer and die in Jerusalem and that those who would be his disciples must be prepared to go along with him on that journey" (Byrne, *Lifting the Burden*, 136).

48. For a detailed exegesis of Matt 17:1–8, see Heil, *Transfiguration*, 201–21.

49. "Glory must not be proclaimed apart from destiny to suffer" (Byrne, *Lifting the Burden*, 136).

50. "The appearance of Elijah with Jesus evidently brings to their minds the current scribal interpretation of Mal. 4:5–6 on the coming of Elijah as a herald of messianic times and the day of the Lord. Since Elijah had just appeared, they evidently wonder why Jesus still must suffer in Jerusalem and why the restoration spoken of by Malachi must be delayed" (Turner, *Matthew*, 421).

51. "Once again, the disciples have grown in their newfound realm of discipleship

When Jesus and the three disciples (17:1) came to the crowd, a man approached him, "falling on his knees" (γονυπετῶν) in a posture for supplicatory worship (17:14), and voiced an intercessory prayer, "Lord, have mercy on my son" (17:15a; cf. 9:27; 15:22).[52] His son had seizures and suffered badly, for he often fell into the fire and into the water (17:15b). The man had brought him to the disciples, but they could not heal him (17:16; cf. 10:1, 8). Jesus then declared, "O faithless and perverse generation [cf. LXX Deut 32:5], how much longer will I be with you? How much longer will I endure you? Bring him here to me" (17:17). In view of Jesus' prediction of the divine necessity for him to be killed (16:21), he will not be with his disciples much longer. Hence the need for them to have the faith to heal when he is no longer with them. Jesus then answered the man's prayer, as he rebuked the demon causing his son's suffering so that it came out of him and he was healed "from that hour" (17:18; cf. 8:13; 15:28), that is, from the time the man presented Jesus with his intercessory prayer of supplicatory worship.

Then the disciples approached Jesus privately and asked him why they were unable to cast out the demon (17:19). He explained that it was because of their "little faith" (cf. 6:30; 8:26; 14:31; 16:8), for if they would have faith the size of a tiny mustard seed, nothing would be impossible for them (17:20).[53] As they were then gathering together in Galilee, Jesus told them that he as the Son of Man is to be betrayed into the hands of men (17:22). He then reiterated that they will kill him, but on the third day he will be raised (17:23a; cf. 16:21). And they were greatly saddened (17:23b). They thus hear that he will be killed, but do not appreciate that God will raise him from the dead.[54] This increases the suspense as to whether the disciples will heed the voice of God from the bright cloud to attentively "listen" to Jesus (17:5) and have the faith not only to heal (17:19-20) but the faith that God will raise Jesus from dead. In contrast to the disciples, the members of the audience

---

understanding, though the process is far from finished, for throughout the Passion Narrative their ignorance will be evident" (Osborne, *Matthew*, 650).

52. "Falling on the knee is frequently an expression of homage and of petition toward human beings and gods. It is frequent as a posture of prayer" (Nützel, "γόνυ," 258).

53. "As the smallest seed to produce a large plant (ten to twelve feet high), the mustard seed was proverbial for one's potential greatness (13:31-32)" (Osborne, *Matthew*, 657). "Jesus challenges them with hyperboles for both the minuscule size (mustard seed) and the huge potential (moving mountains) of their faith" (Turner, *Matthew*, 425).

54. "The disciples understand the fact of his death but not the import. Yet at the same time they refuse to accept death and cannot begin to comprehend his coming resurrection" (Osborne, *Matthew*, 662).

are to have the faith that the risen Jesus remains as "God with us" (1:23), who can answer their supplicatory prayers of intercession (17:14–18).[55]

The Assurance that Communal Prayers Will Be Answered (Matt 17:24—18:35)

When the collectors of the temple tax asked Peter whether "your teacher pays the temple tax," he answered "yes" (17:24-25a; cf. Exod 30:11-16).[56] Jesus then asked Peter, "From whom do the kings of the earth take tolls or taxes—from their sons or from foreigners?" (17:25b). When he said, "From foreigners," Jesus said to him, "Then the sons are free" (17:26). This indicates that neither Jesus, the "Son" of God (17:5), nor Peter, a representative of the disciples as one of the "sons" (υἱοί) of the kingdom of heaven (5:45; 9:15; 13:38), in which there is "something greater than the temple" (12:6), needs to pay for the upkeep of the sacrificial worship in the Jerusalem temple.[57] The "something greater than the temple" that is now here with Jesus and the arrival of the kingdom of heaven includes the compassionate mercy that God desires as the ethical worship that complements sacrificial worship in the temple (9:13; 12:7).

But in order that "we may not offend" (μὴ σκανδαλίσωμεν) or lead astray the collectors of the temple tax (17:27a), and thus possibly prevent them from believing in Jesus and entering into the kingdom of heaven, Jesus directed Peter to pay the temple tax for both of them.[58] Reaffirming, however, that Jesus and Peter, as "sons" in the kingdom of heaven, need not pay the temple tax (17:25-26), God provided for the payment in the form of

---

55. "In the time that is coming (that of the Church) Jesus will no longer be physically present with them (as indeed he has been physically absent for a time on the mountain). But he and the divine power that attends him will be 'with them' (1:23; 28:20), granted the all-important condition of faith" (Byrne, *Lifting the Burden*, 137).

56. "The tax in question is the half-shekel tax that, until 70 CE, devout Jews sent to the Temple yearly to defray the cost of the sacrifices" (Byrne, *Lifting the Burden*, 138).

57. "Jesus, as the unique Son of God, is greater than the temple and is exempt from paying this tax to his Father's house (cf. 12:6; 21:12-13). The plural υἱοί [sons] includes the disciples (5:9, 45; 6:9, 26)" (Turner, *Matthew*, 429).

58. "Since Jesus expects to cause offence by the important dimension of who he is and does (11:6; 15:12), the concern here must be to avoid offence based on misunderstanding. . . . for him to refuse payment would be to send a quite different message: disapproval of the temple and refusal to participate in its corporate worship" (Nolland, *Matthew*, 727). "Jesus justifies his decision to pay the temple tax—even though he actually is free from it—by explaining that he does not wish to *give offense* (Matt 17:27). That is, he wants to prevent the tax collectors from having any reason not to believe in him" (Giesen, "σκανδαλίζω," 248; emphasis original).

a coin worth twice the temple tax that, as Jesus promised, Peter will find in the mouth of a fish that he will catch (17:27b). This incident (17:24-27) thus serves as an exemplary model for the members of the audience. It encourages them to rely upon divine assistance in not offending or leading astray potential believers and members of the kingdom of heaven in which there is "something greater than the temple" (12:6). They are rather to extend to such people the compassionate mercy that God desires as a complement to the sacrificial worship in the temple (9:13; 12:7).[59]

When the disciples asked Jesus who is the greatest in the kingdom of heaven (18:1), he called to a child whom he had stand in their midst (18:2). He then declared that unless they turn and become like children, that is, lowly and dependent, "you will not even enter the kingdom of heaven" (18:3).[60] This recalls his identical warning that "you will not even enter the kingdom of heaven" unless their righteousness, their doing what is right in accord with God's will as ethical worship, abounds beyond that of the scribes and Pharisees (5:20). Whoever "humbles" (ταπεινώσει) himself, becoming lowly and dependent like this child, is the greatest in the kingdom of heaven (18:4). And whoever receives one such child such as this in Jesus' name as one who is "humble" (ταπεινός) of heart (11:29), totally dependent upon God (11:27), receives Jesus himself (18:5).[61] Jesus then becomes an object of worship as "God with us" (1:23), who identifies himself not only with child-like disciples (10:40) but with children themselves, when they are received with the compassionate mercy God desires as ethical worship (9:13; 12:7).[62]

---

59. "The purpose is undoubtedly to show that the royal Father continues to provide for the needs of his children" (Osborne, *Matthew*, 664). "Its main attention is restricted to God's dealings with his sons and the concern not to cause offence" (Nolland, *Matthew*, 728).

60. Jesus "is presumably as realistic about children's capacity for nastiness as any parent. In a culture where children were doubtless loved and valued within their families but had no social value or status whatsoever, he is making a stark challenge to the will to power that flourishes in any community. The humility required for entrance into the kingdom consists in not expecting or demanding to be treated with any more consideration than a child, in that society, could expect" (Byrne, *Lifting the Burden*, 140).

61. "But here the child is to be welcomed not simply as a child, but 'in Jesus' name,' which implies that the child represents Jesus (just as in 25:40, 45, Jesus' smallest brothers represent him), so that to welcome them is to welcome Jesus himself" (France, *Matthew*, 679).

62. "The notion that in appropriately receiving a child one is receiving Jesus makes the best sense in an early church context where Jesus is no longer physically present. This will be one of the ways in which the 'God with us' language of 1:23 retains its significance in the early church" (Nolland, *Matthew*, 734).

The focus progresses from a concern that "we may not offend" (μὴ σκανδαλίσωμεν) potential believers (17:27) to a concern that no one "may offend" (σκανδαλίσῃ), in the sense of cause to sin, "one of these little ones," that is, a disciple, who already believes in Jesus (18:6a; cf. 10:42). It would be better for one who causes a believer to sin to undergo a gruesome loss of physical life (18:6b). Indeed, it would be better for the person through whom a cause to sin comes into the world (18:7) to suffer the loss of a bodily part that instigates a cause to sin and enter into eternal life rather than suffer eternal punishment (18:8-9; cf. 5:29-30). The disciples are not to despise "one of these little ones"—either a child-like believer or an actual child (18:1-4)—but receive and welcome them in the name of Jesus and thus receive and welcome Jesus himself (18:5).[63] Their being represented before Jesus' heavenly Father by their angels (18:10) indicates their dignity and underscores that it is God's will that they not be despised but rather extended compassionate mercy as the ethical worship that pleases God (9:13; 12:7).

Just as a man who finds one straying sheep rejoices more over it than over ninety-nine that did not stray (18:12-13), so it is not the "will" (θέλημα) of the heavenly Father that "one of these little ones," not only an actual child but especially a child-like believer (18:1-10), should be lost (18:14). This means that doing the "will" (θέλημα) of Jesus' heavenly Father in order to become a member of Jesus' true family (12:50), and in order to enter the kingdom of heaven (7:21), includes pursuing a fellow believer who strays from the community. And restoring a believer who has strayed from the community is part of what disciples are to pray for, when they pray that the "will" (θέλημά) of the Father in heaven be done on earth as in heaven (6:10).

If "your brother," a fellow believer, sins and thus strays from the community, reprove him between you and him alone, and if he listens to you, you have regained your brother (18:15). If he does not listen, take one or two others with you as additional witnesses (18:16; cf. Deut 19:15). If he refuses to listen to them, tell the church, and if he refuses to listen to the church, let him be to you as a Gentile or a tax collector (18:17), that is, as a sinner outside of the community to whom you, like Jesus, are to extend the mercy that God desires by calling him to repentance (9:10-13).[64]

"If two of you agree on earth about anything for which you ask," especially regarding the restoration of a sinning brother, Jesus assures that "what you pray for will be done for you" by his Father in heaven (18:18-19;

---

63. "To 'despise' is the opposite of the 'welcome' in v. 5" (France, *Matthew*, 686).

64. "Jesus himself treated notorious sinners compassionately (5:46-47; 9:10-13; 10:3), and so absolute shunning or total withdrawal from personal contact is not necessarily commanded here" (Turner, *Matthew*, 445).

cf. 7:7–8).[65] Where two or three are gathered together in Jesus' name, whose name signifies that he is the one who will save his people from their sins (1:21), there he is in the midst of them (18:20).[66] Communal prayer, especially for the repentance and restoration of sinners, is another way that the risen Jesus is present to the members of the audience as "God with us" (1:23).[67]

After Jesus told Peter that he should forgive a fellow believer who sins against him not just seven but seventy-seven times, thus an unlimited number of times (18:21–22), he illustrated his point with another parable about the kingdom of heaven, in which a "king," representative of both God (5:35) and Jesus (2:2), wanted to settle accounts with his servants (18:23).[68] One owed him a huge amount (18:24). Since he was unable to pay it, "the lord," a term used previously for both God (1:20, etc.) and Jesus (7:21, etc.), ordered him to be sold along with his family and property in payment of the debt (18:25). Recalling how others "worshiped" (προσεκύνει) Jesus with a prayer of petition (8:2; 9:18; 15:25), the servant "worshiped" (προσεκύνει) the lord and prayed for patience in repaying the debt (18:26).[69] Just as Jesus "had compassion" on the crowds (9:36; 14:14; 15:32), the lord "had compassion" on that servant, released him, and forgave him the debt (18:27). Although the servant prayed only for patience, the lord generously granted forgiveness of the huge debt, portraying the generosity of unlimited forgiveness (18:22).

---

65. "The prayer envisaged in context is likely to be for the restoration of the sinner, but this saying is not framed in such a way as to restrict it to only one kind of prayer" (France, *Matthew*, 697). "It is unlikely that the agreement between the two is already an agreement about the guilt or innocence of the one brought to them by the development in vv. 15–17: it is an agreement about what is to be asked of God" (Nolland, *Matthew*, 749–50).

66. "The 'name' will stand for the person; it is not simply pronouncing the name of Jesus, but in order to worship Jesus" (Morris, *Matthew*, 470).

67. "Particularly striking is the way in which the sense of Jesus Emmanuel, explicit at the beginning (1:23) and end (28:20) of the gospel but pervasive throughout, emerges here in a community context. Where 'two or three' are gathered in Christ's name—whether for worship or solemn declaration, or simply for prayer and life together—there the risen Lord is present in community with them" (Byrne, *Lifting the Burden*, 143).

68. This unlimited forgiveness represents a dramatic reversal of Lamech's unrestrained vengeance in LXX Gen 4:24: "If Cain is avenged seven times, then Lamech seventy times seven." "Jesus' point is not a limit of the times forgiveness must occur (a total of seventy-seven times) but the boundless nature of forgiveness, beyond perfection (as 'seventy-seven' is beyond 'seven')" (Osborne, *Matthew*, 693–94).

69. According to BDAG, 882, when human beings are the object of προσεκυνέω, they "are to be recognized by this act as belonging to a superhuman realm."

When the forgiven servant found a fellow servant who owed him a much smaller amount, he viciously demanded payment (18:28). Although the fellow servant made a prayerful request echoing the prayer of the forgiven servant, "Be patient with me, and I will repay you" (18:29; cf. 18:26), the forgiven servant refused and threw him in prison until he repaid the debt (18:30).[70] Previously the disciples "were greatly saddened" (ἐλυπήθησαν σφόδρα) that Jesus would be killed by people who failed to appreciate him as God's agent for bringing about the kingdom of heaven (17:23). And now fellow servants "were greatly saddened" (ἐλυπήθησαν σφόδρα) that the forgiven servant failed to appreciate the divine forgiveness he received from the lord since he did not extend it to his fellow servant, and so they reported it to their lord (18:31). Although the lord had forgiven the servant since "you beseeched [παρεκάλεσάς] me" with a prayerful request (18:32), the servant himself did not extend even the slightest patience much less forgiveness to his fellow servant who "beseeched" (παρεκάλει) him with a similar prayer (18:29).

The lord then forced the forgiven servant to realize his failure to appreciate the divine forgiveness he received by extending it to his fellow servant: "Was it not necessary for you to have mercy [ἐλεῆσαι] on your fellow servant, as I also had mercy [ἠλέησα] on you?" (18:33). This recalls how Jesus answered prayers for mercy (9:27; 15:22; 17:15) and exhibited the "mercy" (ἔλεος) God desires as the ethical worship that complements ritual worship (9:13; 12:7). That the lord handed him over to the torturers until he should repay the whole "debt [τὸ ὀφειλόμενον]" (18:34) indicates his loss of the divine forgiveness of his whole "debt [ὀφειλήν]" (18:32) that he failed to extend to his fellow servant. It reaffirms Jesus' teaching to pray that God "forgive us our debts [ὀφειλήματα], as we forgive our debtors [ὀφειλέταις]" (6:12), and that "if you forgive others their transgressions, your heavenly Father will also forgive you, but if you do not forgive others, neither will your Father forgive your transgressions" (6:14–15).

In answer to Peter's question of how many times "I should forgive" when "my brother" sins against me (18:21), Jesus drew out the consequence of the parable of the unforgiving servant (18:23–34) as an explanation of his call for unlimited forgiveness (18:22): Thus also my Father will do to "you," not just Peter but the whole community of believers he represents, unless "you forgive" each one "his brother" from "your hearts" (18:35). To forgive from "your hearts" means to forgive like the lord of the parable, who generously forgave from his compassion (18:27) and mercy (18:33) in answer

---

70. "Imprisonment was often done in cases of heavy debt as a way to force the family to pay it" (Osborne, *Matthew*, 696).

to an act of supplicatory worship (18:26). It means to perform an act of authentic ethical worship from a "heart" that is not far from God (15:8). The unforgiving servant of the parable did not take the forgiveness he received to heart, so that he was not able to forgive from his heart (18:32–33). Thus each member of the audience risks the loss of God's forgiveness, if he does not forgive a fellow believer as a heartfelt response to the same generous, merciful, compassionate, and unlimited forgiveness he receives in praying to God (6:12, 14–15).[71]

Summary on Matthew 14–18

In contrast to the death-bringing meal celebrated by Herod the "king" (14:1–12), Jesus, the true shepherd-king, empowered his disciples to provide the crowds with a celebratory meal of life-giving overabundance (14:13–21). Jesus' act of worship in "taking" the five "loaves," looking up to heaven, "blessing" and "breaking" the "loaves" he "gave to the disciples" (14:19) reminds the audience of the eucharistic meals that are part of their communal worship. Jesus' overabundant feeding of the crowds teaches the audience that in the Eucharist they have a life-giving spiritual overabundance available to them. It reminds them that their celebration of the Eucharist anticipates the overabundance awaiting them at the final banquet in the kingdom of heaven (cf. 8:11; 26:29). And it assures them that their celebration of the Eucharist can equip them to fulfill their responsibility to enable those who are hungry physically, as well as those who hunger and thirst for righteousness, to be "satisfied" (14:20; cf. 5:6).

After Jesus identified himself as the one with the unique divine power to walk on the sea (14:26–27), Peter wanted to participate in it, as he asked Jesus to command him to come to Jesus on the water (14:28). When Jesus issued the command for him to come, Peter got out of the boat, walked on the water, and came to Jesus (14:29). But, seeing the strong wind, and beginning to sink, he performed an act of supplicatory worship as he cried out, "Lord, save me!" (14:30). Peter received an immediate answer to his prayer as Jesus, stretching out his hand, took hold of him and saved him from sinking, as he said, "O you of little faith, why did you doubt?" (14:31). This recalls that at

---

71. On Matt 18:21–35, see Carter and Heil, *Matthew's Parables*, 116–22; Schneider, "Barmherzigkeit," 161–78. "What this parable brings out is the sense that those grasped by the kingdom must realize that the sea of divine forgiveness in which they have been plunged must now so penetrate and mold their lives that they extend it graciously and without measure to those who offend against them. What God wants from *them* is 'mercy not sacrifice' (Hos 6:6; Matt 9:13; 12:7)" (Byrne, *Lifting the Burden*, 145; emphasis original).

a previous storm on the sea Jesus similarly addressed the disciples as those of "little faith," before he calmed the storm (8:26) and thus answered their prayer, "Lord, save, we are perishing!" (8:25). Jesus' answer to Peter's prayer provides a model for every individual in the audience, assuring them that Jesus has the divine power to likewise answer their prayers to be saved from any and all dangers.

After Jesus miraculously empowered his disciples to feed the crowds with an overabundance, remarkably there was no response to this, either by the crowds or the disciples (14:13–21). But when Jesus and Peter got into the boat and the wind ceased (14:32), the disciples remaining in the boat "worshiped" Jesus, saying, "Truly you are the Son of God!" (14:33). Whereas others have "worshiped" Jesus (2:11; 8:2; 9:18), the disciples, in contrast to the demons (8:29), are the first humans to worship him with an acknowledgment of his unique divine Sonship. In accord with his prayer (11:25–27; 14:23), Jesus has revealed to his disciples his unique divine Sonship by first empowering them to miraculously feed the crowds and then by walking on the sea, demonstrating his absolute power to save.

Pharisees and scribes came to Jesus from Jerusalem (15:1) and accused his disciples of transgressing the tradition of the elders by not washing their hands when they eat a meal (15:2), implying that they are thereby ritually unclean and thus prevented from properly partaking in an act of worship. Their merely human tradition (15:3) allowed them to declare any financial support which would be due to their parents as a gift dedicated to God, and thus as an act of worship (15:5). But this amounts to inauthentic worship as it nullifies the word of God (15:6) that calls for the authentic ethical worship of honoring parents (15:4). Isaiah aptly prophesied about their hypocritical worship (15:7), speaking on behalf of God: "This people honors me with their lips, but their heart is far away from me; in vain they worship me, teaching as doctrines precepts of human beings" (15:8–9; cf. Isa 29:13).

Jesus' teaching about the centrality of the "heart" for authentic worship (15:1–20) reaffirms for the audience his exhortation for them to learn from him, who is meek and humble of "heart" (11:29), to practice the loving mercy God desires as the ethical worship that complements cultic worship (Hos 6:6 in Matt 9:13; 12:7). They are to keep their "heart" focused on heavenly treasure (6:21), the kingdom of heaven which is like a treasure (13:44), so as to authentically worship God rather than earthly wealth (6:24). They are to be those who are the clean of "heart," those who help the unfortunate with the honesty, sincerity, and integrity required to truly worship God (Psalm 15; 24:3–6), for then they will see God (Matt 5:8) as the goal of their worship (Ps 42:3).

Jesus' healing of the daughter of the Canaanite woman (15:21–28) presents the audience with an outstanding model for their own supplicatory and intercessory worship. They are encouraged to have the great faith of the Canaanite woman that Jesus will provide for their own needs, as well as the needs of those for whom they pray to him, because of his divine compassion and power to provide an overabundance of salvific benefits. This unnamed Gentile woman reaffirms that "in his name the Gentiles will hope" (12:21), as she demonstrates for the audience that, regardless of their ethnic origin or gender, they may be confident that the compassionate Jesus will answer their prayers when they pray with faith for him to help them.

With their eucharistic allusions the two overabundant meals (14:13–21; 15:32–39) reinforce for the audience that in the Eucharist they have a life-giving spiritual overabundance available to them, and that their celebration of the Eucharist anticipates the overabundance awaiting them at the final banquet in the kingdom of heaven (cf. 8:11; 26:29). These two complementary miraculous meals for both Jewish and Gentile crowds assure the audience that their celebration of the Eucharist can equip them to fulfill their responsibility to enable those who are hungry to be "satisfied" (14:20; 15:33, 37) regardless of their ethnic origins. They call for the audience to join the disciples in worshiping Jesus as the divine Son of God (14:33).

As spokesman for the disciples (16:15), Peter performed what amounts to an act of confessional worship, as he declared to Jesus, "You are the Christ, the Son of the living God!" (16:16). This complements and develops the worship the other disciples performed when Peter was reentering the boat with Jesus (14:32), as they declared to him, "Truly you are the Son of God!" (14:33). Peter developed the identification of Jesus by the other disciples in their worship, and the identification of Jesus by others as a prophetic figure (16:14), when he became the first to explicitly worship Jesus as "the Christ" (cf. 2:4, 11). And Peter went beyond the confession of the other disciples by worshiping Jesus as the Son of the "living" God, underlining the life-giving power of God, while subtly alluding to the previously implied resurrection of Jesus by the living God (cf. 12:40).

To worship Jesus as the Christ includes worshiping him as the Christ whom God will raise to life after his suffering and death (16:21). When Peter rebuked Jesus for announcing that he "must"—as a divine necessity—undergo suffering, death, and resurrection (16:22), Jesus in turn said to Peter, "Go behind me, Satan! You are an obstacle to me, for you are not thinking the things of God but the things of human beings" (16:23). On the one hand, Jesus told Peter to go "behind me" in the sense of "get out of my way." But at the same time he renewed his initial call for Peter to be his disciple, when he said, "Come behind me" (4:19). Indeed, whoever does not take up his cross and follow "behind me" is not worthy of being a disciple of Jesus (10:38). In not thinking the things of God, Peter is contradicting what Jesus taught his disciples to pray, namely, that God's will, the things of God, be done on earth as in heaven (6:10).

When the disciples heard the voice of God from the bright cloud (17:5), they "fell upon their face and were greatly frightened" (17:6), suggesting that they were in a posture for worship. After Jesus was briefly transfigured on a high mountain, giving the disciples a temporary view of his future coming in heavenly glory (17:1–2), he approached and touching them, said, "Arise and do not be afraid" (17:7; cf. 14:26–27). Raising their eyes, the disciples "saw no one but him, Jesus alone" (17:8). This underscores that Jesus alone, not Moses or Elijah (17:3), is worthy of having a "tent" (17:4) where he may be an object of worship as a human being who will attain heavenly glory. But the disciples as well as the audience must heed the voice of God and "listen" to Jesus (17:5), who has announced the divine necessity of his suffering, death, and resurrection (16:21) before his coming in the glory of his heavenly kingdom (16:28). Only then will they be able to properly worship Jesus as "the Christ, the Son of the living God!" (16:16; cf. 16:20).

When Jesus and the three disciples (17:1) came to the crowd, a man approached him, "falling on his knees" in a posture for supplicatory worship (17:14), and voiced an intercessory prayer, "Lord, have mercy on my son" (17:15a; cf. 9:27; 15:22). The man had brought him to the disciples, but they could not heal him (17:16; cf. 10:1, 8). Jesus then declared, "O faithless and perverse generation, how much longer will I be with you? How much longer will I endure you? Bring him here to me" (17:17). In view of Jesus' prediction of the divine necessity for him to be killed (16:21), he will not be with his disciples much longer. Hence the need for them to have the faith to heal when he is no longer with them. Jesus then answered the man's prayer, as he rebuked the demon causing his son's suffering so that it came out of him and he was healed "from that hour" (17:18; cf. 8:13; 15:28), that is, from the time the man presented Jesus with his intercessory prayer of supplicatory worship.

In order that "we may not offend" or lead astray the collectors of the temple tax (17:27a), and thus possibly prevent them from believing in Jesus and entering the kingdom of heaven, Jesus directed Peter to pay the temple tax for both of them. Reaffirming, however, that Jesus and Peter, as "sons" in the kingdom of heaven, need not pay the temple tax (17:25–26), God provided for the payment in the form of a coin worth twice the temple tax that, as Jesus promised, Peter will find in the mouth of a fish that he will catch (17:27b). This incident (17:24–27) thus serves as an exemplary model for the members of the audience. It encourages them to rely upon divine assistance in not offending or leading astray potential believers and members of the kingdom of heaven in which there is "something greater than the temple" (12:6). They are rather to extend to such people the compassionate mercy that God desires as a complement to the sacrificial worship in the temple (9:13; 12:7).

When the disciples asked Jesus who is the greatest in the kingdom of heaven (18:1), he called to a child whom he had stand in their midst (18:2). He then declared that unless they turn and become like children, "you will not even enter the kingdom of heaven" (18:3). Whoever "humbles" himself, becoming lowly and dependent like this child, is the greatest in the kingdom of heaven (18:4). And whoever receives one such child such as this in Jesus' name as one who is "humble" of heart (11:29), totally dependent upon God (11:27), receives Jesus himself (18:5). Jesus, then, becomes an object of worship as "God with us" (1:23), who identifies himself not only with child-like disciples (10:40) but with children themselves, when they are received with the compassionate mercy God desires as ethical worship (9:13; 12:7).

Just as a man who finds one straying sheep rejoices more over it than over ninety-nine that did not stray (18:12–13), so it is not the "will" of the heavenly Father that "one of these little ones," not only an actual child but especially a child-like believer (18:1–10), should be lost (18:14). This means that doing the "will" of Jesus' heavenly Father in order to become a member of Jesus' true family (12:50), and in order to enter the kingdom of heaven (7:21), includes pursuing a fellow believer who strays from the community. And restoring a believer who has strayed from the community is part of what disciples are to pray for, when they pray that the "will" of the Father in heaven be done on earth as in heaven (6:10).

"If two of you agree on earth about anything for which you ask," especially regarding the restoration of a sinning brother, Jesus assures that "what you pray for will be done for you" by his Father in heaven (18:18–19; cf. 7:7–8). Where two or three are gathered together in Jesus' name, there he is in the midst of them (18:20). Communal prayer, especially for the repentance and restoration of sinners, is another way that the risen Jesus is present to the members of the audience as "God with us" (1:23).

In answer to Peter's question of how many times "I should forgive" when "my brother" sins against me (18:21), Jesus drew out the consequence of the parable of the unforgiving servant (18:23–34) as an explanation of his call for unlimited forgiveness (18:22): Thus also my Father will do to "you," not just Peter but the whole community of believers he represents, unless "you forgive" each one "his brother" from "your hearts" (18:35). To forgive from "your hearts" means to forgive like the lord of the parable, who generously forgave from his compassion (18:27) and mercy (18:33) in answer to an act of supplicatory worship (18:26). It means to perform an act of authentic ethical worship from a "heart" that is not far from God (15:8). Each member of the audience risks the loss of God's forgiveness, if he does not forgive a fellow believer as a heartfelt response to the same generous, merciful, compassionate, and unlimited forgiveness he receives in praying to God (6:12, 14–15).

8

Worship and the Coming Kingdom of Heaven (Matthew 19–25)

Self-Sacrificial Worship in the Kingdom according to the Will of God (Matthew 19–20)

"WHEN JESUS FINISHED THESE words," that is, the words of the discourse regarding community relations (17:24—18:35), he left Galilee, where he had gathered with his disciples before the discourse (17:22), and came to the region of Judea across the Jordan (19:1). "Great crowds" followed him, and he "healed" them there (19:2). This recalls and complements how "great crowds" likewise came to him in Galilee (15:29) and placed the many sick among them at his feet in a gesture suggestive of supplicatory worship and, in answer to their implicit prayer, he "healed" them (15:30).

The Pharisees then approached and, "testing" him (cf. 16:1), asked if "it is permitted" (ἔξεστιν), that is, in accord with God's will/law and thus pleasing to God as ethical worship, for a man to divorce his wife for any cause (19:3).[1] Jesus replied that from the beginning the Creator "made them male and female" (19:4; cf. Gen 1:27). In accord with God's will, then, a man "will be joined" by God (divine passive) to his wife, and the two will become one flesh (19:5; cf. Gen 2:24). What God has joined together let no human being separate (19:6). Although Moses allowed divorce (19:7; cf. Deut 24:1–4) because of "hardness of heart," that is, sinful resistance to God, this was not God's will from the beginning (19:8).[2] Jesus then issued

---

1. "It is permitted" (ἔξεστιν) occurs also outside the NT "to indicate what is permitted or forbidden according to law or the divine will" (Balz, "ἔξεστιν," 5).

2. "The Deuteronomic legislation is a response to human failure, an attempt to

the warning that whoever divorces his wife, except for "sexual immorality" (πορνείᾳ), and marries another commits adultery (19:9; cf. 5:31–32).³ This reinforces the teaching that for a man to remain married to his wife for life, so that they continue to be one flesh in accord with God's plan from the beginning of creation, constitutes ethical worship pleasing to God.⁴

The disciples replied, "If this is the case of a man with a wife, it is better not to marry" (19:10). Jesus then pointed out that not all can accept this word that it is better not to marry, but only those to whom "it has been given" by God (divine passive) (19:11). Some were born as eunuchs, some were made eunuchs by others, but some, in what amounts to an act of ethical self-sacrificial worship, made themselves eunuchs for the sake of the kingdom of heaven; let whoever can accept this, accept it (19:12). Thus, in addition to the self-sacrifice involved in forgoing divorce in favor of lifelong faithfulness in marriage (19:3–9), celibacy for the sake of the kingdom of heaven is another way to offer ethical self-sacrificial worship pleasing to God.⁵

The verb "to bring to" or "offer" (προσφέρω) was used previously to refer to the bringing or offering of gifts as an act of worship (2:11; 5:23–24; 8:4).⁶ It was also used previously to refer to the bringing or offering of sick people to Jesus as an implicit act of supplicatory worship for him to heal them (4:24; 8:16; 9:2, 32; 12:22; 14:35). And now children "were brought to" (προσηνέχθησαν) him as an implicit act of supplicatory worship for him to lay his hands on them and pray, but the disciples rebuked them (19:13).⁷

---

bring order to an already unideal situation caused by human 'hardness of heart.' This familiar biblical term refers not so much to people's attitude to one another (cruelty, neglect, or the like) as to their attitude to God, whose purpose and instructions they have set aside" (France, *Matthew*, 719–20).

3. "Sexual immorality" (πορνεία) "is a broad term meaning sexual immorality of any type, but a growing number have argued that it does not mean 'adultery' here and that if Matthew had intended such he would have used μοιχεία. They contend that the term here refers to incestuous or illicit marriages along kinship lines, forbidden in Lev 18:6–18 but allowed in Gentile circles" (Osborne, *Matthew*, 200).

4. "Lifelong faithfulness in marriage is a sign and manifestation of the kingdom— the basis of the later sense of marriage as sacrament" (Byrne, *Lifting the Burden*, 148).

5. Jesus thus "endorses celibacy as a state of life some believers are called and gifted to undertake for the sake of the kingdom. As in the cases of the person who discovered the treasure in the field (13:44) and the merchant who has at last come upon the pearl of great value (13:45–46), a glimpse of the kingdom has set them free from other attachments in order to devote themselves more intensively to its service" (Byrne, *Lifting the Burden*, 148). Jesus is not "saying that celibacy is to be preferred or is a higher calling. The only point is that it is a valid calling and should be considered by disciples who serve the kingdom" (Osborne, *Matthew*, 707).

6. Schenk, "προσφέρω," 177–78.

7. The gesture of the laying on of hands here "is a sign of prayer by which the

Jesus, however, said, "Allow the children and do not prevent them to come to me, for the kingdom of heaven belongs to such as these" (19:14). After placing his hands on them and presumably praying for them in answer to the supplicatory gesture that he do so (19:13), he went away (19:15). Jesus here not only reaffirmed his appeal that "unless you become like children, you will not enter into the kingdom of heaven" (18:3), but presents the audience with a model of praying for children as those in need of and worthy of God's blessing and thus of participation in communal worship.[8]

A man then approached Jesus and asked, "Teacher, what good must I do to have life eternal?" (19:16). This recalls how it would be worth sacrificing a part of one's body in order to enter into "the life" (18:8–9), and that narrow is the gate and constricted the way that leads to "the life," and few are those who find it (7:14). Having or entering into "the life"—life eternal (cf. 19:17)—is synonymous with entering into the kingdom of heaven, which requires becoming like children (18:3), as well as doing the righteousness, what is right according to the will of God, that surpasses that of the scribes and Pharisees (5:20). Jesus' reply sharpened the focus from doing good in general to keeping the commandments of God, the only one who is good (19:17).[9] Although the young man claimed to have observed all the commandments Jesus enumerated (Exod 20:12–16; Deut 5:16–20; Lev 19:18 in Matt 19:18–19), he asked, "What do I still lack?" (19:20). This indicates to the audience that he senses the need to do the greater righteousness, which goes beyond mere observance of the commandments, as taught by Jesus (5:21–48).

To the young man who voiced his need to do more than merely observe the commandments (19:20) in order to enter into life eternal/the kingdom of heaven (19:16–17), Jesus asked if he wished to be "complete" (τέλειος) (19:21a). This recalls Jesus' appeal for all of his followers to be "complete" (τέλειοι) as their heavenly Father is "complete [τέλειός]" (5:48),

---

one who prays identifies the person prayed for. It is, therefore, a profoundly religious action" (Tipei, *Laying On of Hands*, 177). "Presumably the fruit of prayer is concretely applied to the recipient by the laying on of hands" (Nolland, *Matthew*, 784).

8. "In 18:2–4 Jesus had taken a child and made that little one a symbol of the humility that should prevail in the community of the kingdom. Now when children are brought to him he no longer speaks of them symbolically but, in the face of contrary inclinations from the disciples (v. 13b), insists that children have a central place in the community's life and worship" (Byrne, *Lifting the Burden*, 149).

9. "The man was centering on his own good works rather than centering on God, who alone can grant eternal life. The criterion for life is not in the works themselves but in the only true 'good' there is, the goodness of God . . . Turning to God demands not just good works but obedience to God's commandments" (Osborne, *Matthew*, 717).

by loving not just their neighbor but even their enemies (5:43-47).[10] Jesus then challenged the young man to go beyond loving just his neighbor as himself (19:19) to loving also the poor by performing an act of compassionate mercy for them, an act of ethical self-sacrificial worship that the "good" and "complete" God desires (9:13; 12:7). He is to go and sell his possessions and give the money to the poor, and he will have treasure in heaven, and then he may follow Jesus (19:21b). But when the young man heard this he went away saddened, for he was one "having" (ἔχων) many possessions (19:22), which he was unable to sacrifice in order that "I may have" (σχῶ) life eternal in the kingdom of heaven (19:16).[11]

A rich young man could not sell his many possessions (19:22) and give to the poor in order to have "treasure in heaven" (19:21) and life eternal (19:16). This reinforces Jesus' exhortation to store up "treasures in heaven" (6:20), "for where your treasure is, there will be also your heart" (6:21), the "heart" that is central to the authentic worship of God rather than money (6:24; 15:8). The failure of the rich young man to follow Jesus by worshiping with his heart God rather than riches serves as a negative example for the audience.[12] It calls them to go beyond loving their neighbor and be "complete" like God (5:48) by loving not only their enemies (5:43-47) but also the poor (19:21). They are to perform the ethical self-sacrificial worship of giving from their wealth to the poor as an act of the compassionate mercy that the good and generous God desires (9:13; 12:7; 19:17). Such self-sacrificial worship is thus part of taking up one's cross, denying oneself, and following Jesus in order to save one's life (10:38-39; 16:24-25) and enter into life eternal/the kingdom of heaven.

---

10. "He wants to be 'perfect,' a word that denotes not so much moral flawlessness as completeness, full maturity. And that is what Jesus wants for him too, as he does for all his disciples according to 5:48.... which there sums up the theme of a righteousness greater than that of the scribes and Pharisees (5:20)" (France, *Matthew*, 734). "'Complete (τέλειος)' is the counterpart to 'lack,' but also echoes the requirement of 5:48 to be 'complete ... just as your heavenly Father is complete'" (Nolland, *Matthew*, 792).

11. "The grief that accompanies his departure (v. 22) shows that in his deepest self he wants to take up Jesus' invitation, but his many possessions in fact possess him. Unlike the man who found the treasure in the field (13:44), or the pearl-dealing merchant (13:45-46), he lacks the freedom to 'sell all' in order to obtain the kingdom" (Byrne, *Lifting the Burden*, 150).

12. "His possessions have clearly become his god and have thus replaced God in his life. Therefore, the only recourse is to do what must be done with all idols: get rid of them. Moreover, if he is truly to 'love his neighbor,' he must sell the idolatrous possessions and then give the money 'to the poor' ... Jesus is not talking about almsgiving but about idolatry" (Osborne, *Matthew*, 718). "He had made a god of his wealth, and when faced with the challenge he could not forsake that god" (Morris, *Matthew*, 492).

After a rich young man was unable to perform the ethical sacrificial worship of selling his many possessions and giving to the poor (19:16–22), Jesus told his disciples that it will be difficult for a rich person to enter into the kingdom of heaven (19:23). Indeed, with a rhetorical exaggeration he declared, "It is easier for a camel to go through the eye of a needle than for a rich person to enter into the kingdom of God!" (19:24).[13] Since it is generally presumed that the rich have the resources to fulfill the requirements for salvation, the disciples were greatly astonished and asked, "Who then is able to be saved?" (19:25).[14] Jesus had exhorted his disciples to "look at" the birds of the sky that the heavenly Father takes care of (6:26), and now he "looked at" them and said, "For human beings this is impossible, but for God all things are possible" (19:26).[15] If they, as well as the audience, have faith to seek first the kingdom of God and his righteousness, God will give them everything they need (6:33), and the God for whom all things are possible will enable them to practice the ethical sacrificial worship God desires.

As spokesman for the disciples, Peter then asked Jesus what there will be for the disciples who have performed the ethical sacrificial worship of having left everything and followed Jesus (19:27). Jesus assured them that in the renewed age with its final judgment they will join him in judging the people of Israel (19:28). And everyone who has performed the ethical sacrificial worship involved in following Jesus by leaving house, family members, and lands "for the sake of [ἕνεκεν] my name will receive a hundred times more and will inherit life eternal" (19:29), the life eternal which the rich young man failed to enter by sacrificing his many possessions and following Jesus (19:16–22).[16] This reinforces the previous appeals for everyone in the audience who wishes to follow Jesus to "lose his life" in ethical self-sacrificial worship "for the sake of" (ἕνεκεν) Jesus in order to find it (10:39; 16:25). Many who are first in society, like the rich young man, will be last in

---

13. "The saying about the camel and the needle should not be watered down, but understood as comic exaggeration meant to shock the hearers out of complacency" (Byrne, *Lifting the Burden*, 150–51).

14. "Here the astonishment is caused by the general Jewish belief that riches actually signified favor with God, who blessed the piety of the family with earthly rewards. So for them the rich young man with his superficial piety was in reality one of God's chosen.... If it is impossible for such a one to enter the kingdom, who can?" (Osborne, *Matthew*, 720).

15. That these are the only two occurrences of the verb "look at" (ἐμβλέπω) in Matthew enhances this connection. "Jesus is not condemning riches but the idolatrous coveting of riches. Only by the sovereign grace of God can such idolatry be overcome" (Turner, *Matthew*, 473).

16. "Only by turning to God and 'following,' i.e., living entirely for him, can anyone 'enter' eternal life" (Osborne, *Matthew*, 722–23).

the kingdom of heaven, and the last, like the disciples who have left everything and followed Jesus, will be first in the kingdom of heaven (19:30).[17]

After asserting that "many who are first will be last, and the last first" (19:30), Jesus then further illustrated this with another parable: "For the kingdom of heaven is like a householder, who went out early in the morning to hire workers for his vineyard" (20:1).[18] This recalls that in a previous parable a "householder" (οἰκοδεσπότης) characterized God (13:27; cf. 21:33), suggesting the same for this parable. Agreeing with the workers for a "denarius," the usual daily wage, he sent them into his vineyard (20:2). Going out about the third hour (9 a.m.), he saw others standing in the marketplace idle (20:3), and so he told them to go into his vineyard also, and he will give them what is just (20:4). He went out again at the sixth (noon) and ninth hour (3 p.m.) and did the same (20:5). Going out about the eleventh hour (5 p.m.), he found others standing around and asked why they were standing around all day idle (20:6). They told him that no one had hired them, and so he told them to go into the vineyard also (20:7).

When it was evening, the "Lord" (κύριος) of the vineyard, a reference to the "householder" in accord with his characterization as God (cf. 13:27), said to his manager, "Call the workers and pay them the wages, beginning from the last until the first" (20:8).[19] The term "wages" (μισθός) here is the same term used previously to refer to a "reward/recompense" in heaven given by the heavenly Father (5:12; 6:1), suggesting that the payment of the "wages," the denarius, symbolizes entrance into the kingdom of heaven as the divine reward or recompense. That the workers will be paid from last to first prepares the audience for another example of how "the first will be last, and the last first" (19:30). Those coming around the eleventh hour, the last hired (20:6), received each a denarius (20:9), symbolic of their being given entrance into the kingdom of heaven. Influenced by the mindset of an earthly economic system, those who came first thought they would receive more, but they also received each a denarius (20:10), symbolic of their being given entrance into the kingdom of heaven, just like those who had come last.

---

17. Jesus is calling people "to make sacrifices indeed, but to make sacrifices in a worthwhile cause, and one that in the end will bring a rich reward. He is not suggesting that they serve him simply in order to obtain a reward; if they do, they have not escaped the worldliness he calls them to abandon" (Morris, *Matthew*, 496).

18. "The opening 'for' confirms that this parable refers to the issue of rewards and of first and last which has taken up vv. 27–30" (France, *Matthew*, 749).

19. "The use of ὁ κύριος ('the Lord/master') makes a further contribution to finding God in the story" (Nolland, *Matthew*, 812).

When the first hired received the denarius, they grumbled against the householder/God (20:11), saying, "These last ones worked one hour, and you have made them equal to us who bore the burden and heat of the day" (20:12). The householder/God then pointed out to one of them that he has not done wrong to him, as he agreed to work for a denarius (20:13). He is to take what is his and go (20:14a), content with his being given entrance into the kingdom of heaven. The householder/God then stated, "I desire [θέλω] to give this last one the same as you" (20:14b), since "I am permitted to do what I desire [θέλω] with what is mine" (20:15a).[20] This resonates with the previous scriptural quotation, heard twice by the audience, in which God stated, "Mercy I desire [θέλω] and not sacrifice" (Hos 6:6). Just as Jesus performed the ethical worship of extending the mercy God desires to sinners (Matt 9:13) and hungry disciples (12:7), so the householder/God extended divine mercy to those who were hired last and thus worked less than others by generously granting them entrance into the kingdom of heaven.

The householder/God then asked one of the first hired, those who grumbled against him because they thought they would receive more than the last hired (20:8–12), "Is your eye evil/greedy [πονηρός] because I am good/generous [ἀγαθός]?" (20:15b). This recalls Jesus' statement that only one, God, is "good/generous [ἀγαθός]" (19:17), and that if "your eye is evil/greedy [πονηρός]" (6:23), it means that your heart is focused on earthly rather than heavenly treasure (6:19–21), but you cannot serve and thus authentically worship both God and money (6:24). Those first who thought they would receive more than the last were worshiping money rather than the just, merciful, and generous God.[21] In the kingdom of heaven "the last will be first, and the first last" (20:16; cf. 19:30), no matter when or how much one did to enter it.[22] The parable calls for the audience not to resent but to appreciate and celebrate God's merciful generosity to all who enter

---

20. "And he says he wants *to give* (δοῦναι), not 'to pay'" (Morris, *Matthew*, 503; emphasis original).

21. I give the word "evil" (πονηρός) in 20:15 the connotation of "greedy" rather than "envious," as in some translations, because the first are not so much envious of the last as greedy for more. "They thought that they would receive more" (20:10). Ironically, they want more than the denarius symbolic of their being given entrance into the kingdom of heaven, but the householder/God told them to take what is theirs and go (20:14). They are to be content with their gift of entrance into the kingdom of heaven and not greedily want more than what is given to others.

22. "The first reversal pronouncement in 19:30 is more of a promise to the disciples than a warning; the rich young man and the poor disciples will experience role reversal, as it were. The repetition of the pronouncement in 20:16 is more of a warning against the simplistic assumption that reward is an automatic entitlement of disciples (cf. 20:20–28)" (Turner, *Matthew*, 479–80).

the kingdom of heaven. They will thereby be properly worshiping the generous God who graciously extends to them and others the mercy he desires (9:13; 12:7).[23]

Previously Jesus began to show his disciples that it was necessary that he go to Jerusalem and suffer many things from the elders, chief priests, and scribes, and be killed, but on the third day be raised (16:21). Rebuking him (16:22), Peter not only seemed to ignore Jesus' prediction of his resurrection, but failed to understand the significance of the divine necessity for his suffering and death. When Jesus predicted that he was going to be given over into the hands of men (17:22), and they will kill him, but on the third day he will be raised, the disciples were greatly saddened (17:23), indicating their failure to grasp the significance of his death and resurrection. On his way to Jerusalem Jesus told the twelve disciples (20:17) that he will be given over to the chief priests and scribes, and they will condemn him to death (20:18), and will give him over to the Gentiles to be mocked, scourged, and crucified, but on the third day be raised (20:19). There was no immediate response from them. This adds to the tension of their continuing failure to understand the significance of his death and resurrection.

The mother of the sons of Zebedee (cf. 4:21; 10:2) then approached Jesus with her two sons and performed an act of petitionary worship, as she was "worshiping [προσκυνοῦσα] and asking something from him" (20:20).[24] After he asked her, "What do you want?," she requested that he command that her two sons sit, one at his right and the other at his left, in his kingdom (20:21), thus in the top or first places of preeminence. Replying to both the mother and her sons, Jesus told them that they do not know what they are asking and thus praying to him for (20:22a). In answer to his question to them, the sons affirmed that they can "drink the cup" he is going to drink, a metaphorical allusion to his suffering and death (20:22b).[25] Jesus

23. The parable's primary concern "is to illustrate God's generous provision for those who have done less work and to warn those who have done more not to resent this generosity" (Eubank, "Divine Recompense," 249). "The parable dramatically reinforces the sense of a God desirous to be as generous as possible with the gift of salvation, continuing in this way the sense of divine 'goodness' that underpinned Jesus' interaction with the young man (19:16–22). In the long run God gives salvation as an unmerited free gift. Whether human beings have 'worked' long or little for it is not ultimately decisive" (Byrne, *Lifting the Burden*, 153–54). "The parable emphasizes the place of grace" (Morris, *Matthew*, 505).

24. "In Matthew προσκυνέω is directed preeminently toward Jesus (2:2, 8, 11; 8:2; 9:18; 14:33; 15:25; 28:9, 17)" (Turner, *Matthew*, 486n1).

25. "The 'cup' is the cup of suffering as a result of God's wrath (Ps 75:8; Isa 51:17; Jer 51:7; et al.) and fulfilled in Jesus' death, but they think it the golden goblet of glory and power. When Jesus says 'I am about' (μέλλω) to drink it, this reflects the passion prediction of 17:22 and divine necessity as well as the imminence of the event" (Osborne, *Matthew*, 739–40).

admitted that they will indeed drink his cup, but sitting at his right and left is not his to give, rather it is for those for whom it has been prepared by his Father (20:23). This inappropriate act of petitionary worship thus reinforces Jesus' teaching to pray not for the accomplishment of one's own will, but rather that the will of the heavenly Father be done (6:9-10).

The other ten disciples were indignant that the two brothers wanted the first places of preeminence over them (20:24). Jesus told them that unlike the Gentiles whose great ones exercise authority over the others (20:25), whoever among his disciples wants to be great will be their servant (20:26), and whoever wants to be "first" among them will be their slave (20:27), and thus "last," another example of how the "first will be last, and the last first" (cf. 19:30; 20:16). Jesus did not come to be served but to serve and "to give his life [ψυχήν] as a ransom for many" (20:28), an act of ethical self-sacrificial worship.[26] This further explains the significance of the divine necessity for Jesus' suffering, death, and resurrection, which the disciples have failed to understand (16:21-22; 17:22-23; 20:17-19). It underlines the inappropriateness of praying for the first places of preeminence in the kingdom of heaven (20:20-23). And it reinforces Jesus' previous exhortations that whoever "loses his life [ψυχήν]" for the sake of Jesus in ethical self-sacrificial worship will find it (10:39; 16:25).[27]

As Jesus and his disciples left Jericho, a turning point for going up to Jerusalem, a large crowd followed him (20:29). When two blind men sitting by the way heard that Jesus was passing by, they performed an act of supplicatory worship, saying to him, "Have mercy on us, Lord, Son of David!" (20:30; cf. 9:27-31). After the crowd rebuked them to be silent, they intensified their act of worship, reiterating to him, "Have mercy on us, Lord,

---

26. "λύτρον ('ransom') is used in secular sources primarily of manumission of slaves and release of prisoners of war, but also of an offering to a god to gain release from a curse, an omen, or a state of servitude brought on by one's offences" (Nolland, *Matthew*, 824). "The final phrase 'for many' (to recur in the eucharistic words over the cup [26:28]) once again ascribes to Jesus the role of the Isaianic Servant, this time alluding explicitly to the ending of the Fourth Song (Isa 53:10-12), where the Servant's suffering 'bears' the sins of others (literally, in Semitic idiom, 'of many' [53:10, 12])" (Byrne, *Lifting the Burden*, 155-56). "The use of 'many' derives from the Isa 53 background, and sets up a contrast between the one who dies and the many who benefit. A theology of 'limited atonement' is far from the intention of the passage and would be anachronistic in this context" (France, *Matthew*, 763). "'Many' (πολλοί) refers to all who turn to God and his Messiah and accept the ransom payment, becoming part of the kingdom community" (Osborne, *Matthew*, 743).

27. "The death of the Son of Man is therefore portrayed here as the supreme example of unselfish service; he will give himself for others. His specific role as a 'ransom in place of many' is of course unique; what is to be imitated is the spirit of self-giving which inspires it" (France, *Matthew*, 761).

Son of David!" (20:31). Resonating with his question to the mother of the sons of Zebedee, "What do you want [θέλεις]?" (20:21a), Jesus asked them, "What do you want [θέλετε] me to do for you?" (20:32). The mother had inappropriately requested that her two sons be "first" in the kingdom of heaven (20:21b), indicating a metaphorical "blindness" to appreciating the significance of Jesus' suffering and death as an act of ethical self-sacrificial worship. In contrast, the two blind men appropriately requested that their eyes be opened (20:33), praying for physical sight and implicitly for insight into "seeing" in order to properly follow Jesus.

In contrast to the unsympathetic crowd who wanted to silence the two blind men (20:30-31), Jesus had compassion on them in answer to their double prayer for mercy. He touched their eyes, and immediately they received their sight and "followed" (ἠκολούθησαν) him (20:34), thus joining the crowd who "followed" (ἠκολούθησεν) him (20:29), to his suffering, death, and resurrection in Jerusalem (20:17-19).[28] After his first prediction of his suffering, death, and resurrection (16:21), Jesus exhorted his disciples that if anyone wants to come after him, let him deny himself, take up his cross, and "follow" (ἀκολουθείτω) him (16:24). For whoever wants to save his life will lose it, but whoever loses his life in ethical self-sacrificial worship for the sake of Jesus will find it (16:25; cf. 10:38-39). In contrast to the inappropriate prayer of the mother for her two sons (20:20-23), the appropriate, intensified prayer of the two blind men presents the audience with a model for how they are to pray to Jesus for the insight to be able to "see" and properly "follow" him by imitating his self-sacrificial service for others (20:28).[29]

In the Temple Jesus Teaches Authentic Worship (Matthew 21-23)

When Jesus sent two disciples to procure a donkey and her colt for his entrance into Jerusalem (21:1-3), it happened so that what was spoken

---

28. "In Matthew this following puts them on a par with the crowd in v. 29: they have not necessarily become disciples in a more developed sense, but like the crowd they have behaved in a way that points towards discipleship. Given, however, the rather symbolic handling of sight, the juxtaposition of 'gained their sight' and 'followed' may well hint at more" (Nolland, *Matthew*, 830).

29. "Twice the men cry out to the Son of David in terms reminiscent of the Christian liturgy: 'Lord . . . have mercy on us' (v. 30; v. 31). . . . The quasi-liturgical appeals and the location of the scene after so many instances of the disciples' 'blindness' to the cost of following Jesus suggest that it has an intentional symbolic meaning in regard to the later Church" (Byrne, *Lifting the Burden*, 156).

through the prophet might be fulfilled (21:4): "Say to the daughter of Zion [Isa 62:11], 'Behold, your king is coming to you, meek and mounted on a donkey and on a colt, the offspring of a beast of burden' [Zech 9:9]" (Matt 21:5).[30] The prophetic quotation announces to "the daughter of Zion," that is, to the people of Jerusalem, that their king is now coming to them.[31] The only previous explicit reference to Jesus as "king" was when the Gentile magi came to Jerusalem seeking the newborn messianic "king" of the Jews in order to worship him (2:1–4, 11). That Jesus was now coming to the people of Jerusalem as their "king" gave them the opportunity to complement the worship of Jesus by the magi. But Jesus is to be worshiped as a different kind of "king," one who is meek and whose humility is accentuated by his coming on animals that are beasts of burden rather than on a military warhorse.[32]

In accord with the fulfillment of God's salvific plan as recorded in scripture (21:4), Jesus is coming to the people of Jerusalem as their messianic king who is "meek [πραΰς]" (21:5). This recalls and corresponds with Jesus' exhortation to "learn from me, for I am meek [πραΰς] and humble of heart" (11:29). This exhortation occurred shortly after Jesus' pronouncement that "no one knows the Father except the Son and anyone to whom the Son wishes to reveal him" (11:27). Jesus revealed the will of the Father regarding the kind of ethical worship God desires when Jesus directed the Pharisees to "learn" (μάθετε) the meaning of the divine scriptural quotation: "Mercy I desire and not [simply] sacrifice [Hos 6:6]" (Matt 9:13; 12:7). Jesus' coming to the people of Jerusalem as their messianic king who is "meek and humble of heart" will thus give them, as well as the audience, the opportunity to "learn" (μάθετε) from him more of what God desires with regard to their worship.

The two disciples (21:1) who procured the animals as Jesus had ordered (21:6) performed a worshipful gesture of homage and honor when

---

30. Matthew's mention of a second donkey is due "to a typically Jewish interest in the *form* of the text, so that even though he knew it referred to only one animal, its wording nonetheless lent itself to the mention of the other. . . . and its expansive poetic wording has given Matthew scope for adding a further creative twist to his concept of 'fulfillment'" (France, *Matthew*, 778–79; emphasis original). By having Jesus ride two animals Matthew "makes the event more striking to accentuate its prophetic symbolic character" (Nolland, *Matthew*, 837).

31. "The term 'daughter of Zion' is a common biblical expression that refers to Jerusalem and its inhabitants" (Turner, *Matthew*, 494–95).

32. "Thus the entry into Jerusalem is the antithesis of 'triumphal' in the way meant by the pilgrims who acclaim him Messiah. They are thinking of the conquering victor, while Jesus intends it of the suffering Servant of Isa 53 by riding a donkey rather than a warhorse" (Osborne, *Matthew*, 755). A "donkey is no warhorse but merely a beast of burden and a means of transport" (Nolland, *Matthew*, 836).

they placed their cloaks on the donkey and on the colt for Jesus to sit upon (21:7). The very large crowd added to this worshipful gesture as they spread their own cloaks on the road, while others contributed to it as they cut branches from the trees and spread them on the road (21:8).[33] The crowds preceding him and those following then performed an act of laudatory worship, as they were crying out with praise, "Hosanna to the Son of David! Blessed is he who comes in the name of the Lord! Hosanna in the highest heights! [Ps 118:25–26]" (Matt 21:9).

With the double "hosanna" they first praise Jesus as the royal messianic Son of David and then God, the Lord in whose name Jesus is coming, "in the highest heights" (ἐν τοῖς ὑψίστοις), that is, in heaven (21:9; cf. LXX Ps 148:1).[34] This complemented the acts of supplicatory worship performed by the two blind men who twice had cried out, "Have mercy on us, Lord, Son of David!" (20:30, 31). Although Jesus has been festively acclaimed and praised as the royal messianic Son of David who has "come" in the name of the Lord God (21:9), in contrast to Gentile rulers (20:25), he has not "come" to be served but to serve and to give his life in ethical self-sacrificial worship as a ransom for many (20:28).

When Jesus entered into Jerusalem "all" (πᾶσα) the city "was shaken" (ἐσείσθη), saying, "Who is this?" (21:10). This resonates with and intensifies how King Herod "was troubled" (ἐταράχθη) and "all" (πᾶσα) Jerusalem with him (2:3), when they heard from the magi that there was a newborn king of the Jews whom they had come to worship (2:2). In answer to the question of Jesus' identity by all the city of Jerusalem, the crowds were identifying him as "the prophet Jesus, the one from Nazareth of Galilee" (21:11). This recalls what Jesus had said when the people of Nazareth, his native place (13:54), took offense at him: "A prophet is not without honor except in his native place and in his own house" (13:57; cf. 16:14). The honor that has been given

---

33. "The spreading of garments and palm branches on the road marks the festive acknowledgement of Jesus's kingship" (Turner, *Matthew*, 496). "Matthew pictures the entry as a 'red carpet' ride into Jerusalem. Truly the royal Messiah is coming, but not in the way the crowds think" (Osborne, *Matthew*, 756).

34. "'Hosanna!' and 'Blessed is he who comes in the Lord's name!' both derive from Ps 118 (vv. 25 and 26 respectively), which was the last and longest of the Hallel psalms (113–118) traditionally chanted at the major festivals in Jerusalem. The latter part of Ps 118 apparently describes a joyful pilgrimage (with green branches, v. 27) into the temple, led by the king (the 'one who comes in the Lord's name'), and it is from those verses that the crowd's shouts are drawn" (France, *Matthew*, 780). Hosanna "is literally a cry for help ('Save!') but idiomatically expresses jubilant praise" (Turner, *Matthew*, 496). See also Rebell, "ὡσαννά," 509. The addition of "in the highest heights" in the second Hosanna clause is "a reverent way of speaking of God in heaven" (France, *Matthew*, 780). LXX Ps 148:1: "Praise the Lord from the heavens; praise him in the highest heights [ἐν τοῖς ὑψίστοις]."

to the prophet Jesus at his entrance into Jerusalem was ironically ominous in view of the tradition that prophets were destined to be persecuted and killed by their own people (5:10–12; 23:29–39). At the same time it prepares the audience to expect prophetic gestures and teaching of the word and will of God by Jesus, especially regarding matters of worship.

After being identified as a "prophet" (21:11), Jesus performed a dramatic prophetic gesture when he entered into the temple and drove out all those selling and buying animals for sacrificial worship, and he overturned the tables of the moneychangers and the chairs of those selling doves (21:12).[35] In accord with his prophetic role he declared to them the scriptural word of God: "My house will be called a house of prayer [Isa 56:7], but you are making it a den of robbers [Jer 7:11]" (Matt 21:13). "My house," that is, God's temple, was intended by God to be known as a "house of prayer," that is, a place for true and authentic worship of God. But those engaged in the commercial business of the sacrificial system in the temple were robbing the people not only financially by taking their money, but spiritually by promoting sacrificial rituals that have become inadequate and incomplete for a full and proper worship of God. "Something greater than the temple is here" (12:6) with Jesus, who taught that God desires mercy and not simply sacrifice (9:13; 12:7).[36]

Twice previously two blind men performed an act of supplicatory worship as they prayed for Jesus as the messianic Son of David to have mercy on them (9:27; 20:30–31). Each time Jesus answered their prayer for mercy by healing them (9:29–30; 20:33–34). When the blind and the lame approached Jesus in the temple, he again demonstrated the mercy God desires as ethical worship (9:13; 12:7), as he healed them (21:14), his final and climactic act of healing in Matthew. Jesus thereby enabled them to worship in the temple from which they had been prohibited access since the time of David, when he pronounced that "the blind and the lame shall not enter into the house of the Lord" (LXX 2 Sam 5:8).[37]

---

35. On overthrowing the tables of cultic perversion as a symbol of divine wrath toward sacrificial abuse and its subsequent substitution by a new moral order, see Huys, "Turning the Tables," 137–61. "Most of the pilgrims carried pagan coins with idolatrous likenesses of the emperor on them. These had to be exchanged for Tyrian silver" (Osborne, *Matthew*, 762).

36. "The two activities of Jesus in the Temple—expulsion and healing—neatly give expression once more to the divine preference: 'What I want is mercy, not sacrifice' (Hos 6:6; Matt 9:13; 12:7)" (Byrne, *Lifting the Burden*, 159).

37. Heil, "Healing Miracles in Matthew," 283–84. "Jesus uses the healings to display what the temple should look like as a 'house of prayer'" (Osborne, *Matthew*, 763). "Jesus removes the barrier to their full participation in God's house of prayer" (Turner, *Matthew*, 500).

When the chief priests and the scribes, those who will be responsible for putting Jesus to death (16:21; 20:18), saw the wonderful things that he did and the boys crying out in the temple and saying, "Hosanna to the Son of David!," they were indignant (21:15). For the audience the wonderful things that Jesus did include not only his amazing expulsion of those engaged in the commercial business of sacrificial worship (21:12-13), but also his miraculous healing of the blind and lame (21:14). Although Herod had put to death all "the boys" (τοὺς παῖδας) in Bethlehem and its vicinity because of the birth there of Jesus as the messianic Son of David (2:16), in ironic contrast, "the boys" (τοὺς παῖδας) in the temple were crying out in praise of Jesus as the Son of David. Their act of laudatory worship of Jesus not only echoes that of the crowds when he entered into Jerusalem (21:9), but complements it as praise for Jesus' merciful healing of the blind and lame (21:14) to enable them to participate in temple worship.

The indignant chief priests and scribes (21:15) asked Jesus if he heard the act of laudatory worship with which the boys were addressing him in the temple and he answered affirmatively (21:16a). He then asked them if they have never read in the scriptural word of God: "Out of the mouth of infants [νηπίων] and nurslings you have prepared praise for yourself [Ps 8:3]" (Matt 21:16b). This recalls and resonates with Jesus' praise of his heavenly Father for having hidden from the wise and intelligent what he has revealed to "infants" (νηπίοις), the childlike (11:25). By means of this scriptural reference Jesus has thus indicated that in praising him in the temple the boys represent the "infants" from whose mouths God has prepared praise for himself. By their act of laudatory worship of Jesus in the temple the boys were actually praising God and thus present the audience with a model of the authentic worship God desires to take place in the temple as God's "house of prayer" (21:13).[38]

When Jesus was returning to Jerusalem in the morning after spending the night in Bethany (21:17), he was hungry (21:18). Seeing a fig tree on the way, he found nothing on it except leaves, so he said to it, "Never again will there be fruit from you!" And immediately the fig tree withered (21:19). This characterized how Jesus cleansed the temple of its commercial business when he found no "fruit," that is, no authentic worship of God in it, as it had become a "den of robbers" rather than God's "house of prayer [προσευχῆς]" (21:12-13).[39] The disciples were amazed at how the fig tree withered imme-

---

38. "The most striking feature of this quotation, however, is the bold assumption by Jesus that what the psalm says about the praise of *God* is applicable to the children's praise of *him*" (France, *Matthew*, 789; emphases original).

39. "Jesus is deliberately staging a symbolic act that uses an OT image in which the fig tree symbolizes Israel (Isa 28:4; Hos 9:10) and a barren fig tree symbolizes sin and

diately (21:20). Jesus told them that if they have faith and do not doubt, not only will they do what was done to the fig tree, but even if they say to this mountain, "Be lifted up and thrown into the sea, it will be done" (21:21; cf. 17:20).[40] He then declared, "And everything, whatever you ask for in prayer [προσευχῇ], believing, you will receive" (21:22). By praying with faith in God, the audience, as a community of believers, can become God's "house of prayer" that the Jerusalem temple failed to become.[41]

That whatever "you ask for" in prayer while believing, "you will receive" (21:22) develops Jesus' pronouncement that if two of his followers agree on earth about anything for which "they ask, it will be done" for them by Jesus' Father in heaven (18:19), just as if they pray for something with faith, "it will be done" (21:21). With this emphasis on "believing," Jesus developed his pronouncement that "everyone who asks receives" (7:8). Jesus told the Gentile centurion who prayed for his servant's healing with faith not found in Israel (8:10) that "as you have believed, let it be done for you" (8:13). Two blind men answered yes when Jesus asked if they believed that he can heal them (9:28). He then told them, "According to your faith let it be done for you" (9:29). To the Canaanite woman who prayed for Jesus to heal her daughter (15:22), Jesus said, "Great is your faith! Let it be done for you as you wish" (15:28). These are models that encourage the audience to pray with faith (21:21), for "*everything*, whatever you ask for in prayer, *believing*, you will receive" (21:22).[42]

When Jesus again entered the temple, the chief priests and the elders of the people, who will be among those responsible for putting him to death (16:21), approached him as he was teaching, asking, "By what authority are you doing these things, and who gave you this authority?" (21:23). "These things" refers to both Jesus' cleansing of the temple (21:12-13) and his healing of the blind and lame, which led to the boys addressing him with an act

---

corruption in the nation. . . . So this symbolic action is intended by Jesus as a further explication of his actions in the temple the previous day" (Osborne, *Matthew*, 770). "'Fruit' has been, and will continue to be in this gospel, a prominent metaphor for the sort of behavior God requires of his people" (France, *Matthew*, 792).

40. "This is simply a metaphor for accomplishing great things" (Osborne, *Matthew*, 771).

41. "Jesus had found the Temple wanting as a 'house of prayer' (v. 13); the community of the Church he is 'building' is to be, in its stead, a 'house' of truly efficacious prayer" (Byrne, *Lifting the Burden*, 160). That the term "prayer" (προσευχή) in Matthew occurs only in 21:13 and 21:22 enhances this connection.

42. "The accent here is on both 'everything' (first for emphasis) and the dynamic present tense 'believing' . . . So here believing once again means a total dependence on God and union with his will and purposes. It is not a formula for getting what we want but a God-centeredness for wanting what he wants" (Osborne, *Matthew*, 771).

of laudatory worship in the temple (21:14-15). The answers to their questions can be readily supplied by the audience: Jesus is doing these things by the divine authority given to him by his heavenly Father (7:29; 9:6, 8). Jesus then reaffirmed his divine authority with his own question to them (21:24, 27), cleverly compelling them to admit their failure to repent and believe in John the Baptist based on his divine authority. If they admit to Jesus that John's authority was from heaven, they indict themselves for not believing him (21:25), and they cannot claim his authority was from humans as they fear the crowd, since all hold John as a prophet with divine authority (21:26).[43]

With a parable about a man, representative of God, who told his two sons to work in his vineyard Jesus accentuated the failure of the chief priests and the elders to repent (21:28-32). They were forced to admit that the first son, who at first refused but later repented, rather than the second, who at first agreed but never went, did the will of his father/God (21:31). They characterize the unrepentant second son. Even when they saw that tax collectors and prostitutes repented and believed in John, and so entered into the kingdom of heaven, they did not later, like the first son, repent and believe in him (21:32). In not doing the will of the father/God, the chief priests and the elders failed to repent and thus receive the mercy of God in contrast to the tax collectors (9:10) who repented and received divine mercy in accord with Jesus' pronouncement that God's will is mercy not sacrifice (9:13). They remind the audience of the need to participate in the ethical worship God desires not only by extending mercy to others but by repenting and receiving it themselves.[44]

Jesus then told the chief priests and the elders of the people (21:23) another parable in which a "householder," representative of God (cf. 20:1, 11), planted a vineyard, representative of Israel as the chosen people of God, put a fence around it, dug a wine press in it, and built a tower (cf. Isa 5:1-7).[45] He then leased it to "tenants" (γεωργοῖς), representative of the leaders of the people (LXX Joel 1:11), and went on a journey (Matt 21:33). When the proper time for the "fruits" (καρπῶν) drew near, he sent his "ser-

---

43. "The very question Jesus asks contains the answer to their two questions, for Jesus' ministry and authority are tied closely to that of John the Baptist" (Osborne, *Matthew*, 776).

44. "The lesson of this passage is that today's disciples must not assume the permanence of either their own supposed righteous standing before God or the unrighteous status of notorious sinners" (Turner, *Matthew*, 510). "There is also for the audience the challenge and warning to continue to be among those who do the will of God" (Carter and Heil, *Matthew's Parables*, 159).

45. "As in Isa 5 the emphasis is on the incredible effort the man put into his vineyard to make it productive and viable" (Osborne, *Matthew*, 787).

vants" (δούλους), representative of the prophets (LXX Jer 25:4; Amos 3:7), to the tenants to receive its "fruits [καρπούς]" (Matt 21:34). This recalls and resonates with Jesus' cursing of the fig tree for its failure to produce "fruit [καρπός]" (21:19), symbolic of the temple's failure to produce the "fruit" of authentic worship by becoming God's "house of prayer" (21:13). In other words, the householder/God expected the tenants/leaders of the temple to give to his servants/prophets the "fruits" of the authentic worship of God that have been produced by their leadership of the people.[46]

But, receiving God's servants/prophets, the tenants/leaders beat one, killed one, and stoned another (21:35). When God sent other servants/ prophets, more than the first, they did the same to them (21:36). Finally, he sent his son, representative of Jesus as the Son of God (3:17; 11:27; 17:5), thinking they would respect his son (21:37). But when they saw the son, they threw him out of the vineyard and killed him in order to have his inheritance (21:38-39), prefiguring the fulfillment of Jesus' predictions that the Jewish leaders will be among those who kill him (16:21; 17:22-23; 20:18-19). When Jesus asked the Jewish leaders what the "Lord" of the vineyard will do to those tenants when he comes (21:40), they ironically condemned themselves by declaring that he will utterly destroy the evil men and lease the vineyard to other tenants/leaders who will give him the "fruits" of the authentic worship God desires at the proper times (21:41).

Jesus then asked the Jewish leaders if they have never read in the scriptures that the "stone" (representative of the Son of God, Jesus) the "builders" (οἰκοδομοῦντες) (representative of the Jewish leaders of the temple) rejected by killing him has become the cornerstone of a new place for authentic worship. This has been done by the Lord, who will raise Jesus from the dead, and "it is wonderful in our eyes" (21:42; cf. LXX Ps 117:22-23).[47] This indicates that through his death and resurrection Jesus will become the foundational cornerstone of the church, developing his assertion that "I will build [οἰκοδομήσω] my church" on the rock that is Peter, the leader of the disciples (16:18). Therefore the kingdom of God will be taken away from the Jewish leaders and given to a nation that will produce its "fruits" (21:43) of authentic worship, the church led by the disciples, as the community of

---

46. Note "the insistent repetition of the word 'fruit' (vv. 34 [bis], 41, 43) to describe the life which God requires of his people (3:8, 10; 7:16-20; 12:33; 13:8, 23, 26), and the lack of fruit has most recently in 21:18-20 symbolized the current failure of the temple regime" (France, *Matthew*, 810).

47. "The addition of this quotation thus points us beyond the death of Jesus to his resurrection, which is the amazing thing which the Lord will do. In that case the new 'nation' of v. 43 may be understood as the people who follow the risen Jesus" (France, *Matthew*, 811).

those who pray with faith in God (21:21-22). It will become the place for the true and authentic worship of God, God's "house of prayer" (21:13), that the Jewish temple failed to become.[48]

When the chief priests and the Pharisees heard Jesus' parables, they knew he was speaking about them (21:45).[49] They thus knew that they represented the second, unrepentant son in the parable of the two sons (21:28-32). And they knew that they represented the tenants who failed to produce the "fruits" of authentic worship and that they will be among those who will kill Jesus, God's Son, as indicated in the parable about the vineyard (21:33-43). Although they were seeking to arrest Jesus, they feared the crowds, who held him, as they did John the Baptist, to be a prophet (21:46; cf. 21:26). Indeed, after the crowds identified Jesus as a prophet (21:11), he prophetically cleansed the temple that failed to be God's house of true worship (21:12-13). He then healed the blind and the lame in the temple, which resulted in an act of true worship in the temple (21:14-16). After he cursed a fig tree for failing, like the temple, to produce the "fruit" symbolic of authentic worship, he taught his disciples the authentic worship of praying with faith (21:17-22), as members of the church whose "cornerstone" is the risen Jesus (21:42-43).

After the two previous parables to the Jewish leaders (21:28-32; 21:33-46) Jesus told them a third (22:1), beginning, "The kingdom of heaven is like a king" (cf. 18:23), who gave a wedding banquet for his son (22:2). Representative of God, like the householder with the vineyard in the previous parable (21:33), the king twice sent his servants, representative of the prophets (cf. 21:34. 36), to call those who have been invited to the banquet, but they did not come (22:3-4). Some ignored and went away (22:5), but the rest killed the servants (22:6), just as the tenants representative of the Jewish leaders killed the servants in the previous parable (21:35-36). Whereas in the previous parable the tenants predicted that the Lord would "destroy" the murderers and lease his vineyard to other tenants who will give him the fruits of authentic worship at the proper times (21:41), in this parable the king actually "destroyed" the murderers and burned their city (22:7). Since

---

48. "The parable is targeting the Jerusalem leadership, not the Jewish people as a whole. While 'the nation' to whom the kingdom will be given (v. 43) seems unmistakably to be the Church as the mixed community of Jewish and Gentile believers, the parable leaves open the relationship between the Christian Church and that part of Israel (the Jewish people) that did not come to faith in Jesus as Messiah" (Byrne, *Lifting the Burden*, 163).

49. Matt 21:44 is usually considered to be an accretion to the text, an early interpolation from Luke 20:18; see Metzger, *Textual Commentary*, 47.

those called were not worthy (22:8), the king then sent his servants to call whomever they find to the wedding banquet (22:9).

After the king/God sent his servants/prophets to call to the wedding banquet whomever they find (22:9), they gathered all they found, "bad and good" (22:10). This recalls the gracious inclusivity of God who causes the sun to rise on the "bad and good" (5:45). Jesus continued this inclusivity as he extended the mercy God desires to the bad, sinners, whom he called (9:13) to repent in order to enter into the kingdom of heaven (21:28-32). One of the invited "bad and good" was not clothed with a wedding garment (22:11-12), symbolic of the repentance expected of one receiving God's mercy, and so was thrown out of the wedding banquet (22:13).[50] The parable encourages the audience, as among the "many" (all) who are called to receive God's mercy and repent, to be among the "few" (ὀλίγοι) who prove that they are chosen (22:14), the "few" (ὀλίγοι) who find the difficult way to eternal life (7:14).[51] To enter the kingdom of heaven they are to clothe themselves with the "wedding garment" by doing the greater righteousness (5:20), producing the fruit worthy of repentance (3:8), that pleases God as ethical worship.[52]

The Pharisees then took counsel in order to entrap Jesus in speech (22:15) to implement the counsel they took to destroy him (cf. 12:14). They sent to him their own disciples along with the Herodians, Jewish supporters of the local Roman rulers.[53] They began to set their trap by deceitfully acknowledging what they really did not believe, namely, that Jesus is truthful and teaches the way of God in truth, not caring about the favor of anyone, for he does not take notice of the status of human beings (22:16).[54] With

---

50. "Even though this man belongs to the new group of invitees, he is one who produces no fruit, and so is no less liable to forfeit his new-found privilege than those who were excluded before him" (France, *Matthew*, 827).

51. Meyer, "Many," 89–97. "The chosen are the new tenants who will produce the fruit, who, as we have seen in the last parable, may be Jewish or Gentile; their chosenness does not depend on their racial origin but on their response to God's summons and their readiness to give God his due" (France, *Matthew*, 828).

52. "The man without a wedding garment represents all those who accepted the invitation but did not, within that calling, undergo the conversion of life required for entrance into the final kingdom.... they will be found lacking the 'wedding garment' of good works and suffer the exclusion described" (Byrne, *Lifting the Burden*, 165). The wedding garment symbolizes "the better righteousness and perfection which is demanded of all those who receive the call of God" (Charette, *Recompense*, 149).

53. "The name assures us that they were people attached to the Herods, and we are probably right in assuming that when many opposed that dynasty these people supported it" (Morris, *Matthew*, 555).

54. "The Pharisees don't believe a word of what they are saying, but they are unconsciously stating absolute truth" (Osborne, *Matthew*, 808).

this insincere address they enticed Jesus to give them his opinion regarding whether "it is lawful," that is, in accord with God's will, to give tax to Caesar, the Roman emperor, or not (22:17). Their malicious intention was to place Jesus in a dilemma. If he answered yes, he would discredit himself with the disciples of the Pharisees, as he would appear to be a sympathizer of the oppressive Roman regime the Jewish religious leaders opposed. But if he answered no, he would discredit himself with the Herodians, who could accuse him of political rebellion against the Roman regime.

Aware of their wickedness, Jesus began to unmask their trap as a testing of him by hypocrites (22:18). He demonstrated their hypocrisy when he asked them to show him the coin for the tax, a Roman denarius, thus revealing their complicity with the Roman regime (22:19).[55] When he asked whose "image" (εἰκών) and inscription was on the coin (22:20), they answered "Caesar's," prompting Jesus' powerful pronouncement: "Then give to Caesar what belongs to Caesar and to God what belongs to God!" (22:21). What belongs to God is every human being, made in the "image" (εἰκόνα) and likeness of God (LXX Gen 1:26–27). Furthermore, their possession of the coin, which bore the image of the emperor with the inscription, "Tiberius Caesar, son of the divine Augustus," associated them with idolatrous worship in violation of the divine law: "Do not act lawlessly and make for yourselves an engraved likeness, any image [εἰκόνα], a likeness of male or female" (LXX Deut 4:16).[56]

Jesus' dramatic and emphatic pronouncement to "give" (ἀπόδοτε) to Caesar what belongs to Caesar but to God what belongs to God (22:21) calls for the audience, as among the "other tenants who will give [ἀποδώσουσιν]" to the householder/God the "fruits" of authentic worship at the proper times (21:41), to give themselves entirely to God as part of the authentic worship God desires.[57] Like all human beings, they belong to God, since they were made in God's image and likeness (Gen 1:26–27). Jesus has indeed taught "the way of God in truth" (22:16).[58] To be God's "house of prayer" that the

---

55. "By calling for *them* to produce a coin with Caesar's image on it he shows his adversaries up as people who carry around the offensive coinage, while he does not" (Byrne, *Lifting the Burden*, 166; emphasis original).

56. See also Osborne, *Matthew*, 809.

57. "Jesus first agrees that it is right to pay the Roman head tax; we have a duty to Caesar. Yet he qualifies it carefully by hinting that the greater obligation is to God. The absence of the secular-sacred dichotomy in the ancient world means that Caesar's realm is actually part of God's realm" (Osborne, *Matthew*, 810). "The obligation to God covers all of life; we must serve Caesar in a way that is honoring to God" (Morris, *Matthew*, 558).

58. "Jesus does not support the Pharisees by opposing Caesar's tax, but neither does he support the Herodians by affirming total loyalty to Rome. Ironically, Jesus has

temple failed to be (21:13), the members of the audience are not only to pray with faith (21:21–22), but to give their own lives (rather than animal sacrifices; cf. 21:12) completely to God in a self-sacrificial way as the ethical worship that belongs to and pleases God.

On that day Sadducees, who with the Pharisees had previously tested Jesus (16:1, 6, 11, 12), now questioned him with regard to resurrection from the dead, which they firmly denied (22:23). They pointed out that, as Moses said in giving the law of the levirate marriage (Deut 25:5–6), if a man dies without having children, his brother is to marry his wife and "raise up" descendants for his brother (Matt 22:24).[59] They then presented Jesus with a case, probably theoretical, in which there were seven brothers among them. The first one married and died, and having no descendants, left his wife to his brother (22:25). The same happened successively with each of the remaining brothers (22:26), and finally the wife also died (22:27). With obvious ridicule regarding resurrection from the dead, they tried to stump Jesus when they asked him whose wife she will be in the resurrection, since all of the brothers had married her (22:28).[60]

Jesus replied to the Sadducees who attempted to ridicule resurrection from the dead (22:23–28) that they are led astray since they do not know the "scriptures" (γραφάς) or the power of God (22:29).[61] This recalls for the audience the previous reference to a quotation in the "scriptures [γραφαῖς]" (21:42), which alluded to the Lord God raising up Jesus, the "stone/son" that the "builders/leaders" rejected by killing him, to become the foundational cornerstone, through his death and resurrection, of a new temple/household to be God's "house of prayer" (21:13) for authentic worship. Jesus then rendered their ridicule of resurrection from the dead based on the practice of levirate marriage ridiculously irrelevant, since in the resurrection people

---

truly taught the way of God despite the insincere flattery of his questioners" (Turner, *Matthew*, 529).

59. "Raise up" echoes "resurrection" and indicates that "the production of an heir is the only sort of 'resurrection' of the dead brother that their theology allows" (France, *Matthew*, 838).

60. "Accepting only the Five Books of Moses (the Pentateuch) as authentic Scripture and finding in them no trace of life after death, they refused to believe in any kind of human immortality save the continuance of an individual's name in the family line. Hence, from the Torah's prescription requiring a man to raise up offspring for a brother who has died (Deut 25:5–6; cf. Gen 38:8) they have conjured up a quibble (vv. 24–28) that seems to make belief in life after death ridiculous" (Byrne, *Lifting the Burden*, 166).

61. "Their ignorance of 'the power of God' refers to their denial of his ability to raise the dead, indeed, to prepare a final harvest of eschatological blessing for his people in heaven" (Osborne, *Matthew*, 817).

neither marry nor are given in marriage, but are like angels in heaven (22:30).[62]

Jesus then asked the Sadducees ridiculing resurrection from the dead (22:23-28) whether they have not read what was spoken to them by God himself (22:31) in the Pentateuch, the only part of scripture they accept as normative: "I am the God of Abraham and the God of Isaac and the God of Jacob [Exod 3:6]" (Matt 22:32a).[63] If God still identifies himself as the God of the patriarchs Abraham, Isaac, and Jacob, who had died long before God made this pronouncement, then this means that God will surely raise them from the dead to heavenly life. Jesus then concluded that "he is not the God of the dead but of the living!" (22:32b).[64] He is the God of those living now and those who will live after being raised from the dead. That he is not the God of the dead reinforces that the sacrifices of dead animals are not the authentic worship God wanted in the temple as God's "house of prayer" (21:13). Authentic worship is giving to God what belongs to God (22:21)—the living human being, and worshiping the God who will raise believers to eternal life, just as he will raise the patriarchs after raising Jesus from the dead.

Hearing Jesus' powerful pronouncement that God is not the God of the dead but of the living (22:32), "the crowds were astonished at his teaching" (22:33). This recalls that when Jesus finished his sermon on the mount, "the crowds were astonished at his teaching" (7:28), for he taught them not as their scribes but as one having divine authority (7:29). This means having the divine authority not only to teach authentic worship but to be an object of worship. After the crowds worshiped Jesus as the messianic Son of David at his entrance into Jerusalem (21:9), he was identified by the crowds as the prophet from Nazareth of Galilee (21:11). As a prophet revered by the crowds (21:46), Jesus taught the authentic worship of praying with faith (21:21-22) instead of sacrificing dead animals (21:12-13), of giving to God

---

62. "Since no one dies any more (being in this respect 'like the angels in heaven') there is no longer any need for procreation, and hence no need for marriage, the institution designed to supply it" (Byrne, *Lifting the Burden*, 166).

63. "By introducing Exod 3:6 with 'what was spoken . . . by God' (cf. 1:22; 2:15), Jesus emphasizes the divine inspiration behind the passage, thus a double indictment (ignorance of God as well as Scripture). In v. 24 they asserted 'Moses said,' so now Jesus trumps that by saying, 'in actuality God said'" (Osborne, *Matthew*, 817-18).

64. "This description—'I *am*,' not 'I was'—implies an ongoing divine relationship with the three and hence their continuing personal existence. The relationship God seeks to forge with human beings here and now is one that transcends death" (Byrne, *Lifting the Burden*, 167; emphasis original). "Those with whom the living God identifies himself cannot be truly dead, and therefore they must be alive with him after their earthly life is finished" (France, *Matthew*, 840-41).

what belongs to God (22:21)—one's entire life as a living human being, and of worshiping the God of the living (22:32) who raises the dead to eternal life in the kingdom of heaven.

After Jesus silenced the Sadducees, the Pharisees gathered together (22:34) for another attempt to implement their plan to entrap Jesus in speech (22:15) to destroy him (12:14). One of them, an expert in the Mosaic law, to test him (cf. 16:1; 19:3) asked him which commandment in the law is the greatest (22:35–36). He thus challenged Jesus to name a single commandment that embraces and sums up all the others.[65] Jesus quoted the scriptural basis for the Shema prayer used commonly in Jewish liturgical worship: "You shall love the Lord your God with all your heart and with all your soul and with all your mind [Deut 6:5]" (Matt 22:37).[66] This resonates with the importance of a whole-hearted, interior commitment required for the authentic worship of God (15:9), as indicated by a previous quotation by Jesus: "This people honors me with their lips, but their heart is far away from me [Isa 29:13]" (Matt 15:8). This first and greatest commandment (22:38) thus reinforces and develops the need to give to God what belongs to the God of the living (22:21, 32)—the entire, living human being—by loving God whole-heartedly.

But to the first and greatest commandment to love God whole-heartedly (22:37–38), Jesus added a second like it: "You shall love your neighbor as yourself [Lev 19:18]" (Matt 22:39; cf. 19:19).[67] Thus, not on just one, but on the combination of these two commandments the whole law and the prophets "hangs" (22:40), that is, is summed up and embraced by them.[68] This develops Jesus' previous pronouncement that doing to others what you want them to do to you, which amounts to loving them as yourself, is the law and the prophets (7:12) by adding the commandment to love God whole-heartedly. But Jesus already extended the commandment to love your neighbor to include loving your enemy and thus be "perfect," completely inclusive in loving all human beings, like the heavenly Father (5:43–48).

---

65. "Any answer must risk pleasing some at the expense of alienating others, and therein perhaps is the element of 'test' from an unsympathetic dialogue partner, particularly in view of the suspicion already noted in 5:17 that Jesus had come to 'abolish' the law" (France, *Matthew*, 842).

66. "The Shema was recited every morning and evening and summed up Jewish faith and practice" (Osborne, *Matthew*, 822–23).

67. "It is 'like' Deut 6:5 not only in that it is equally important, but also in the formal sense that it uses the same verbal form, 'you are to love,' and more fundamentally in that it equally insists that one's religious duty is focused outside oneself. It might be possible to think even of love for God as a self-centered spiritual experience, but love for one's neighbor is inescapably practical and altruistic" (France, *Matthew*, 846).

68. Donaldson, "Law That Hangs," 689–709.

For the audience to become God's household of authentic worship that the Jerusalem temple failed to be (21:13) they are not only to pray to God with faith (21:21-22) and confess their whole-hearted love of God in liturgical worship, but also to practice the ethical worship of loving all of their fellow human beings.[69]

After the Pharisees had gathered together to test Jesus with a question (22:34-35), while they were still gathered together, Jesus questioned them (22:41) as to their opinion on whose son is the Christ, to which they replied, "David's" (22:42). He then asked how then does David by the Spirit call him "Lord," when he says (22:43), "The Lord said to my Lord, 'Sit at my right, until I place your enemies under your feet'" [Ps 110:1]? (Matt 22:44).[70] If David calls the Christ "Lord," how can the Christ be the Son of David? (22:45).[71] No one was able to answer him a word, and from that day no one dared to question him any longer (22:46). The audience, however, may provide the answer that the Christ is not only the Son of David but David's divine Lord as the Son of God. Having taught the disciples and audience how to offer authentic worship to God (21:13, 21-22; 22:21, 32, 37-40), Jesus now reminds them that as the Christ he is a worthy object of worship himself not only as the messianic Son of David (9:27; 15:22; 20:30-31; 21:9, 15) but as the divine Son of God (14:33; 16:16; cf. 3:17; 11:27; 17:5).[72]

Jesus then spoke to the crowds and to his disciples (23:1) about the scribes and Pharisees as those who "sit on the chair of Moses" (23:2).[73] This means that they are in a position to control access to the Mosaic law, so that they know and can tell others what Moses said.[74] Therefore the

---

69. "Without erasing the distinction between them, Jesus reaches here for a radical unity in the two commandments. To love God with all one's heart and soul and mind (that is, with one's whole being and life-energy) is inseparable from an active love of those whom God loves in the way God loves them, that is, with a love that is compassionate and extends even to the hostile" (Byrne, *Lifting the Burden*, 168).

70. "So the quote establishes two things: the royal glory and power of the Messiah ('sit at my right hand') and the victory of the Messiah over his enemies (as demonstrated in Jesus' victory in the controversy narratives of 21:23-22:46)" (Osborne, *Matthew*, 829).

71. "The problem presupposes the conventional attribution of the Psalms to David and also the messianic understanding of the psalm in question" (Byrne, *Lifting the Burden*, 168).

72. "The inability of the Pharisees to reply leaves an answer hanging in the air: the Messiah is David's son, yes, but he must also be more than David's son. He must be, as we readers and the disciples know, the Son of *God*" (Byrne, *Lifting the Burden*, 168; emphasis original).

73. "The chair or seat of Moses may be a metaphor or may refer to such a seat in synagogues where authoritative teaching occurred" (Turner, *Matthew*, 546).

74. Powell, "What Moses Says," 419-35.

crowds and disciples are to do and observe whatever they tell them, but not act according to their works, for they do not practice what they speak about the Mosaic law (23:3), especially about how to properly worship God. They tie up heavy "burdens" (φορτία), hard to bear, and place them on the shoulders of people, but they are not willing to lift a finger to move them (23:4).[75] This recalls Jesus' invitation for all who labor and are "burdened" (πεφορτισμένοι) to come to him for rest (11:28), for his "burden" (φορτίον) is light (11:30). They are to learn from him (11:29) that God desires mercy not simply sacrifice (9:13; 12:7). Rather than going to the unmerciful scribes and Pharisees, they are to come to Jesus not only to receive divine mercy but to learn how to extend mercy to others as the ethical worship that pleases God.

The scribes and Pharisees do all their works "to be seen" (πρὸς τὸ θεαθῆναι) by people, for they widen their phylacteries, the small leather cases containing scripture verses that they wore on their arm and forehead while praying, and lengthen the tassels of their garments (23:5). They "love" (φιλοῦσιν) the place of honor at banquets and the seats of honor in the synagogues (23:6) and the greetings in the marketplaces and to be called by people "Rabbi" (23:7), an honorary title for outstanding teachers of the Mosaic law.[76] This recalls and resonates with how the hypocrites "love" (φιλοῦσιν) to pray while standing in the synagogues and on the street corners, so that they may be seen by people (6:5). But Jesus exhorted his followers not to perform their righteousness, works that are righteous in accord with God's will, and are thus intended to please God as acts of worship, "to be seen" (πρὸς τὸ θεαθῆναι) by people, otherwise they will have no reward from their Father in heaven (6:1). Such behavior may win honor from human beings, but it is not the proper way to worship God.

The followers of Jesus are not to be called "Rabbi," for they have one "teacher" (διδάσκαλος), and they are all brothers (23:8). Their one teacher is of course Jesus himself. When he was previously addressed by various Jewish leaders as "teacher [διδάσκαλε]" (22:16, 24, 36), he taught how to properly worship God. People are to give to the God of the living, not dead sacrificial animals (cf. 21:12-13), but themselves as living persons made in the image and likeness of God (22:21, 32). They are to complement their liturgical worship in which they confess their wholehearted love of the one God with their ethical worship of loving their neighbor as themselves

---

75. "The way these experts 'lay heavy burdens' on others is presumably through making and imposing interpretations of the Torah in which, contrary to the interpretation of Jesus, priority is not given to mercy or love as the supreme criterion of what God wants" (Byrne, *Lifting the Burden*, 171).

76. BDAG, 902.

(22:37-40). They are not to call anyone on earth their father, for their one Father is the heavenly one (23:9). This reaffirms Jesus' teaching to pray to "our Father in heaven" (6:9). Nor are they to be called "instructors," for their one instructor is "the Christ" (23:10), Jesus, who not only teaches proper worship, but who, as "the Christ" who is both the Son of David and the Son of God, is worthy to be properly worshiped (22:42-45).

In contrast to the scribes and Pharisees, who exalt themselves and seek to be served and honored as great ones by human beings (23:5-10), the greatest among the followers of Jesus will be their "servant [διάκονος]" (23:11), and whoever will exalt himself will be humbled by God, but whoever "will humble himself" (ταπεινώσει ἑαυτόν) will be exalted by God (23:12). This recalls Jesus' previous teaching that whoever "will humble himself" (ταπεινώσει ἑαυτόν) like a child is the greatest in the kingdom of heaven (18:4). And it recalls that whoever wishes to be great among his disciples will be their "servant [διάκονος]" (20:26). Jesus himself provides the model for this. As the Son of Man, he did not come "to be served" (διακονηθῆναι) but "to serve" (διακονῆσαι) and to give his life as a ransom for many (20:28), an act of self-sacrificial worship. Similarly, the followers of Jesus are to humble themselves, like Jesus who is "humble" (ταπεινός) in heart (11:29), and serve one another as an act of ethical self-sacrificial worship for which they will be exalted by God.

Jesus then directly addressed the scribes and Pharisees with a series of seven "woes" (23:13, 15, 16, 23, 25, 27, 29; cf. 11:21; 18:7), prophetic laments with a threat of divine condemnation.[77] They lock the kingdom of heaven before human beings and do not enter it themselves (23:13). Their converts are destined for eternal punishment twice as much as themselves (23:15).[78] As "blind guides," they abuse sacred items meant for the proper worship of God, as they make casuistic distinctions between swearing by the temple sanctuary or the gold of the sanctuary, by the altar or the gifts on the altar (23:16-20).[79] But all such swearing is ultimately swearing by, and thus offending rather than properly worshiping, God himself (23:21-22), since swearing invokes God to be the guarantor of the truthfulness of human dealings. This woe reaffirms Jesus' previous teaching against swear-

---

77. In the NT "woe" (οὐαί) "is an expression of both compassion and regret. We are not to understand it as a way of exulting over the fate of evildoers . . . at least in some places the word contains something of appeal. Surely they will turn from their evil way?" (Morris, *Matthew*, 578-79). See also Balz, "οὐαί," 540.

78. On Matt 23:14 as a later interpolation derived from Mark 12:40 or Luke 20:47, see Metzger, *Textual Commentary*, 50.

79. "Although the leaders view some oaths as binding and others as nonbinding, Jesus rejects this as empty casuistry" (Turner, *Matthew*, 555).

ing at all and replacing it with being truthful in all that one says or does (5:33–37). Such behavior will not only avoid abusive references to aspects of ritual worship, but serve as ethical worship pleasing to God.[80]

With the fourth woe Jesus accused the hypocritical scribes and Pharisees of tithing the smallest of herbs in accord with the law (Deut 14:22–29; Lev 27:30–33), in order to support the priests and Levites in charge of temple worship (Num 18:8–32), but neglecting the more important matters of the law, namely, justice and mercy and faithfulness (Matt 23:23). As "blind guides," they meticulously strain out a small unclean gnat to ritually cleanse a liquid yet ironically swallow a large unclean camel (23:24; cf. Lev 11:4, 41–44), a rhetorical exaggeration underlining their neglect of the more important matters. In neglecting "justice" (κρίσιν) they stand in contrast to Jesus as God's beloved servant, who will proclaim divine "justice" (κρίσιν) to the Gentiles (Matt 12:18) and bring divine "justice" (κρίσιν) to victory (12:20). Their neglect of "mercy" (ἔλεος) stands in noteworthy contrast to how Jesus has faithfully practiced it. It recalls and reaffirms God's desire for the practice of "mercy" (ἔλεος) to complement ritual, sacrificial worship as the ethical worship that pleases God (9:13; 12:7).[81]

With the fifth woe Jesus charged the hypocritical scribes and Pharisees with ritually cleansing the outside of cup and dish, but inwardly they themselves are morally unclean, full of greed and self-indulgence (23:25). A "blind Pharisee" should first cleanse the inside of the cup, so that the outside may also become ritually clean (23:26).[82] And with the sixth woe Jesus

---

80. "Of course, for followers of Jesus it is not necessary to swear an oath at all, and he has already made it clear that they are expected to tell the truth at all times without the necessity of an oath to enforce truth (5:33–37)" (Morris, *Matthew*, 582). "Since every oath by nature centers on God and is made in relation to God, there is no need to swear by anything, but instead a 'yes' is a 'yes' and a 'no' is a 'no' because all promises are made before the throne of God and will be judged by God" (Osborne, *Matthew*, 850).

81. "In view of the function of tithing to support the sacrificial system, we are not at all far here from the sentiment of Hos 6:6 ('What I want is mercy, not sacrifice'), cited twice earlier in the gospel (9:13; 12:7). The sense of mercy *before* (not in place of) ritual observance is of a piece with the priorities running through the six illustrative rulings in the Great Sermon (5:21–48, especially 5:23–24)" (Byrne, *Lifting the Burden*, 174; emphasis original). "Matthew at the end wants it to be quite clear that a prophet-like focus on issues of justice and mercy is not to be thought of as antithetical to even the minutiae of cultic practice" (Nolland, *Matthew*, 938).

82. "The contrast here between 'outside' and 'inside' is clearly concerned with more than the two physical surfaces of the vessel, for what Jesus says is on the 'inside' is not the sort of ritual uncleanness which washing was designed to remove but moral uncleanness—cf. the things which 'come out of the heart,' which 'make a person unclean' (15:18–19). So the inside (=contents) and outside of the vessel is being used as a metaphor for the inside and outside of the person, just as the inside and outside of the tomb will be in vv. 27–28" (France, *Matthew*, 874–75).

compared them to tombs whitewashed to warn people from inadvertently touching them and becoming ritually unclean (Num 19:11–22); they appear beautiful outwardly, but inwardly are full of the bones of the dead and every uncleanness (Matt 23:27). Similarly, the scribes and Pharisees outwardly appear to people to be righteous, but inwardly they are full of hypocrisy and the "lawlessness [ἀνομίας]" (23:28) that excludes one from the kingdom of heaven (7:23; 13:41). They may, however, cleanse themselves inwardly of the moral uncleanness of selfishness and lawlessness by altruistically and generously extending to others the mercy they neglect (23:23) but that God desires as the ethical worship the complements ritual worship (9:13; 12:7).[83]

With the seventh woe Jesus warned that the hypocritical scribes and Pharisees, despite building tombs for the prophets and adorning memorials for the righteous, are completing their ancestors' mission of murdering the prophets (23:29–32). Reiterating John the Baptist's derogatory address of them for their lack of repentance (3:7–8), Jesus called them a "brood of vipers" who will not be able to flee divine condemnation (23:33; cf. 12:34). Some of the prophets, wise men, and scribes Jesus will send, with whom the disciples may identify themselves (5:11–12; 7:24; 10:16; 13:52), they will kill, crucify, scourge in synagogues, and persecute (23:34; cf. 10:17, 23, 28). Consequently, as part of this evil and unfaithful generation (23:36), there will come upon them all the righteous blood shed on earth, from the blood of the righteous Abel to that of the prophet Zechariah, whom they murdered between the temple sanctuary and the altar (23:35).[84] They thus abused and desecrated sacred places intended for the proper worship of God.

Having been previously identified to the city of Jerusalem as the prophet from Nazareth of Galilee (21:10–11), Jesus addressed the people of the city with a prophetic lament: "Jerusalem, Jerusalem, who kill the prophets and stone those sent to her, how often I wanted to gather your children together, as a hen gathers her young under her wings, but you were

---

83. "The Pharisees were punctilious in observing the law as they understood it. But their concentration on the externals to the neglect of demands like justice and mercy and faithfulness meant that in the last resort they followed their own inclinations, not the law of God. They rejected the divine demands in the place where those demands were most significant, in the region of the heart. Because in their innermost being they refused to submit to the law of God, in the fullest sense of the term they were lawless" (Morris, Matthew, 585).

84. "The idea of 'blood coming upon you' is an OT idiom for responsibility and guilt for the death of others" (Osborne, Matthew, 856). "The final woe and its allusion to Zechariah (23:35; cf. 2 Chron. 24:21) assume that Jesus is the climactic prophet of God. Abel and Zechariah were the first and last martyrs of the Hebrew Bible, which ends not with Malachi but with 2 Chronicles" (Turner, Matthew, 558).

unwilling!" (23:37).[85] Consequently, "your house," the temple that failed to be God's "house" of prayer (21:13), will be left to them deserted (23:38).[86] When Jesus entered Jerusalem, the crowds worshiped him as the messianic Son of David with the words of a scriptural psalm: "Blessed is he who comes in the name of the Lord [LXX Ps 117:26]!" (Matt 21:9). But now Jesus solemnly promised that the people of Jerusalem will not see him again until he comes a final time at the end of the world to bring to completion the kingdom of heaven he inaugurated. Then they will worship him, triumphantly vindicated by being raised from the dead by the Lord God, with the very same words: "Blessed is he who comes in the name of the Lord!" (23:39).[87]

Worship in View of the Final Coming of Jesus (Matthew 24–25)

In accord with his prophetic pronouncement to Jerusalem that "your house will be left to you deserted" (23:38), Jesus left the temple (24:1). To his disciples, impressed with all the buildings they see in the temple, Jesus declared that there will not ever be left here a "stone" upon a "stone" which will not be thrown down (24:2). This stands in ironic contrast to Jesus' previous declaration to the chief priests and Pharisees that the "stone" (Jesus) which the builders (Jewish leaders) rejected has become the cornerstone of a new edifice for worship (Christian community), accomplished by the Lord God raising Jesus from the dead (21:42). Whereas the temple with its ritual sacrifices of dead animals failed to be God's house of prayer (21:12–13), Jesus taught his followers to pray with faith (21:22) and give themselves entirely to the living God (22:21, 32). They are to complement their liturgical worship of loving God with their ethical worship of loving their neighbor

---

85. "The imagery of the protective wings of a mother bird is applied to God in the OT and Jewish tradition. On the lips of Jesus its use involves a claim to be in a position to act in the place of God" (Nolland, *Matthew*, 950–51).

86. "This connotes both abandonment by God (Ezek 8:6; 11:23) and destruction" (Osborne, *Matthew*, 863). "[T]here is a sad irony in that what was described in 21:13 as God's house is now '*your* house,' and it has been left 'to you' because God has abandoned it, as Jesus himself is about to do in 24:1" (France, *Matthew*, 883–84; emphasis original).

87. "Throughout the long indictment Jesus has spoken in the denunciatory tones of the prophets of Israel. The prophets denounced Israel's unfaithfulness, indicated the punishment it would endure as a result, and pointed to a restoration to come because of the saving faithfulness of God. Within such a tradition even the woes, for all the sharpness of their expression, can be understood as warnings rather than condemnations" (Byrne, *Lifting the Burden*, 176).

(22:36-40), as with Jesus, an object of worship as the messianic Son of God (22:45), "something greater than the temple is here" (12:6).[88]

The disciples then approached Jesus as he was sitting on the Mount of Olives and asked him what will be the sign of his final coming and of the end of the age (24:3). Jesus warned them not to let anyone mislead them (24:4). For many will come in his name, saying, "I am the Christ," and they will mislead many (24:5). If anyone says to them, "Here is the Christ," they are not to believe it (24:23). False Christs and false prophets will arise and give great signs and wonders to mislead, if possible, even the elect (24:24). But the sign of the coming of the true Christ as the Son of Man at the end of the age will be readily apparent to everyone (24:27-30). In the meantime, while they are awaiting the final coming of Jesus, there is a sense in which the Christ is still with them. If two or three of them agree on earth about any matter for which they ask, it will be granted to them by Jesus' Father in heaven (18:19). For where two or three are gathered together in the name of Jesus, and thus within a context of communal prayer, "there am I in the midst of them" (18:20).

Jesus also warned his disciples that before his final coming many false prophets will arise and will mislead many (24:11), and because lawlessness will be increased, the love of many will grow cold (24:12). But the one who perseveres to the end will be saved (24:13; cf. 10:22). This encourages the audience, as they await the final coming of Jesus, to persevere in their wholehearted love of God that they profess in their liturgical worship (22:37), which is to be complemented by their love of their neighbor as themselves (22:39), ethical worship pleasing to God. Loving their neighbor includes loving even their enemies (5:43-44), and extending to them the mercy God desires as the ethical worship that complements ritualistic, sacrificial worship (9:13; 12:7).[89]

In the parable of the wise and foolish maidens (25:1-13), after the bridegroom arrived, characterizing the final coming of Jesus (cf. 9:15), the

---

88. "Now, having entered the temple dramatically and controversially in 21:12-16, he leaves it with an equally emphatic and more far-reaching statement about its future. He is abandoning it, never to return, and after that it has no future except to be destroyed. What has been hitherto the earthly focus of the presence of God among his people is so no longer. There is a direct sequence from 23:38: the 'house' which is now being left deserted (by God and by Jesus) is ripe for demolition, to make way for 'something greater than the temple' (12:6)" (France, *Matthew*, 886).

89. "'Lawlessness' refers, presumably, to failure to keep the Torah in the sense of its interpretation by Jesus in which 'justice, mercy, and faith' are the determining or 'weightier' matters (23:23) and the 'greatest commandment' is the double commandment of love (22:34-40). It is not surprising, then, that lawlessness should lead to a cooling of love" (Byrne, *Lifting the Burden*, 183).

wise maidens, who were ready, entered the wedding feast with him, symbolic of entering the kingdom of heaven, and then the door was locked (25:10). Later the foolish maidens came and said, "Lord, Lord, open for us!" (25:11). But replying he said, "Amen I say to you, I do not know you!" (25:12). This recalls Jesus' previous warning that not everyone who says to him, "Lord, Lord," will enter the kingdom of heaven, only the one who does the will of his Father in heaven (7:21; cf. 12:50). Despite the claims of all that they did in his name (7:22), he will declare to them, "I never knew you!" (7:23). The parable thus exhorts the audience to be ready for the unknown time of Jesus' final coming (25:13) by doing the will of God, so that they, like the wise maidens, may enter into the kingdom of heaven. The "will" (θέλημα) of God includes especially extending to others the mercy that "I [God] will" (θέλω) as the ethical worship that complements ritualistic worship (9:13; 12:7).[90]

In the parable of the talents (25:14–30) the servant who received five talents and the one who received two talents gained another five talents and another two talents respectively (25:16–17).[91] This resonates with how the disciples, as "sowers" who are to "sow" the word of the gospel, can expect to yield a remarkably abundant harvest of people for the kingdom of heaven (13:8, 23). The servant who received one talent hid it in the ground (25:18, 25), although he knew that his lord "reaps where he does not sow and gathers where he does not scatter" (25:24, 26). The Lord Jesus "reaps" a harvest where he does not "sow" the seed and "gathers" (3:12; 13:30) a harvest where he does not "scatter" the seed, because he has entrusted his disciples with his ministry of "scattering" and "sowing" (13:3) the seed, the word of the gospel, that God will cause to produce an abundant harvest of people for the kingdom of heaven (13:3–8, 18–23). They are his workers who are to gather for him the "harvest" of people (9:37–38) with the healing and preaching authority he gave them (10:1, 7–8).

Jesus previously explained that the disciples, but not the crowds, have been given by God to know the mysteries of the kingdom of heaven as they are expressed in the parables discourse (13:11). He then promised that whoever has this knowledge, "it will be given to him and he will abound," but whoever does not have it, "even what he has will be taken from him" (13:12). This promise is now confirmed and developed. The one talent has been taken away from the servant because he did not risk working with it to experience the mystery of God causing him to produce abundantly. For to everyone who has, that is, the servant who has taken the risk to double

---

90. For a more detailed discussion of Matt 25:1–13, see Carter and Heil, *Matthew's Parables*, 193–96.

91. A "talent" (τάλαντον) was a unit of coinage of considerable value; see BDAG, 988.

his talents, "it will be given and he will abound," but the one servant who does not have, "even what he has will be taken from him" (25:29). For the audience to be ready for the unknown day and hour of Jesus' final coming (25:13), they must creatively use whatever talents they have been given by God to gain people for the kingdom of heaven. This is ethical worship pleasing to God, as it assures their entrance into "the joy of your Lord" (25:21, 23).[92]

The climactic parable of universal judgment (25:31-46) urges the audience to be ready for the unknown time of Jesus' final coming (25:13) by attending to the provocative way that Jesus is still with them in the "least brothers" with whom he identifies himself (25:40, 45). The members of the audience are urged to become the righteous "sheep" rather than "goats" (25:31-33) by extending to Jesus' needy least brothers the mercy God desires (9:13; 12:7) as ethical worship. This includes such compassionate practices as feeding the hungry, giving drink to the thirsty, welcoming strangers, clothing the naked, caring for the sick, and visiting prisoners (25:35-40). Furthermore, these practices are not merely optional but absolutely necessary, as indicated by the condemnation of the "goats" for not doing them (25:41-46). Loving Jesus, who is "God with us" (1:23), in his least brothers serves as ethical worship pleasing to God, as confirmed when Jesus told the righteous "sheep": "Come, you who are blessed by my Father, inherit the kingdom prepared for you from the foundation of the world" (25:34; cf. 5:20).[93]

But the audience may find themselves in the situation of being needy "least brothers" of Jesus, as disciples, "these little ones" (10:42; 18:6, 10, 14), who humble themselves like a child, believe in Jesus, and do the will of his Father as "brothers" in the true family of Jesus (12:49-50). In their mission

---

92. "Some, through fear, may think they can get by simply by avoiding wrongdoing and giving back to God what they have received on a basis of strict justice (cf. the third slave). But those who appreciate God as Jesus reveals God to be have the freedom to live in the creative and adventurous way that is truly appropriate (cf. the first two). They seek to carry out 'what God wants': an enterprising, even risk-taking practice of the 'weightier matters of the Torah: justice, mercy and faith' (23:23). Hence they stand to receive at the judgment the invitation 'Enter into the joy of your master' (vv. 21, 23)" (Byrne, *Lifting the Burden*, 191-92). For a more detailed discussion of Matt 25:14-30, see Carter and Heil, *Matthew's Parables*, 196-200.

93. "In this self-identification, spanning the 'distance' between the divine and 'the least' of the human, Jesus' two-part response to the question about which commandment of the Torah is the 'greatest' (22:34-40) acquires new depth. In loving and serving one's neighbor in the way described here one is actually loving and serving Christ, and in loving and serving Christ one is loving and serving 'God with us.' The two commandments making up the 'greatest commandment of the Torah' come together on this christological base" (Byrne, *Lifting the Burden*, 193).

as disciples they may be in need of food or drink (10:9, 42), strangers seeking to be hospitably welcomed into the homes of others (10:11-13), in need of clothing (10:10), and sick or imprisoned because of the expected hardship and possibility of being persecuted during their mission (10:16-23). They may take the risk of becoming Jesus' "least brothers," however, since they can be assured that there will be righteous "sheep" who will take care of them and be rewarded with entrance into the kingdom of heaven for doing so (25:34). They are to be encouraged, then, that becoming needy "least ones" and enduring such hardships as disciples amounts to ethical worship pleasing to God, since Jesus, "God with us" (1:23), identifies himself with "these least brothers of mine" (25:40, 45).[94]

Summary on Matthew 19-25

Testing Jesus, the Pharisees asked if "it is permitted," that is, in accord with God's will/law and thus pleasing to God as ethical worship, for a man to divorce his wife for any cause (19:3). Jesus replied that although Moses allowed divorce (19:7) because of "hardness of heart," that is, sinful resistance to God, this was not God's will from the beginning (19:8). Jesus then issued the warning that whoever divorces his wife, except for "sexual immorality," and marries another commits adultery (19:9; cf. 5:31-32). This reinforces the teaching that for a man to remain married to his wife for life, so that they continue to be one flesh in accord with God's plan from the beginning of creation, constitutes ethical worship pleasing to God.

Jesus pointed out that not all can accept that it is better not to marry, but only those to whom "it has been given" by God (19:10-11). Some, in what amounts to an act of ethical self-sacrificial worship, have made themselves eunuchs for the sake of the kingdom of heaven (19:12). Thus, in addition to the self-sacrifice involved in forgoing divorce in favor of lifelong faithfulness in marriage (19:3-9), celibacy for the sake of the kingdom of heaven is another way to offer ethical self-sacrificial worship pleasing to God.

Children were brought to Jesus for him to lay his hands on them and pray, but the disciples rebuked them. Jesus, however, placed his hands on them, presumably praying for them in answer to the supplicatory gesture that he do so (19:13). Jesus not only reaffirmed his appeal that "unless you become like children, you will not enter into the kingdom of heaven" (18:3), but presents the audience with a model of praying for children as those in

---

94. For a more detailed discussion of Matt 25:31-46, see Carter and Heil, *Matthew's Parables*, 200-8; Heil, "Double Meaning," 3-14.

need of and worthy of God's blessing and thus of participation in communal worship.

A rich young man could not sell his many possessions (19:22) and give to the poor in order to have "treasure in heaven" (19:21) and life eternal (19:16). This reinforces Jesus' exhortation to store up "treasures in heaven" (6:20), "for where your treasure is, there will be also your heart" (6:21), the "heart" that is central to the authentic worship of God rather than money (15:8; 6:24). The failure of the rich young man to follow Jesus by worshiping with his heart God rather than riches serves as a negative example for the audience. It calls them to go beyond loving their neighbor and to be "complete" like God (5:48) by loving not only their enemies (5:43–47) but also the poor (19:21). They are to perform the ethical self-sacrificial worship of giving to the poor as an act of the compassionate mercy that the good and generous God desires (9:13; 12:7; 19:17). Such self-sacrificial worship is thus part of taking up one's cross, denying oneself, and following Jesus in order to save one's life (10:38–39; 16:24–25) and enter into life eternal/the kingdom of heaven.

In the parable of the workers in the vineyard (20:1–16), those hired first, who thought they would receive more than those hired last, were worshiping money rather than the just, merciful, and generous God. In the kingdom of heaven "the last will be first, and the first last" (20:16; cf. 19:30), no matter when or how much one did to enter it. The parable calls for the audience to appreciate and celebrate God's merciful generosity to all who enter the kingdom of heaven. They will thereby be properly worshiping the generous God who graciously extends to them and others the mercy he desires (9:13; 12:7).

The other ten disciples were indignant that the sons of Zebedee wanted the first places of preeminence (20:24). Jesus told them that unlike the Gentiles whose great ones exercise authority over the others (20:25), whoever among his disciples wants to be great will be their servant (20:26), and whoever wants to be "first" among them will be their slave (20:27). Jesus did not come to be served but to serve and "to give his life as a ransom for many" (20:28), an act of ethical self-sacrificial worship. This reinforces Jesus' previous exhortations that whoever "loses his life" for the sake of Jesus in ethical self-sacrificial worship will find it (10:39; 16:25).

In contrast to the unsympathetic crowd who wanted to silence the two blind men (20:30–31), Jesus had compassion on them in answer to their double prayer for mercy. He touched their eyes, and immediately they received their sight and "followed" him (20:34), thus joining the crowd who "followed" him (20:29), to his suffering, death, and resurrection in Jerusalem (20:17–19). In contrast to the inappropriate prayer of the mother for her two sons (20:20–23), the appropriate, intensified prayer of the two blind men presents the audience with a model for how they are to pray to Jesus for the insight to be able to "see" and properly "follow" him by imitating his ethical self-sacrificial worship (20:28).

The two disciples (21:1) who procured the animals as Jesus had ordered (21:6) for his entrance into Jerusalem performed a worshipful gesture of homage and honor when they placed their cloaks on the donkey and on the colt for Jesus to sit upon (21:7). The very large crowd added to this worshipful gesture as they spread their own cloaks on the road, while others contributed to it as they cut branches from the trees and spread them on the road (21:8). The crowds preceding him and those following then performed an act of laudatory worship, as they were crying out with praise, "Hosanna to the Son of David! Blessed is he who comes in the name of the Lord! Hosanna in the highest heights!" (21:9).

After being identified as a "prophet" (21:11), Jesus performed a dramatic prophetic gesture when he entered the temple and drove out all those selling and buying animals for sacrificial worship, and he overturned the tables of the moneychangers and the chairs of those selling doves (21:12). In accord with his prophetic role he declared to them the scriptural word of God: "My house will be called a house of prayer, but you are making it a den of robbers" (21:13). "My house," that is, God's temple, was intended by God to be known as a "house of prayer," that is, a place for true worship. But those engaged in the commercial business of the temple's sacrificial system were robbing the people not only by taking their money, but by promoting sacrificial rituals that have become inadequate and incomplete for proper worship of God. "Something greater than the temple is here" (12:6) with Jesus, who taught that God desires mercy and not simply sacrifice (9:13; 12:7).

The indignant chief priests and scribes (21:15) asked Jesus if he heard the act of laudatory worship with which the boys were addressing him in the temple and he answered affirmatively (21:16a). He then asked them if they have never read in the scriptural word of God: "Out of the mouth of infants and nurslings you have prepared praise for yourself [Ps 8:3]" (Matt 21:16b). This recalls Jesus' praise of his heavenly Father for having hidden from the wise and intelligent what he has revealed to "infants," the childlike (11:25). By means of this scriptural reference Jesus has thus indicated that in praising him in the temple the boys represent the "infants" from whose mouths God has prepared praise for himself. By their act of laudatory worship of Jesus in the temple the boys are actually praising God and thus present the audience with a model of the authentic worship God desires to take place in the temple as God's "house of prayer" (21:13).

When Jesus was returning to Jerusalem in the morning after spending the night in Bethany (21:17), he was hungry (21:18). Seeing a fig tree on the way, he found nothing on it except leaves, so he said to it, "Never again will there be fruit from you!" And immediately the fig tree withered (21:19). This characterized how Jesus cleansed the temple of its commercial business when he found no "fruit," that is, no authentic worship of God in it (21:12–13). Jesus then told his disciples, "Everything, whatever you ask for in prayer, believing, you will receive" (21:22). By praying with faith in God, the audience, as a community of believers, can become God's "house of prayer" that the Jerusalem temple failed to become.

That whatever "you ask for" in prayer while believing, "you will receive" (21:22) develops Jesus' pronouncement that if two of his followers agree on earth about anything for which "they ask, it will be done" for them by Jesus' Father in heaven (18:19), just as if they pray for something with faith, "it will be done" (21:21). Jesus told the Gentile centurion who prayed for his servant's healing with faith not found in Israel (8:10) that "as you have believed, let it be done for you" (8:13). Two blind men answered yes when Jesus asked if they believed that he can heal them (9:28). He then told them, "According to your faith let it be done for you" (9:29). To the Canaanite woman who prayed for Jesus to heal her daughter (15:22), Jesus said, "Great is your faith! Let it be done for you as you wish" (15:28). These are models that encourage the audience to pray with faith (21:21), for "*everything*, whatever you ask for in prayer, *believing*, you will receive" (21:22).

Jesus asked the Jewish leaders if they have never read in the scriptures that the "stone," representative of the Son of God, Jesus, that the "builders," representative of the Jewish leaders of the temple, rejected by killing him has become the cornerstone of a new place for authentic worship. This has been done by the Lord, who will raise Jesus from the dead, and "it is wonderful in our eyes" (21:42). This indicates that through his death and resurrection Jesus will become the foundational cornerstone of the church, developing his assertion that "I will build my church" on the rock that is Peter, the leader of the disciples (16:18). Therefore the kingdom of God will be taken away from the Jewish leaders and given to a nation that will produce its "fruits" (21:43) of authentic worship, the church led by the disciples, as the community of those who pray with faith in God (21:21–22). It will become the place for the true worship of God, God's "house of prayer" (21:13), that the Jewish temple failed to become.

In the parable of the wedding banquet (22:1–14) one of the invited was not clothed with a wedding garment (22:11–12), symbolic of the repentance expected of one receiving God's mercy, and so was thrown out (22:13). The parable encourages the audience, as among the "many" (all) who are called to receive God's mercy and repent, to be among the "few" who prove that they are chosen (22:14), the "few" who find the difficult way to eternal life (7:14). To enter the kingdom of heaven they are to clothe themselves with the "wedding garment" by doing the greater righteousness (5:20), producing the fruit worthy of repentance (3:8), that pleases God as ethical worship.

Jesus' pronouncement to give to Caesar what belongs to Caesar but to God what belongs to God (22:21) calls for the audience to give themselves entirely to God as part of the authentic worship God desires. Like all human beings, they belong to God, since they were made in God's image and likeness. To be God's "house of prayer" that the temple failed to be (21:13), the members of the audience are not only to pray with faith (21:21-22), but to give their own lives (rather than animal sacrifices; cf. 21:12) completely to God in a self-sacrificial way as the ethical worship that belongs to and pleases God.

Hearing Jesus' pronouncement that God is not the God of the dead but of the living (22:32), "the crowds were astonished at his teaching" (22:33). This recalls that when Jesus finished his sermon on the mount, "the crowds were astonished at his teaching" (7:28), for he taught them not as their scribes but as one having divine authority (7:29). This means having the authority not only to teach authentic worship but to be an object of worship. After the crowds worshiped Jesus as the messianic Son of David at his entrance into Jerusalem (21:9), he was identified by the crowds as the prophet from Nazareth of Galilee (21:11). As a prophet revered by the crowds (21:46), Jesus taught the authentic worship of praying with faith (21:21-22) instead of sacrificing dead animals (21:12-13), of giving to God what belongs to God (22:21)—one's entire life as a living human being, and of worshiping the God of the living (22:32) who raises the dead to eternal life in the kingdom of heaven.

To the first and greatest commandment to love God whole-heartedly (22:37-38), Jesus added a second: "You shall love your neighbor as yourself" (22:39; cf. 19:19). Thus, not on just one, but on the combination of these two commandments the whole law and the prophets is summed up and embraced (22:40). But Jesus already extended the commandment to love your neighbor to include loving your enemy and thus be "perfect," completely inclusive in loving all human beings, like the heavenly Father (5:43-48). For the audience to become God's household of authentic worship that the Jerusalem temple failed to be (21:13) they are not only to pray to God with faith (21:21-22) and confess their whole-hearted love of God in liturgical worship, but also to practice the ethical worship of loving all of their fellow human beings.

Jesus spoke to the crowds and to his disciples (23:1) about the scribes and Pharisees as those who "sit on the chair of Moses" (23:2). Therefore they are to do and observe whatever they tell them, but not act according to their works, for they do not practice what they speak about the Mosaic law (23:3), especially about how to properly worship God. They tie up heavy "burdens" and place them on the shoulders of people, but they are not willing to lift a finger to move them (23:4). This recalls Jesus' invitation for all who labor and are "burdened" to come to him for rest (11:28), for his "burden" is light (11:30). They are to learn from him (11:29) that God desires mercy not simply sacrifice (9:13; 12:7). They are to come to Jesus not only to receive divine mercy but to learn how to extend mercy to others as the ethical worship that pleases God.

The parable of the wise and foolish maidens (25:1–13) exhorts the audience to be ready for the unknown time of Jesus' final coming (25:13) by doing the will of God that the foolish maidens failed to do (25:11; cf. 7:21). Then they, like the wise maidens, may enter into the kingdom of heaven. The "will" of God includes especially extending to others the mercy that "I [God] will" as the ethical worship that complements ritualistic worship (9:13; 12:7).

In the parable of the talents (25:14–30) the one talent was taken away from the servant because he did not risk working with it to experience the mystery of God causing him to produce abundantly. For to everyone who has, that is, the servant who has taken the risk to double his talents, "it will be given and he will abound," but the one servant who does not have, "even what he has will be taken from him" (25:29; cf. 13:12). For the audience to be ready for the unknown day and hour of Jesus' final coming (25:13), they must creatively use whatever talents they have been given by God to gain people for the kingdom of heaven. This is ethical worship pleasing to God, as it assures their entrance into "the joy of your Lord" (25:21, 23).

The climactic parable of universal judgment (25:31–46) urges the audience to be ready for the unknown time of Jesus' final coming (25:13) by attending to the provocative way that Jesus is still with them in the "least brothers" with whom he identifies himself (25:40, 45). The members of the audience are urged to become the righteous "sheep" (25:31–33) by extending to Jesus' needy least brothers the mercy God desires (9:13; 12:7) as ethical worship. This includes such compassionate practices as feeding the hungry, giving drink to the thirsty, welcoming strangers, clothing the naked, caring for the sick, and visiting prisoners (25:35–40). Furthermore, these practices are not merely optional but absolutely necessary, as indicated by the condemnation of the "goats" for not doing them (25:41–46). Loving Jesus, who is "God with us" (1:23), in his least brothers serves as ethical worship pleasing to God, as confirmed when Jesus told the righteous "sheep": "Come, you who are blessed by my Father, inherit the kingdom prepared for you from the foundation of the world" (25:34; cf. 5:20).

But the audience may find themselves in the situation of being needy "least brothers" of Jesus, as disciples, "these little ones" (10:42; 18:6, 10, 14), who humble themselves like a child, believe in Jesus, and do the will of his Father as "brothers" in the true family of Jesus (12:49–50). In their mission as disciples they may be in need of food or drink (10:9, 42), strangers seeking to be hospitably welcomed into the homes of others (10:11–13), in need of clothing (10:10), and sick or imprisoned because of the expected hardship and possibility of being persecuted during their mission (10:16–23). They may take the risk of becoming Jesus' "least brothers," however, since they can be assured that there will be righteous "sheep" who will take care of them and be rewarded with entrance into the kingdom of heaven for doing so (25:34). They are to be encouraged, then, that becoming needy "least ones" and enduring such hardships as disciples amounts to ethical worship pleasing to God, since Jesus, "God with us" (1:23), identifies himself with "these least brothers of mine" (25:40, 45).

9

Worshiping the Risen King (Matthew 26–28)

Worship in Preparation for the Death of Jesus (Matt 26:1–56)

WHILE JESUS WAS RECLINING for a meal in the house of Simon the leper in Bethany (26:6), an anonymous woman performed a noteworthy act of devotional worship of Jesus as she poured costly perfumed ointment from an alabaster flask on his head (26:7).[1] To the disciples who objected to what they considered this "waste" (26:8), Jesus explained that she has performed a "good deed" (ἔργον καλόν) toward him (26:10). She thus serves as a model for the followers of Jesus, who are to perform the "good deeds" (καλὰ ἔργα) that inspire people to the doxological worship of glorifying the heavenly Father (5:16).[2]

Jesus explained that in pouring the perfumed ointment upon his body the anonymous woman did it to prepare him for burial (26:12). Her good deed enhances the worthiness of Jesus to be worshiped as the Son of Man who came not to be served but to serve and to give his life as a "ransom" or "redemption" (λύτρον) for many (20:28). His sacrificial death by crucifixion will occur appropriately during the feast of Passover (26:2), which celebrated how God "redeemed" (ἐλυτρώσω) his people in the exodus event (LXX Exod 15:13; cf. 6:6) through the blood of slaughtered lambs (12:1–13).[3]

---

1. "Matthew leaves her unnamed to center on her worshipful act" (Osborne, *Matthew*, 950).

2. "Matthew probably intends an echo of the 'good deeds' of 5:16 which draw others to glorify God" (Nolland, *Matthew*, 1054).

3. "'Passover' (τὸ πάσχα) appears only here [26:2] and in vv. 17–19 in Matthew, and its use here alongside the imminent crucifixion almost certainly enacts Jesus' coming

Just as the Passover was to be a perpetual "memorial" (μνημόσυνον) of this (12:14), so whenever the gospel is proclaimed what the woman has done in worshiping Jesus will be told in "memory" (μνημόσυνον) of her (Matt 26:13). Her good deed not only inspires the audience to glorify God (5:16) but to worship Jesus himself for the precious value of his self-sacrificial death by which the people of God are redeemed.[4]

The disciples objected to the "waste" (26:8) when the anonymous woman poured costly perfumed ointment on the head of Jesus (26:7), because "it could have been sold for much and given to the poor" (26:9). This recalls that indeed Jesus told the rich young man to sell his possessions and "give to the poor" in order to have treasure in heaven (19:21) and gain eternal life (19:16). But what the woman did was a good deed toward Jesus (26:10) while he was still present. Once he is no longer with them physically, they are to give to the poor who will always be with them (26:11; cf. Deut 15:11), just as the followers of Jesus will fast after he is taken away from them (Matt 9:15).[5] But the anonymous woman's act of worshiping Jesus while he is still present inspires the audience to worship Jesus ethically when he is no longer physically present by giving to the poor who will always be with them. In giving to the poor the audience will in effect be worshiping Jesus, "God with us" (1:23), because whatever they do to the "least brothers" of Jesus, they do to him (25:40, 45).[6]

In contrast to the unnamed disciples concerned with what could be "given" (δοθῆναι) to the poor (26:9), a named disciple, one of the Twelve, who was called Judas Iscariot, went to the chief priests (26:14), and asked them what they were willing to "give" (δοῦναι) him if he betrays Jesus to them (26:15; cf. 10:4). The anonymous woman unselfishly performed an act of devotional worship, a good deed toward "me" (ἐμέ), Jesus (26:10), the "me" (ἐμέ) who will not always be physically present (26:11). But Judas selfishly wants to know what they will give "me" (μοι) to betray Jesus (26:15). Whereas the woman expended her very valuable ointment to anoint Jesus

---

death as the paschal lamb" (Osborne, *Matthew*, 945).

4. "She has understood, as the disciples have not, that he is about to perform an infinitely costly 'service' for herself and all humankind. In the name of all who will benefit (the 'many' [20:28; 26:28]) she performs this costly gesture of gratitude and appreciation, one that is possible now but will not be when the community no longer has Jesus physically among them" (Byrne, *Lifting the Burden*, 203).

5. "Jesus's allusion to [Deut] 15:11 in Matt. 26:11 is a reminder of an ongoing responsibility, not a stoic comment about an inevitable situation" (Turner, *Matthew*, 620).

6. "Matthew excludes any thought that religious activity is being given priority here over care of one's neighbour with the recent presence of 25:31–46, with its 'inasmuch as you did it for [even] one of the least of these my brothers or sisters, you did for me'" (Nolland, *Matthew*, 1055).

for burial as an act of worship (26:12), Judas greedily accepted a mere thirty pieces of silver to betray his master to death (26:15), the same contemptuous amount paid as wages to a rejected prophet/shepherd (Zech 11:12), the paltry sum paid for a gored slave (Exod 21:32). Judas, then, exemplifies for the audience how one cannot serve and thus properly worship both God and money (Matt 6:24).[7]

It was already "the first day of the feast of Unleavened Bread" (26:17)—that is, the beginning of the weeklong celebration that coincided with the Passover and commemorated the hasty exit of Israel from Egypt, when they could take only unleavened bread (Exodus 12). Whereas Judas violated his discipleship by submitting himself to the chief priests with his selfish concern for what "you are willing" (θέλετέ) to give "me [μοι]" (Matt 26:15), the rest of the disciples remain in submission to their master with their concern for Jesus, as they ask him where "do you want" (θέλεις) us to prepare for "you" (σοι) to eat the Passover (26:17). This assures the audience that there are still obedient disciples who want to play their part in enabling the sacrificial death of their master, as an act of ethical self-sacrificial worship, to take place appropriately during Passover worship, as Jesus had predicted (26:2).

While the disciples and Jesus were eating the Passover meal, Jesus, as the host of the meal, performed the ritual worship of taking bread, blessing or thanking God for it, breaking it for distribution, and giving it to his disciples (26:26). In the ritual of the Passover meal the role of the host was to pronounce the traditional symbolic interpretations upon the various elements of the meal. This enabled the participants not only to commemorate but to actually share in and sacramentally relive the salvific experience of the original Passover meal, when God liberated his people from slavery in the exodus from Egypt and gave them the hope of future and final salvation.[8] In his last Passover meal with his disciples, Jesus, as their Teacher (26:18), Lord (26:22), and host, transformed the meaning of this meal for them as he placed a new symbolic interpretation upon the bread and wine.

---

7. "'What do you want to give me?' [26:15] is an oriental euphemism expressing somewhat delicately the demand for money" (Nolland, *Matthew*, 1059). "He [Judas] may have taken this action out of greed, since he asks how much the leaders will pay him (cf. Matt 6:19–21, 24)" (Turner, *Matthew*, 622).

8. "The meal itself was characterized by the same hope of eschatological salvation which the exodus came to signify for Judaism, looking to God's final intervention to redeem Israel. The meal then became liturgical, centering on the Father's Passover prayer and the recitation of the Hallel (Pss 113–18). There was the blessing of the festival and wine, then the ritual drinking of the wine and the partaking of the food, followed by the liturgical question-answer response on the significance of the event" (Osborne, *Matthew*, 963).

He thereby instituted the sacrament of the Eucharist, enabling the audience not only to commemorate but to relive the salvific experience of Jesus' last meal, which anticipated his self-sacrificial death.[9]

A particular focus of the Passover meal was the body of the lamb, which was to be eaten whole and entire (Exod 12:9) without any of its bones being broken (Exod 12:46; Num 9:12). After the body of the lamb was served at the Passover meal, Jesus directed the disciples to take and eat the bread he has blessed and broken for them, which he designated as the symbolic and sacramental equivalent of his body: "This is *my* body" (Matt 26:26).[10] The bread thus became the very "body" of Jesus, which "body" had already been anointed for death and burial (26:12). By giving them the Passover bread, which is his body destined for his self-sacrificial death, to eat, Jesus enabled his disciples at this meal, and the audience in the sacramental meal of the Eucharist, to share in his death as the salvific event that climaxes all of the past saving deeds of God for his people that the Passover celebrated. Those who eat the bread that has become the very body of Jesus are united in a special table fellowship with him and thus share in the salvific effect of his death as an act of self-sacrificial worship (20:28).

The ritual gestures of taking, blessing, breaking, and giving that Jesus performed in offering the bread that is his body (26:26) recall the identical gestures he used in both of his previous miraculous meals with the crowds (14:13–21; 15:32–39). The pattern Jesus established by these gestures in the miraculous meals concluded with his disciples distributing the bread to the crowds (14:19; 15:36). This pattern implies that when the disciples "take" the Passover bread/body that Jesus "gives" them, they are not only to feed themselves but to again distribute it to the people in future celebrations of this new Passover meal. The very nature of the traditional Passover meal as a repeatedly celebrated commemoration, as well as the overabundance provided by the miraculous meals (14:20; 15:37), indicate that the disciples are to continually celebrate this new Passover meal in the sacramental meal of the Eucharist. By instituting the Eucharist at his last meal with his disciples,

---

9. "In the case of the Passover, the original anticipated the imminent Exodus as the saving event and subsequent celebrations looked back to the saving event and brought the participants freshly into touch with it. In the case of the Last Supper/Lord's Supper, the original anticipated the imminent Passion as the saving event and subsequent celebrations looked back to the Passion and brought the participants freshly into touch with it" (Nolland, *Matthew*, 1075).

10. "This part occurs a little later in the meal, at the eating of the paschal lamb, i.e., after it is served but before it is eaten" (Osborne, *Matthew*, 966).

Jesus has enabled them, as well as the audience, to feed, satisfy, and unify other people with him and his saving, self-sacrificial death.[11]

Continuing the ritualistic worship at his special Passover meal, Jesus "takes" a cup of wine, "gives thanks" to God for it, and "gives" it to his disciples with the command, "Drink from it, all of you" (26:27). That all of them are to "drink" (πίετε) from the "cup" (ποτήριον) Jesus gives them fulfills for all of the disciples on the literal level the previous promise Jesus made to the disciples James and John that they would "drink [πίεσθε] the cup [ποτήριόν]" (20:23) that he drinks, as a metaphor for sharing in his suffering and death before they enter with him into the heavenly glory of his kingdom (20:20-23). The literal drinking from the cup that Jesus gave all the disciples, then, further deepened their sacramental participation in his self-sacrificial death through this new Passover meal and thus prepared them for their own future sufferings and deaths (10:16-25; 24:9-13).[12]

As he had reinterpreted the Passover bread as his own body destined for death (26:26), so Jesus reinterpreted the cup of wine (26:27) as the symbolic and sacramental equivalent of his own blood about to be shed in his imminent death: "This is *my* blood of the covenant, which will be poured out for many for the forgiveness of sins" (26:28). By designating the cup of wine as "my blood of the covenant," Jesus related the blood to be shed by his death to the sacrificial "blood of the covenant" that Moses poured out upon the altar, representative of God, and upon the people (Exod 24:3-8) with the words, "Behold the blood of the covenant which the Lord has made with you in accordance with all these words" (24:8). The ceremony establishing the covenant concluded with a meal that bonded the people of Israel together in their covenantal relationship with God (24:9-11).

In the biblical tradition "covenant" (διαθήκη) referred to the fundamental relationship uniting God to Israel as his specially chosen people, the promise and pledge of mutual fidelity and loyalty according to which God would be their saving God and they would be his obedient people. By referring to his blood as "my blood of the covenant" (Matt 26:28), Jesus indicated that the blood of his self-sacrificial death will bring about the fulfillment of "*the* covenant," the new and definitive covenant according to which God would unite himself permanently and profoundly with his people in

---

11. "The four verbs concerning the bread ('took,' 'blessed,' 'broke,' 'gave') which we have seen repeated carefully in the accounts of the feeding miracles in 14:19 and 15:36 represent a familiar liturgical sequence, and the further verb 'gave thanks' (as in 15:36) associated with 'took' and 'gave' in relation to the wine completes the range of eucharistic language" (France, *Matthew*, 988).

12. "Jesus has the disciples drink from the same cup, emphasizing the community in unity that has been formed" (Osborne, *Matthew*, 967).

a salvific and liberating relationship.¹³ Jesus thus further transformed the Passover meal, at which he instituted the sacramental meal of the Eucharist, into a covenantal meal, whereby those who drink the wine designated as his blood of *the* covenant are sacramentally and profoundly united into this new and final covenantal relationship that God established with his people through the blood of the salvific self-sacrificial death of Jesus.¹⁴

That Jesus' blood, which effects *the* new covenant with God, "will be poured out for many for the forgiveness of sins" (26:28) emphasizes the nature of Jesus' death as a covenantal sacrifice for the atonement of sins.¹⁵ As the blood of sacrificed animals was "poured out" by priests on the altar as a sin offering to atone for the sins of the people (Lev 4:7, 18, 25, 30, 34), so the blood that will be "shed" or "poured out" by the death of Jesus represents a sacrifice for the atonement of sins for "many," a Semitic expression for "all" people (cf. Matt 20:28).¹⁶ Jesus "will save his people from their sins" (1:21), then, by his self-sacrificial death, which reaffirms how God is to be glorified for giving human beings the divine authority to forgive sins (9:2, 5, 6, 8; cf. 6:12, 14–15). As the commemoration of Jesus' new and unique Passover meal, the sacramental meal of the Eucharist, which includes the drinking of the wine/blood of Jesus, thus celebrates the divine forgiveness of sins that the blood of the salvific sacrificial death of Jesus makes available for all peoples.

That one of the Twelve who is eating with Jesus will betray him to death (26:21) means that Jesus will no longer drink wine, the festive drink produced from the "fruit of the vine": "from now on I shall not drink from this fruit of the vine until that day when I drink it with you new in the kingdom of my Father" (26:29). But the death of Jesus through betrayal by

13. For the promise of the new covenant, see Jer 31:31–34; 32:37–41. Note also the salvific and liberating effect of the "blood" of God's covenant in Zech 9:11: "As for you also, because of the blood of my covenant with you, I will set your captives free from the waterless pit." For more on the role of the blood of Jesus in Matthew, see Heil, "Blood of Jesus," 117–24.

14. "The reference to Exod 24:8 in the saying over the cup can be taken only typologically, i.e., as an indication that the atoning act in the death of Jesus is interpreted as surpassing and corresponding to the OT act of atonement. Thus a renewal of the covenant of Sinai is not intended; instead, the passage speaks of God's surpassing pledge of salvation in 'blood,' i.e., in the death of Jesus" (Hegermann, "διαθήκη," 300).

15. On the relation of Matt 26:28 to 27:25 ("His blood be upon us and upon our children"), see Nicklas, "Versöhnung mit Israel," 17–24.

16. "As in 20:28, 'many,' is Semitic idiom and should be understood in a universal, not a restrictive sense: i.e., 'for all'" (Byrne, *Lifting the Burden*, 205n13). "The purpose and result of his atoning death will be 'for the forgiveness of sins,' echoing both the suffering Servant (Isa 53:11–12) and the new covenant passage (Jer 31:34)" (Osborne, *Matthew*, 968).

one of the Twelve will not bring a definitive conclusion to the festivity of his table fellowship with his followers. On the contrary, on "that day" of God's end-time fulfillment of his salvific activity, after Jesus' triumph over death through his resurrection, he will drink "new" festive wine and thus again be united in joyous meal fellowship with his followers in the heavenly "kingdom of my Father." The sacramental celebration of the Eucharist, then, not only commemorates and makes present for its participants the past saving events of Jesus' life, death and resurrection, but also anticipates the future, final, and festive "wedding" banquet that Jesus, the "bridegroom" (9:15; 22:2), will share with all of his followers in the kingdom of heaven.[17]

The "singing of a hymn" by Jesus and his disciples as they went out to the Mount of Olives (26:30) marks the jubilant conclusion of the unique Passover meal, which enabled the disciples to sacramentally anticipate both his death and his future triumph over it.[18] Peter brashly contradicted Jesus' authoritative prediction that all the disciples will abandon him (26:31–32). He insisted that he will prove the exception (26:33). Jesus then predicted that Peter would instead "deny" (ἀπαρνήσῃ) him three times (26:34). But Peter protested: "Even if I must die with you, I will not deny [ἀπαρνήσομαι] you" (26:35). Peter's failure to deny himself rather than Jesus, as well as his failure to die with Jesus, recalls Jesus' previous pronouncement: "If anyone wishes to come after me, he must deny [ἀπαρνησάσθω] himself, take up his cross, and follow me" (16:24; cf. 10:38). Peter's negative example reminds and reinforces for the audience their need to deny themselves and accept whatever sufferings and persecution they may incur as an act of the ethical self-sacrificial worship required of a follower in imitation of Jesus.

When Jesus and his disciples came to Gethsemane on the Mount of Olives, he told them, "Sit here while I go over there and pray" (26:36). He took along Peter and the two sons of Zebedee (cf. 17:1; 20:20), and began to be saddened and distressed (26:37), telling them, "My soul is very

---

17. "In this way the Eucharist touches no less than five 'moments' in time. (1) Looking 'backward,' so to speak, it recalls and renews the covenant made with the original people of God and the manna with which they were fed in their desert wandering. (2) Less remotely, it recalls the meals in which Jesus celebrated the mercy of God (9:10–13; 11:19) and especially the two occasions when he multiplied the loaves to ensure that the people did not go away faint and hungry (14:13–21; 15:32–39). (3) Now, on the eve of his death, he transforms the Passover, in order that (4) throughout its life the Church may experience saving union with its Emmanuel Lord, as a foretaste and anticipation of (5) union with him in the banquet of the kingdom" (Byrne, *Lifting the Burden*, 205–6).

18. Traditionally the Passover meal included the singing of the "Hallel" Psalms (113–18), which recalled God's liberation of Israel from Egypt and of the individual from death (116:1–9).

sorrowful [cf. LXX Ps 41:6, 12; 42:5], even to death; remain here and watch with me" (Matt 26:38). Jesus' urgent plea for these three disciples to "watch" (γρηγορεῖτε) with him recalls his earlier command for the disciples and for all others to "watch [γρηγορεῖτε]" (24:42; 25:13) in the period after his resurrection and before his final coming (24:36–44). To "watch" means to be awake and alert, ready and prepared for the crucial "day" and "hour" (24:36, 44) introducing God's final and definitive salvation. The situation of the disciples' "watching" with Jesus while he prays thus sets them up as a paradigm for the audience's time of "watching" for the final and triumphant coming of Jesus after his death and resurrection.

Going forward a little, Jesus "fell on his face" (26:39). This accentuates the overwhelming effect of his profound distress and anxiety in view of his imminent death, as it places him in a position for worship (cf. 2:11; 4:9; 17:6). He then prayed, "My Father, if it is possible, let this cup pass from me" (26:39). In direct correspondence to the heavenly proclamations of God himself that "this is my beloved Son with whom I am well pleased" (3:17; 17:5), Jesus relied upon his unique sonship as he affectionately and respectfully begged God as "my" intimate and loving "Father" for deliverance from his approaching death. The deferential preface "if it is possible [δυνατόν]" recalls Jesus' previous assertions that "for God all things are possible [δυνατά]" (19:26) and that "whatever you ask for in prayer with faith, you will receive" (21:22; cf. 17:20). When Jesus introduced his earnest prayer with "if it is possible," he did so knowing and firmly believing that the God who is his loving "Father" is powerful enough to answer the prayer of his "beloved Son" for deliverance from death.

That Jesus ardently prayed for his Father to let this "cup" (ποτήριον) of suffering and death pass by him (26:39) presents the audience with a shocking contradiction not only to his earlier assurance that the two sons of Zebedee would drink the "cup" (ποτήριον) that Jesus drinks and thus share in his suffering and death (20:22–23), but also to the giving of the Passover "cup" (ποτήριον) of his wine/blood, which all the disciples drank as a sacramental participation in his suffering and death (26:27). In accord with his prior lament (26:38), Jesus' plea here for "this cup" to pass from him brought his deep dread and sorrow to a climax.

The dramatic tension between the divine necessity that Jesus suffer and die and his quite human dread of the kind of suffering and death he was to undergo was resolved through the very process of his praying as Jesus uttered the words "but not as I will but as you will!" (26:39). In thus submitting his own will to the sovereign will of his Father, Jesus showed how he is indeed God's obedient and "beloved Son." By so praying, he exemplified the key characteristic of his new "family" of followers: "whoever does the will of my Father in heaven is my brother and sister and mother!" (12:50). For those he calls to follow him on his way to suffering and death, Jesus demonstrated what it means to think "the things of God" rather than the "things of human beings" (16:23) and to "deny oneself" (16:24) in order to take up one's cross and follow him—namely, to deny one's own will in favor of God's sovereign and salvific will.

Jesus' acceptance of God's will over his own will in prayer, even though he knew and believed that God had the power to let this cup of suffering and death pass by him (26:39), developed his previous teaching about prayer. Although the disciples, as well as the audience, are to pray with faith in God's absolute power to grant their request (21:21-22; 18:19-20; 17:20), they must realize that God, although he possesses unlimited power, does not always choose to exercise that power to remove suffering and death. The will of God remains sovereign. But the Gethsemane prayer of Jesus illustrates how one can voice the deepest of human fears and concerns with firm faith that God can alleviate them and yet ultimately submit one's own will to God's sovereign will precisely in and through such prayer.

After Jesus found the disciples sleeping rather than watching with him (26:40), he developed his previous command for them to "watch with me" (26:38), as he commanded them to "watch and pray" (26:41). His addition of the command to pray indicates the significance and power of his own praying. Now that he has prayed (26:39), he can command and empower his disciples likewise to pray. That Jesus prayed precisely while the disciples were sleeping and unable to watch with him indicates that the prayer of Jesus is not only the model for the disciples to emulate in their prayer but is the basis or empowerment for their own praying. The disciples who were sleeping can now "watch and pray" only because Jesus has first successfully watched and prayed. They are a model for the audience to be able not only to "watch" but also to "pray" in order to be ready for the unknown time of Jesus' final coming (24:42; 25:13).

Jesus enjoined his disciples to watch and pray in order that they not "enter the test" (26:41), recalling how he earlier taught them to pray that God, "our Father," not allow "us to enter into the test but to deliver us from the evil one" (6:13). The "test," "trial," or "temptation" (πειρασμός) refers to God's final struggle with and conquering of the powers of evil, which was now reaching a crescendo with the suffering and death of Jesus. The dreaded "test" embraces not only the critical "hour" of Jesus' suffering and death but the future time of the disciples' own persecution, sufferings, and deaths (10:16-25; 24:9-13). Although the praying of the disciples will not guarantee the elimination of their sufferings and distress, the powerful prayer of Jesus has demonstrated how they, as well as the audience, in and through his praying, can deny themselves and conform their own wills to the sovereign will of God through their praying and thus withstand the terrible "test."

The disciples needed to watch and pray because of the fundamental and constant tension that "the spirit is willing but the flesh is weak" (26:41). In other words, although the "spirit," that part of the human person attuned to God and the spiritual, transcendent realm, is "willing" or "eager" to obey God's will, the "flesh," that part of the human person attuned to oneself and the earthly, limited, and mortal realm, is "weak" and thus disinclined to obey the will of God. This basic tension has been demonstrated by Peter and the disciples, whose "spirit" is willing to die with Jesus (26:35) but whose "flesh" prevents them from staying alert and watching (26:40). Jesus illustrated for the audience how to overcome this tension between "spirit" and "flesh" in and through prayer. In his prayer of lament Jesus, distressed and sorrowful over his imminent death (26:38), fully voiced his own concerns of the "flesh" as he begged his Father to let the cup of suffering and death pass by him. But in and through his prayer he allowed his "willing spirit" to predominate over the "weak flesh" as he submitted his own will to that of God (26:39).

When Jesus prayed the first time, he left open that it might be "possible" (δυνατόν) that his Father's will correspond to his own will not to drink the cup of suffering and death (26:39). But in his second prayer, "My Father, if it is not possible that this cup pass without my drinking it, your will be done!" (26:42), he realized that "it is not possible" (οὐ δύναται) for him to escape drinking the "cup," and without any further mention of his own will totally resigned himself to the will of God. His second prayer thus enabled Jesus to accept his Father's will even more fully and absolutely. With an exact echo of the "Our Father" prayer he taught his disciples, "your will be done" (6:10), Jesus not only exemplified how to pray but makes it possible for the disciples and the audience to accept and accomplish God's will on the basis and strength of his prayer.

After Jesus found his disciples still asleep (26:43), he prayed a decisive and definitive "third time," saying the same thing again (26:44), and thus completing his total submission to the will of his Father.[19] Jesus then began to illustrate how his praying has transformed him. Whereas he had begun praying that if it were possible God might allow the cup of his suffering and death to pass by him (26:39), once he had totally submitted his own will to the sovereign will of God through prayer (26:42), he was able to proclaim to his disciples with resolute acceptance, "Behold, the hour has arrived and the

---

19. "In the ancient world, doing something a second time emphasizes it greatly, while a third time makes it superlative or ultimate. So Jesus becomes the ultimate model of intense, persevering prayer" (Osborne, *Matthew*, 981).

Son of Man is betrayed into the hands of sinners" (26:45). He thereby not only indicated his resolved recognition of the divine necessity for his suffering and death but climactically proclaimed that his previous predictions of his betrayal to death were now being fulfilled (17:22; 20:18; 26:2). Now that he has completed his powerful prayer, Jesus' authoritative announcement of his betrayal has set in motion the events leading to his suffering and sacrificial death.[20]

Jesus' exhortation to the disciples, "Get up, let us go!" (26:46), indicated the powerful effect his prayer has had in uniting them to himself. Before he withdrew to pray, Jesus commanded his disciples to "sit here" and "remain here" while he prayed (26:36, 38). But after he had prayed, Jesus empowered his disciples to "get up" from their inert, sleeping position and enabled them to "go" with him—"Let *us* go!" Now that Jesus has been strengthened through his prayer, he and his disciples can "go" together to play their respective roles in God's salvific plan—the bewildered disciples to be "scattered" (26:31, 56) and Jesus to be betrayed. With his climactic exclamation, "Behold, my betrayer has arrived!" (26:46), Jesus not only intensified his announcement, "Behold the hour has arrived!" (26:45) but illustrated his determined readiness—now that he has submitted himself to God's will through prayer—to face his betrayer (26:47-50). He has thus presented the audience with a model of how they, in and through prayer, can play their roles in God's plan of salvation.[21]

Worship and the Death of Jesus (Matt 26:57—27:54)

After the chief priests and the whole Sanhedrin failed to find false witnesses to put Jesus to death, two presumably true witnesses came forward (26:59-60) and testified that they heard Jesus claim, "I have the power to destroy the sanctuary of God and within three days rebuild it" (26:61). While Jesus never explicitly claimed that he himself had the power "to destroy" (καταλῦσαι) the "sanctuary" (ναόν)—the building that contained the Holy of Holies as the place of God's unique presence and of the most important acts of worship, the very epitome of the special sacredness of the entire temple (ἱερόν) complex—he did predict the utter destruction of all the impressive buildings of the temple (24:1): "There will not be left here a stone upon a stone that will not be thrown down [καταλυθήσεται]" (24:2). In so doing, Jesus had hinted at the inadequacy of the many magnificent

---

20. On Jesus' acceptance of his death as a divinely ordained sacrifice, see Huizenga, "Obedience unto Death," 507-26.

21. For a more detailed discussion of Matt 26:1-56, see Heil, *Death*, 23-56.

buildings of the temple, including its central "sanctuary," as a permanent dwelling place of God and locus of authentic worship.

The two true witnesses compounded their accusation by attributing to Jesus the ridiculous boast that within "three days" he would rebuild the destroyed sanctuary (26:61). For the audience this boast proves to be a profound prophecy of the power Jesus will exercise through his death and resurrection. The "three days" recalls the "third day" on which Jesus predicted that he would rise from the dead (16:21; 17:23; 20:19). It is through his death and resurrection, then, that Jesus will "build" a new and superior "sanctuary," constructed by the divine power manifested in his resurrection. This new "sanctuary" will be the new communal edifice God will erect upon the "cornerstone" of the risen Jesus. This had been indicated by Jesus' parable about the wicked tenants in which he revealed that by his death as God's Son he would become the "stone" rejected by the "builders" (21:42), the Jewish leaders in charge of the temple sanctuary. But by raising Jesus from the dead, God would make him the "cornerstone" of a new edifice for authentic worship, the community of Jesus' followers.

As a new "sanctuary," the community of Jesus' followers will practice the authentic worship the old sanctuary failed to achieve. It will be a community characterized as God's familial household of genuine prayer (21:13), a community that prays with faith in God's limitless power to provide for his people (21:22), a community that practices compassion toward fellow human beings, the divine "mercy" that complements "sacrifice" performed in the temple sanctuary (9:13; 12:7). The testimony of the two true witnesses (26:60–61) prompts the audience to probe the profound paradox that it is precisely through the death of Jesus, the aim of their accusation, that he will exercise the divine power of his resurrection to "build" a new and superior "sanctuary" for authentic worship. It will be the communal edifice of Jesus' followers and demonstrate that indeed "something greater than the temple is here" (12:6).[22]

The whole cohort of Gentile soldiers who gathered around Jesus (27:27) performed a cruel parody of a royal investiture. Ironically, they further illustrated Jesus' true kingship and worthiness to be worshiped. After stripping him of his own clothing, the soldiers placed a scarlet military cloak around him, ironically clothing him as one of themselves and thus as their own King (27:28). Their ridicule of the royal reverence due Jesus by

---

22. "Ironically, the two witnesses who eventually come forward and accuse Jesus of claiming to be able to destroy the Temple of God and to build it in three days (v. 61) do, in a fashion, speak the truth. Jesus had not made such a claim in so many words, but readers of the gospel know that he, the One who is 'greater than the Temple' (12:6), had foretold its destruction" (Byrne, *Lifting the Burden*, 209).

"genuflecting" before him foreshadowed and exemplified the genuine worship to be accorded him as the true King.[23] Mimicking the regal acclamation rendered to a Roman emperor or king, the soldiers saluted Jesus with a ridiculing "Hail, King of the Jews!" (27:29). This stands in contrast to the man who approached Jesus, "genuflecting" before him (17:14) as a prelude to his act of supplicatory worship of Jesus (17:15). And it complements the Gentile magi who worshiped Jesus as the newborn King of the Jews (2:2, 8). For the audience the soldiers unwittingly indicated that Jesus is worthy to be worshiped as the true King not only of the Jews but also of the Gentiles.[24]

While on the cross Jesus cried out in a loud voice, quoting an Aramaic version of a scriptural psalm: "Eli, Eli, lema sabachthani?" (Ps 22:1), that is, "My God, My God, why have you forsaken me?" (Matt 27:46). The reporting of Jesus' words in Aramaic along with their translation reinforced the great importance of his prayerful cry. Having endured God's silent abandonment, symbolized by the dismal darkness (27:45) God caused instead of rescuing him from excruciating death at the hands of reviling accusers (27:39-44), Jesus prayed for the reason "why" or "for what purpose" (ἱνατί) God has forsaken him. Although indicative of his experience of intense anguish as he dies radically alone and without divine intervention, Jesus' cry is not one of despair but is a lamentful prayer, uttered with complete confidence and total trust in his God, whom he addressed twice as "my God." With confidence in his Father's sovereign plan for him, he prayed for God to refute the ridicule of his trust as God's Son (27:43) by disclosing the divine purpose of his death.[25]

Some of the bystanders distorted Jesus' lamentful prayer of trust in God into a plea for Elijah to rescue him (27:47).[26] In order to prolong Jesus' life, one of the bystanders offered him a drink from a sponge filled with vin-

---

23. "In the presence of the emperor all supplicants were to fall on their knees in obeisance" (Osborne, *Matthew*, 1031).

24. "In all cases the mockery imposes on Jesus titles and roles that are profoundly true: he *is* 'the King of the Jews' (vv. 29, 37)—though in a way very different from what the foreigners who mock and crucify him suppose" (Byrne, *Lifting the Burden*, 216; emphasis original).

25. "It is not a cry of despair—because Jesus still calls upon God. But it is a cry of dereliction because no answer from God will come until he has shared the lot of all human beings in death" (Byrne, *Lifting the Burden*, 217). "As in Gethsemane Jesus is experiencing the depths of pain in his very soul, but this in no way mitigates his victory there, and Ps 22 is a perfect source for his expression of agony. Beneath his real pain there is still a trust in God, and he knows his deliverance is coming" (Osborne, *Matthew*, 1038).

26. "Here this reflects the belief by many Jews that Elijah was ready to appear from heaven in time of need" (Osborne, *Matthew*, 1038).

egar and placed on a reed (27:48; cf. Ps 69:22). But the rest of the bystanders did not want to delay or interfere with a possible miraculous rescue of Jesus. Their derisive desire to see if Elijah will "save" him (27:49) advanced the malicious mockery of Jesus' divine power to "save" others and to be "saved" himself by God (27:40-43). By twisting his lamentful prayer of trust into a mocked plea for rescue, the bystanders continued to illustrate their stubborn blindness to the divine necessity of Jesus' self-sacrificial death. They do not understand that Jesus was exemplifying his teaching that salvation comes from the God who will ultimately "save" those who entrust themselves completely to him (19:25-26; 24:22), that whoever perseveres to the end "will be saved" (10:22; 24:13), and that whoever wishes to "save" his life will lose it in the ethical worship of self-sacrificial service (10:39; 16:25; 20:28).

Jesus repeated the loud cry of his prayer of lamentful trust in God before he finally "gave up his spirit" (27:50). In response to Jesus' death and as a beginning to the answer of "why" God abandoned him to death (27:46), the veil hanging in the temple sanctuary "was split" by God (divine passive) in two pieces "from top to bottom," totally destroyed from heaven downward (27:51). This destruction of the sanctuary veil, symbolic of the temple cult, indicated the termination of the old temple sanctuary that Jesus had judged inadequate as the place of authentic worship (21:12-17) and pointed to the advent of a new, superior sanctuary. The tearing of the sanctuary veil, indicative of the temple's demise (23:38; 24:1-2), began to fulfill the prophecy attributed to Jesus by the two witnesses at his trial before the Sanhedrin (26:61) and to contradict the mockery of his powerlessness on the cross (27:40). By his death in apparent weakness, Jesus demonstrated his power to destroy the old temple sanctuary and opened the way for his rebuilding of a new one for authentic worship—the community of his followers.[27]

A spectacular chain reaction of events continued God's answer to Jesus' lamentful prayer (27:46): The earth "was shaken" by God (divine passive), which caused the rocks to be split (27:51), which in turn enabled the tombs, made and sealed with rocks, to be opened, so that many bodies of the holy ones who had fallen asleep in death were raised from them (27:52). After Jesus' resurrection these holy ones entered the holy city of Jerusalem and appeared to many (27:53). Now that Jesus' sacrificial blood of the covenant has been poured out for "many" (26:28), it has the life-giving, salvific effect of raising the "many" bodies of the holy ones from the dead, so that they bore witness of God's salvific vindication to the "many" to whom they appeared.

27. "The result will be that access to God will no longer be through the old, discredited cultic system but through Jesus himself, and more specifically through his death as a ransom for many" (France, *Matthew*, 1081).

This triumphant appearance of the vindicated holy ones, after the resurrection of the vindicated Jesus, to the many in the holy city of Jerusalem thus encourages the audience to become holy ones who dedicate themselves to God by practicing the ethical self-sacrificial worship exemplified and made possible by Jesus' self-sacrificial death.

When the Gentile centurion and those with him who were keeping watch over the dying Jesus (27:36) saw the earthquake and the things that happened (27:51-53), they were greatly awed and declared, "Truly this one [οὗτος] was the Son of God!" (27:54).[28] Their climactic confession contradicted the bystanders' misunderstanding that "this one [οὗτος] is calling for Elijah" (27:47). It also transformed their own mockery of the crucified Jesus, namely, that "this one [οὗτός] is Jesus, the King of the Jews" (27:37), into a profession of faith in the crucified Jesus' more profound identity as the divine Son of God. And their confession confirmed that of Jesus himself before the high priest, when he acknowledged that he was "the Christ, the Son of God" (26:63-64).

Through their worshipful confession of the crucified Jesus the Roman soldiers, who represent the Gentile world, became members of the new, communal "sanctuary" of authentic worship that Jesus has the power to build (26:61; 27:40) through his resurrection, now that his death has pointed to God's destruction of the old temple sanctuary (27:51). The climactic confession of Jesus' divine sonship by these Gentile soldiers, "Truly this one [οὗτος] was the Son of God!" (27:54), confirmed God's previous proclamations that "this one [οὗτός] is my beloved Son, with whom I am well pleased" (3:17; 17:5). It reaffirmed and enhanced the disciples' worship of him, when they declared to Jesus, "Truly you are the Son of God!" (14:33), and Peter's worship of him, when he declared to Jesus, "You are the Christ, the Son of the living God!" (16:16).[29] It complemented the Gentile magi's worship of the infant Jesus and underlines for the audience the worthiness of Jesus to be worshiped as the divine Son of God, who died as an act of ethical self-sacrificial worship of God to save his people from their sins (1:21).[30]

---

28. "Like the other centurion we met earlier in the gospel, this officer and his men have displayed faith beyond that of 'anyone in Israel' (8:10), and so they, too, represent the many who will come from east and west to join the Jewish patriarchs in the kingdom of heaven (8:11-12)" (France, *Matthew*, 1085).

29. On the relation between Matt 14:33 and 27:54, see Angel, "Son of God," 299-317.

30. "Jesus has performed the role signified by his name ('to save the people from their sins' [1:21b; cf. 26:28]) not only for Israel but for the entire world, represented here by the Gentile soldiers, who are the first to acknowledge his true identity as disclosed by the supernatural events" (Byrne, *Lifting the Burden*, 219). For a more detailed discussion of Matt 26:57-27:54, see Heil, *Death*, 57-89.

Worship of the Risen Jesus (Matt 27:55—28:20)

Quickly going away from the tomb with fear and "great joy [χαρᾶς]" (cf. 2:10), the women ran to announce to the disciples (28:8) the angel's message that Jesus has been raised from the dead and can be seen in Galilee (28:7). But suddenly the risen Jesus met them, saying, "Hail" or "Rejoice [χαίρετε]" (28:9a; cf. 5:12), thus reinforcing their great joy.[31] The earlier tension raised by the women's lack of response to the death of Jesus (27:55-56), which stood in sharp contrast to the worshipful confession of the dead Jesus by the centurion and those with him (27:54), was then dramatically resolved. The women approached, grasped the feet of Jesus, and "worshiped" (προσεκύνησαν) him (28:9b).[32] This silent gesture of worship of the risen Jesus by these Jewish followers, the Galilean women, complemented the exuberant confession of worship by the Gentile soldiers that the crucified Jesus was truly the Son of God (27:54). It also complemented the gesture of worship of the child Jesus as the newborn King of the Jews by the Gentile magi, who, falling down, "worshiped" (προσεκύνησαν) him (2:11).

The eleven disciples went to Galilee to the mountain to which Jesus had ordered them (28:16; cf. 26:32). When they saw Jesus, they worshiped, but some doubted (28:17).[33] That some of the disciples "doubted" expresses the attitude of "little faith" (cf. 14:31) that characterizes the disciples in Matthew (6:30; 8:26; 16:8; 17:20) and that is oriented to an increase in faith through a deeper experience of Jesus' divine power and status. This salutary "doubt" on the part of some of the disciples before the risen Jesus contrasts sharply with the lack of any such doubt regarding the spread of a false interpretation of the empty tomb on the part of the faithless characters in the previous scene (28:11–15). That the eleven disciples "worshiped" (προσεκύνησαν) the risen Jesus complemented the women who likewise "worshiped" (προσεκύνησαν) the risen Jesus (28:9). And it reinforces for the audience the previous worship of the disciples after they saw Jesus performing the uniquely divine activity of walking on the sea: Those in the boat "worshiped" (προσεκύνησαν) him, saying, "Truly you are the Son of God!" (14:33).

---

31. "There is double meaning in Jesus' 'greetings' (χαίρετε), which on one level is a cheerful 'Hello' (the Greek greeting) but at another level echoes the women's 'great joy' (χαρᾶς μεγάλης) in v. 8; Jesus has now lifted their 'joy' to a new magnitude" (Osborne, *Matthew*, 1068).

32. "To take hold of the feet is at one and the same time intimate and profoundly self-subordinating" (Nolland, *Matthew*, 1252). "Grasping the feet is often used of petition but here is an act of worship" (Osborne, *Matthew*, 1069).

33. For the translation of οἱ δέ as "some" rather than "all" of the disciples in Matt 28:17, see van der Horst, "Once More," 27–30.

The risen Jesus then approached the disciples and declared, "To me has been given all authority in heaven and on earth" (28:18; cf. LXX Dan 7:14). That to Jesus has been given by God (divine passive) all "authority" (cf. 11:27) reaffirms that God gave Jesus the "authority" (21:23) not only to cleanse the temple of its sacrificial worship for failing to be God's house of true prayer (21:12-13), but to heal the blind and the lame in the temple, which prompted the boys there to worship him as the messianic Son of David (21:14-16).[34] At that time Jesus exercised his divine authority to teach the disciples that whatever they ask for in prayer with faith they will receive (21:22). It recalls that, as the Son of Man, Jesus has "authority" on earth to forgive sins (9:6), which prompted the crowds to perform an act of doxological worship, as they glorified God who had given such "authority" to human beings (9:8). And that Jesus has been given all authority "in heaven and on earth" reaffirms his authority to teach his disciples to pray that God's will be done "on earth as in heaven" (6:10).

The risen Jesus then directed his disciples to go and make disciples of all the nations by "baptizing them into the name of the Father and of the Son and of the Holy Spirit" (28:19).[35] This recalls that when Jesus was baptized by John, "he saw the Spirit of God descending like a dove and coming upon him" (3:16). And then the voice of his Father from heaven declared, "This is my beloved Son with whom I am well pleased" (3:17). That Jesus was equipped with the Spirit of God at his baptism enabled him to fulfill John's promise that Jesus "will baptize you with the Holy Spirit and fire" (3:11). After having been given the Spirit at his baptism, Jesus was led by the Spirit into the wilderness to have his divine sonship tested by the devil (4:1). Equipped with the Spirit of God, Jesus demonstrated that he indeed was the beloved Son of his divine Father, as he resisted the temptation to worship the devil rather than God, proclaiming, "The Lord your God shall you worship and him alone shall you serve" (4:10).

The command of the risen Jesus to make disciples of all the nations by baptizing them into the name of the Father and of the Son and of the Holy Spirit (28:19) reminds the audience that their own baptism was a ritual,

---

34. "The divine passive 'has been given' (ἐδόθη) shows this authority/power comes from God himself" (Osborne, *Matthew*, 1078).

35. "Not only does the postresurrection Jesus launch the universal mission; he also launches baptism as the primary sacrament of initiation into the Christian faith" (Osborne, *Matthew*, 1080). "[F]or 'the Son' to take his place as the middle member, between the Father and the Holy Spirit, in a threefold depiction of the object of the disciple's allegiance is extraordinary. The human leader of the disciple group has become the rightful object of their worship. And the fact that the three divine persons are spoken of as having a single 'name' is a significant pointer toward the Trinitarian doctrine of three persons in one God" (France, *Matthew*, 1118).

sacramental act of worship by which they became beloved sons and daughters of God and thus brothers and sisters of Jesus. The brothers and sisters of Jesus are characterized as those who do the will of Jesus' heavenly Father (12:50), as taught and exemplified by Jesus. Equipped like Jesus with the Holy Spirit at their baptism, the members of the audience are enabled to do God's will, which includes resisting false worship for the true worship of God. They are also enabled by the Holy Spirit to make disciples of all the nations by baptizing them into the divine family, so that they may engage in the true worship not only of the divine Father but of Jesus, his divine beloved Son (3:16–18; 4:10).[36]

Jesus' ministry customarily included teaching, preaching, and healing (4:23; 9:35). But when he gave his twelve disciples authority to preach and heal (10:1, 7–8), he did not yet give them his divine authority to teach (7:29; 21:23; 22:16). It was only after the disciples experienced the ethical worship of Jesus' self-sacrificial death that the risen Jesus gave them the authority to make disciples of all the nations by "teaching them to observe all that I have commanded you" (28:20a). With regard to worship, Jesus taught and exemplified not only the liturgical, ritual worship of how to pray (6:6–13; 14:23; 19:13; 26:36–44) but the ethical worship of extending mercy to others. He taught people to "learn" that God desires the ethical worship of practicing mercy and love for others that complements ritual sacrificial worship (9:13; 12:7; 22:34–40; 23:23). The risen Jesus has thus given his disciples as well as the audience the divine authority to teach all the nations to practice the ethical worship that complements ritual worship, the holistic, authentic worship that they themselves are to exemplify.[37]

The risen Jesus concluded his instructions to his disciples and thus to the audience by assuring them, "And behold, I am with you all days until the end of the age" (28:20b). Jesus thus promised to continue to be "God

36. "Following his [Jesus'] baptism at the hands of John 'to fulfill all righteousness' (3:15), the Spirit descended upon him and he heard the Father's affirmation, 'This is my beloved Son, in whom I am well pleased' (3:17). To be baptized 'into the name of the Father and of the Son and of the Holy Spirit' is to be drawn into that same divine-human communion; it is to become a beloved son or daughter upon whom the Father's favor rests" (Byrne, *Lifting the Burden*, 228). "Matthew's story has been about the action of the Father through the Son and by means of the Holy Spirit. And that is what the baptized are joined to" (Nolland, *Matthew*, 1269).

37. "The final element of 'discipling' the nations is teaching them to 'observe' all that Jesus has commanded his own disciples (v. 20a). One thinks here especially of the teaching contained in the Great Sermon, that is, of the Torah as authoritatively interpreted by Jesus, where the supreme criterion is what God wants: 'mercy, not sacrifice' (Hos 6:6; cf. Matt 9:13; 12:7), where 'justice, mercy, and faith' are the 'weightier matters' (23:23) and where love, in its 'double direction' (love of God/love of neighbor) is the 'greatest commandment' of the Torah (22:34–40)" (Byrne, *Lifting the Burden*, 228).

with us" (1:23) in both our liturgical, ritual worship as well as in our ethical worship. Whoever welcomes a child in the name of Jesus welcomes Jesus himself (18:5), and thus worships him ethically. In a liturgical gathering together for prayer in the name of Jesus (18:19–20a) he promised that "there I am in the midst of them" (18:20b). And with regard to the ethical worship that it is necessary for disciples to practice by extending the mercy and love God desires to others, Jesus promised to be with us always by provocatively identifying himself with the least among us, when he declared as the criterion for final judgment, "Whatever you did to one of these least brothers of mine, you did to me" (25:40, 45). Jesus not only taught and exemplified how we are to practice a true and holistic worship, but became, as the beloved Son of God (3:17; 17:5), an always present object of our authentic worship of God.[38]

Summary on Matthew 26–28

Jesus explained that in pouring the perfumed ointment upon his body the anonymous woman did it to prepare him for burial (26:12). Her good deed inspires the audience to glorify God (5:16) for the precious value of Jesus' self-sacrificial death. It also enhances the worthiness of Jesus to be worshiped as the Son of Man who came not to be served but to serve and to give his life as a "ransom" or "redemption" for many (20:28). His sacrificial death by crucifixion will occur appropriately during the feast of Passover (26:2), which celebrated how God "redeemed" his people in the exodus event (LXX Exod 15:13; cf. 6:6) through the blood of slaughtered lambs (12:1–13). Just as the Passover was to be a perpetual "memorial" of this (12:14), so whenever the gospel is proclaimed what the woman has done in worshiping Jesus will be told in "memory" of her (Matt 26:13). She not only inspires the audience to glorify God but to worship Jesus himself for the precious value of his self-sacrificial death by which the people of God are redeemed.

While the disciples and Jesus were eating the Passover meal, Jesus, as the host of the meal, performed the ritualistic worship of taking bread, blessing or thanking God for it, breaking it for distribution, and giving it to his disciples (26:26). In the ritual of the Passover meal the role of the host was to pronounce the traditional symbolic interpretations upon the various elements of the meal. This enabled the participants not only to commemorate

---

38. "And by this stage in Matthew's story, the manner in which Jesus manifests God's presence is clearly such that the only proper response involves worship of Jesus" (Nolland, *Matthew*, 1271). See also McDonald, "I Am with You Always," 66–86. For a more detailed discussion of Matt 27:55—28:20, see Heil, *Death*, 91–110.

but to actually share in and sacramentally relive the salvific experience of the original Passover meal. In his last Passover meal with his disciples, Jesus, as their Teacher (26:18), Lord (26:22), and host, transformed the meaning of this meal for them as he placed a new symbolic interpretation upon the bread and wine. He thereby instituted the sacrament of the Eucharist, enabling the audience not only to commemorate but to relive the salvific experience of Jesus' last meal, which anticipated his self-sacrificial death.

A particular focus of the Passover meal was the body of the lamb, which was to be eaten whole and entire (Exod 12:9) without any of its bones being broken (Exod 12:46; Num 9:12). After the body of the lamb was served at the Passover meal, Jesus directed the disciples to take and eat the bread he has blessed and broken for them, which he designated as the symbolic and sacramental equivalent of his body: "This is *my* body" (Matt 26:26). The bread thus became the very "body" of Jesus, which "body" had already been anointed for death and burial (26:12). By giving them the Passover bread, which is his body destined for his self-sacrificial death, to eat, Jesus enabled his disciples at this meal, and the audience in the sacramental meal of the Eucharist, to share in his death as the salvific event that climaxes all of the past saving deeds of God for his people that the Passover celebrated. Those who eat the bread that has become the very body of Jesus are united in a special table fellowship with him and thus share in the salvific effect of his death as an act of self-sacrificial worship (20:28).

As he had reinterpreted the Passover bread as his own body destined for death (26:26), so Jesus reinterpreted the cup of wine (26:27) as the symbolic and sacramental equivalent of his own blood about to be shed in his imminent death: "This is *my* blood of the covenant, which will be poured out for many for the forgiveness of sins" (26:28). By designating the cup of wine as "my blood of the covenant," Jesus related the blood to be shed by his death to the sacrificial "blood of the covenant" that Moses poured out upon the altar, representative of God, and upon the people (Exod 24:3–8) with the words, "Behold the blood of the covenant which the Lord has made with you in accordance with all these words" (24:8). The ceremony establishing the covenant concluded with a meal that bonded the people of Israel together in their covenantal relationship with God (24:9–11).

That one of the Twelve who is eating with Jesus will betray him to death (Matt 26:21) means that Jesus will no longer drink wine, the festive drink produced from the "fruit of the vine": "from now on I shall not drink from this fruit of the vine until that day when I drink it with you new in the kingdom of my Father" (26:29). On "that day" of God's end-time fulfillment of his salvific activity, after Jesus' triumph over death through his resurrection, he will drink "new" festive wine and thus again be united in joyous meal fellowship with his followers in the heavenly "kingdom of my Father." The sacramental celebration of the Eucharist not only commemorates and makes present for its participants the past saving events of Jesus' life, death and resurrection, but also anticipates the future, final, and festive "wedding" banquet that Jesus, the "bridegroom" (9:15; 22:2), will share with all of his followers in the kingdom of heaven.

When Jesus and his disciples came to Gethsemane on the Mount of Olives, he told them, "Sit here while I go over there and pray" (26:36). He took along Peter and the two sons of Zebedee (cf. 17:1; 20:20), and began to be saddened and distressed (26:37), telling them, "My soul is very sorrowful, even to death; remain here and watch with me" (26:38). Jesus' urgent plea for these three disciples to "watch" with him recalls his earlier command for the disciples and for all others to "watch" (24:42; 25:13) in the period after his resurrection and before his final coming (24:36–44). To "watch" means to be awake and alert, ready and prepared for the crucial "day" and "hour" (24:36, 44) introducing God's final and definitive salvation. The situation of the disciples' "watching" with Jesus while he prays thus sets them up as a paradigm for the audience's time of "watching" for the final and triumphant coming of Jesus after his death and resurrection.

Going forward a little, Jesus "fell on his face" (26:39), accentuating the overwhelming effect of his profound distress and anxiety in view of his imminent death, as it places him in a position for worship (cf. 2:11; 4:9; 17:6). He then prayed, "My Father, if it is possible, let this cup pass from me" (26:39). Jesus relied upon his unique sonship (3:17; 17:5) as he affectionately and respectfully begged God as "my" intimate and loving "Father" for deliverance from his approaching death. The deferential preface "if it is possible" recalls Jesus' previous assertions that "for God all things are possible" (19:26) and that "whatever you ask for in prayer with faith, you will receive" (21:22; cf. 17:20). When Jesus introduced his earnest prayer with "if it is possible," he did so knowing and firmly believing that the God who is his loving "Father" is powerful enough to answer the prayer of his "beloved Son" for deliverance from death.

The dramatic tension between the divine necessity that Jesus suffer and die and his quite human dread of the kind of suffering and death he was to undergo was resolved through the very process of his praying as Jesus uttered the words "but not as I will but as you will!" (26:39). In thus submitting his own will to the sovereign will of his Father, Jesus showed how he is indeed God's obedient and "beloved Son." By so praying, he exemplified the key characteristic of his new "family" of followers: "whoever does the will of my Father in heaven is my brother and sister and mother!" (12:50). For those he calls to follow him on his way to suffering and death, Jesus demonstrated what it means to think "the things of God" rather than the "things of human beings" (16:23) and to "deny oneself" (16:24) in order to take up one's cross and follow him—namely, to deny one's own will in favor of God's sovereign and salvific will.

Jesus' acceptance of God's will over his own will in prayer, even though he knew and believed that God had the power to let this cup of suffering and death pass by him (26:39), developed his previous teaching about prayer. Although the disciples, as well as the audience, are to pray with faith in God's absolute power to grant their request (21:21–22; 18:19–20; 17:20), they must realize that God, although he possesses unlimited power, does not always choose to exercise that power to remove suffering and death. The will of God remains sovereign. But the Gethsemane prayer of Jesus illustrates how one can voice the deepest of human fears and concerns with firm faith that God can alleviate them and yet ultimately submit one's own will to God's sovereign will precisely in and through such prayer.

After Jesus found the disciples sleeping rather than watching with him (26:40), he developed his previous command for them to "watch with me" (26:38), as he commanded them to "watch and pray" (26:41). His addition of the command to pray indicates the significance and power of his own praying. Now that he has prayed (26:39), he can command and empower his disciples likewise to pray. That Jesus prayed precisely while the disciples were sleeping and unable to watch with him indicates that the prayer of Jesus is not only the model for the disciples to emulate in their prayer but is the basis or empowerment for their own praying. The disciples who were sleeping can now "watch and pray" only because Jesus has first successfully watched and prayed. They are a model for the audience to be able not only to "watch" but also to "pray" in order to be ready for the unknown time of Jesus' final coming (24:42; 25:13).

When Jesus prayed the first time, he left open that it might be "possible" that his Father's will correspond to his own will not to drink the cup of suffering and death (26:39). But in his second prayer, "My Father, if it is not possible that this cup pass without my drinking it, your will be done!" (26:42), he realized that "it is not possible" for him to escape drinking the "cup," and without any further mention of his own will totally resigned himself to the will of God. His second prayer thus enabled Jesus to accept his Father's will even more fully and absolutely. With an exact echo of the "Our Father" prayer he taught his disciples, "your will be done" (6:10), Jesus not only exemplified how to pray but makes it possible for the disciples and the audience to accept and accomplish God's will on the basis and strength of his prayer.

Jesus' exhortation to the disciples, "Get up, let us go!" (26:46), indicated the powerful effect his prayer has had in uniting them to himself. Before he withdrew to pray, Jesus commanded his disciples to "sit here" and "remain here" while he prayed (26:36, 38). But after he had prayed, Jesus empowered his disciples to "get up" from their inert, sleeping position and enabled them to "go" with him—"Let *us* go!" Now that Jesus has been strengthened through his prayer, he and his disciples can "go" together to play their respective roles in God's salvific plan—the bewildered disciples to be "scattered" (26:31, 56) and Jesus to be betrayed. With his climactic exclamation, "Behold, my betrayer has arrived!" (26:46), Jesus not only intensified his announcement, "Behold the hour has arrived!" (26:45) but illustrated his determined readiness—now that he has submitted himself to God's will through prayer—to face his betrayer (26:47-50). He has thus presented the audience with a model of how they, in and through prayer, can play their roles in God's plan of salvation.

At the trial of Jesus two presumably true witnesses came forward (26:59-60) and testified that they heard Jesus claim, "I have the power to destroy the sanctuary of God and within three days rebuild it" (26:61). This prompts the audience to probe the profound paradox that it is precisely through the death of Jesus, the aim of their accusation, that he will exercise the divine power of his resurrection to "build" a new and superior "sanctuary" for authentic worship. It will be the communal edifice of Jesus' followers and demonstrate that indeed "something greater than the temple is here" (12:6).

Although indicative of his experience of intense anguish as he dies radically alone and without divine intervention, Jesus' cry, "My God, my God, why have you forsaken me?" (27:46; cf. Ps 22:1), is not one of despair but is a lamentful prayer. It was uttered with complete confidence and total trust in his God, whom he addressed twice as "my God." With confidence in his Father's sovereign plan for him, he prayed for God to refute the ridicule of his trust as God's Son (27:43) by disclosing the divine purpose of his death.

In response to Jesus' death and as a beginning to the answer of "why" God abandoned him to death (27:46), the veil hanging in the temple sanctuary "was split" by God (divine passive) in two pieces "from top to bottom" (27:51). This destruction of the sanctuary veil, symbolic of the temple cult, indicated the termination of the old temple sanctuary that Jesus had judged inadequate as the place of authentic worship (21:12-17) and pointed to the advent of a new, superior sanctuary. By his death in apparent weakness, Jesus demonstrated his power to destroy the old temple sanctuary and opened the way for his rebuilding of a new one for authentic prayer and worship—the community of his followers.

Through their worshipful confession of the crucified Jesus the Roman soldiers, who represent the Gentile world, became members of the new, communal "sanctuary" of authentic worship that Jesus has the power to build (26:61; 27:40) through his resurrection, now that his death has pointed to God's destruction of the old temple sanctuary (27:51). The climactic confession of Jesus' divine sonship by these Gentile soldiers, "Truly this one was the Son of God!" (27:54), confirmed God's previous proclamations that "this one is my beloved Son, with whom I am well pleased" (3:17; 17:5). It underlines for the audience the worthiness of Jesus to be worshiped as the divine Son of God (14:33; 16:16), who died on the cross as an act of ethical self-sacrificial worship of God to save his people from their sins (1:21).

The eleven disciples went to Galilee to the mountain to which Jesus had ordered them (28:16; cf. 26:32). When they saw Jesus, they worshiped, but some doubted (28:17). That the eleven disciples "worshiped" the risen Jesus complemented the women who likewise "worshiped" the risen Jesus (28:9). And it reinforces for the audience the previous worship of the disciples after they saw Jesus performing the uniquely divine activity of walking on the sea: Those in the boat "worshiped" him, saying, "Truly you are the Son of God!" (14:33).

The command of the risen Jesus to make disciples of all the nations by baptizing them into the name of the Father and of the Son and of the Holy Spirit (28:19) reminds the audience that their own baptism was a ritual, sacramental act of worship by which they became beloved sons and daughters of God and thus brothers and sisters of Jesus. The brothers and sisters of Jesus are characterized as those who do the will of Jesus' heavenly Father (12:50), as taught and exemplified by Jesus. Equipped like Jesus with the Holy Spirit at their baptism, the members of the audience are enabled to do God's will, which includes resisting false worship for the true worship of God. They are also enabled by the Holy Spirit to make disciples of all the nations by baptizing them into the divine family, so that they may engage in the true worship not only of the divine Father but of Jesus, his divine beloved Son (3:16–18; 4:10).

When Jesus gave his twelve disciples authority to preach and heal (10:1, 7–8), he did not yet give them his divine authority to teach (7:29; 21:23; 22:16). It was only after the disciples experienced the ethical worship of Jesus' self-sacrificial death that the risen Jesus gave them the authority to make disciples of all the nations by "teaching them to observe all that I have commanded you" (28:20a). With regard to worship, Jesus taught and exemplified not only the liturgical, ritual worship of how to pray (6:6–13; 14:23;

19:13; 26:36-44) but the ethical worship of extending mercy to others. He taught people to "learn" that God desires the ethical worship of practicing mercy and love for others that complements ritual sacrificial worship (9:13; 12:7; 22:34-40; 23:23). The risen Jesus has thus given his disciples as well as the audience the divine authority to teach all the nations to practice the ethical worship that complements ritual worship, the holistic, authentic worship that they themselves are to exemplify.

The risen Jesus concluded his instructions to his disciples and thus to the audience by assuring them, "And behold, I am with you all days until the end of the age" (28:20b). Jesus thus promised to continue to be "God with us" (1:23) in both our liturgical, ritual worship as well as in our ethical worship. Whoever welcomes a child in the name of Jesus welcomes Jesus himself (18:5), and thus worships him ethically. In a liturgical gathering together for prayer in the name of Jesus (18:19-20a) he promised that "there I am in the midst of them" (18:20b). And with regard to the ethical worship that it is necessary for disciples to practice by extending the mercy and love God desires to others, Jesus promised to be with us always by provocatively identifying himself with the least among us, when he declared as the criterion for final judgment, "Whatever you did to one of these least brothers of mine, you did to me" (25:40, 45). Jesus not only taught and exemplified how we are to practice a true and holistic worship, but also became, as the beloved Son of God (3:17; 17:5), an always present object of our authentic worship of God.

10

Conclusion

DETAILED SUMMARIES CAN BE found at each of the conclusions of chapters 2–9 above. This final chapter will provide a synthetic overview of the various key dimensions of the theme of worship in the Gospel of Matthew.

Jesus as Object of Worship

Jesus as Object of Reverential Worship

Before his birth in Bethlehem of Judea Jesus was introduced to the audience as the Christ (Matt 1:1, 16–18) whose primarily Jewish genealogy as son of David and son of Abraham (1:1) included Gentile women (1:5). His conception was from the Holy Spirit (1:18, 20) and he will come to be known as "God with us" (1:23). This indicated to the audience of Matthew that he has the divine status that makes him a worthy object of worship by all peoples, whether they are Jews or Gentiles. The Gentile magi who came to Jerusalem from the east when Jesus was born (2:1) provide the audience with a first model for the reverential worship of Jesus. In Bethlehem they "fell down" and "worshiped" the infant Jesus (2:11) as the newborn messianic King of the Jews (2:2, 4).

After they were saved from possible death in a sea storm through Jesus' uniquely divine power to walk upon the sea, the disciples in the boat "worshiped" him with the words, "Truly you are the Son of God!" (14:33). Peter, who was returning to the boat after his failed attempt to come to Jesus on the water (14:28–31) when the other disciples worshiped Jesus, later complemented and enhanced their worship, when he declared to Jesus,

"You are the Christ, the Son of the living God!" (16:16). When three of the disciples, Peter, James, and John, heard the voice of God from the bright cloud declaring Jesus, whom they had just seen transfigured into a heavenly being (17:2), as his beloved Son (17:5), they "fell upon their face and were greatly frightened" (17:6), which placed them in a posture for the reverential worship of Jesus. This underscored for the audience that Jesus alone is worthy of having a "tent" (17:3–4) where he may be an object of worship as the beloved Son of God who will attain heavenly glory only after the divine necessity of his suffering, death, and resurrection (16:21).

The crowds preceding and those following Jesus as he rode into Jerusalem on a donkey and its colt (21:7) performed an act of reverential worship, as they cried out with praise, "Hosanna to the Son of David! Blessed is he who comes in the name of the Lord! Hosanna in the highest heights! [Ps 118:25–26]" (Matt 21:9). In contrast to Gentile rulers (20:25), however, Jesus has not "come" to be served but to serve and to give his life as a ransom for many (20:28).

When the chief priests and the scribes, who were among those responsible for putting Jesus to death (16:21; 20:18), saw the boys crying out in the temple and saying, "Hosanna to the Son of David!," they were indignant (21:15). Jesus then asked them if they have never read in the scriptural word of God: "Out of the mouth of infants and nurslings you have prepared praise for yourself [Ps 8:3]" (Matt 21:16b). By their act of reverential worship of Jesus in the temple the boys were actually praising God and thus present the audience with a model of the authentic worship God desires to take place in the temple as God's "house of prayer" (21:13).

While Jesus was reclining for a meal in the house of Simon the leper in Bethany (26:6), an anonymous woman performed a noteworthy gesture of reverential worship of Jesus as she poured costly perfumed ointment from an alabaster flask on his head (26:7). Jesus explained that she did this to prepare him for burial (26:12). Whenever the gospel is proclaimed what the woman has done in worshiping Jesus will be told in memory of her (26:13). Her "good deed," like the good deeds of Jesus, not only inspires the audience to glorify God (5:16; 9:8; 15:31), but to worship Jesus himself for the precious value of his self-sacrificial death by which the people of God are redeemed (20:28).

When the Gentile centurion and those with him who were keeping watch over the dying Jesus (27:36) saw the earthquake and the things that happened (27:51–53), they were greatly awed and performed an act of reverential worship of Jesus, declaring, "Truly this one was the Son of God!" (27:54). These Roman soldiers, who represent the Gentile world, thus became members of the new, communal sanctuary of authentic worship that

Jesus has the power to build (26:61; 27:40) through his resurrection, now that his death has pointed to God's destruction of the old temple sanctuary (27:51). Their climactic confession of Jesus' divine sonship reaffirmed and enhanced the Jewish disciples' worship of him as the Son of God (14:33; 16:16). It complemented the Gentile magi's worship of the infant Jesus as the newborn King of the Jews (2:2, 11) and underlines for the audience the worthiness of the crucified Jesus to be worshiped as the divine Son of God.

After the women at the tomb ran to announce to the disciples (28:8) the angel's message that Jesus has been raised from the dead and can be seen in Galilee (28:7), suddenly the risen Jesus met them. They approached, grasped the feet of Jesus, and "worshiped" him (28:9). The reverential worship of the risen Jesus by the Jewish women was complemented by that of the eleven Jewish male disciples, who went to Galilee to the mountain to which Jesus had ordered them (28:16; cf. 26:32). When they saw the risen Jesus, even though some of them doubted, they "worshiped" (28:17). The women and the disciples thus provide a model for the audience's reverential worship of the risen Jesus.

Jesus as Object of Supplicatory Worship

A Jewish leper, a man with a contagious skin disease which was not only personally painful but rendered him ritually unclean and thus excluded him from the worshiping community, approached and "worshiped" Jesus, expressing the faith that Jesus can heal him: "Lord, if you will, you can make me clean" (8:2). Jesus' answer to the leper's act of supplicatory worship by healing and restoring him to the worshiping community (8:3–4) presents the audience with a model for their own supplicatory worship. They are called to imitate the remarkable faith of the leper in their own praying to Jesus. His answer to the leper's prayer indicates his divine will and power to eliminate whatever personal difficulties may prevent one from a full participation in communal worship.

A Gentile centurion performed an act of intercessory supplicatory worship as he prayed to Jesus (8:5) on behalf of his paralyzed servant (8:6). Jesus answered his intercessory prayer in accord with his great faith (8:10), as at the mere word of Jesus his servant was healed (8:13). Jesus' healing of the centurion's servant presents the audience with a model for their own intercessory prayer. They are called to pray for others in need with the great faith of the centurion. The answer to his prayer indicates that Jesus has the divine power, as "God with us" (1:23), to help those for whom we pray.

A Jewish ruler came to Jesus and "worshiped" him with an intercessory prayer of supplication: "My daughter has just died, but come, lay your hand on her, and she will live" (9:18). Jesus' raising of the dead daughter, as if she were only sleeping (9:24-25), to life in answer to the intercessory supplicatory worship of the ruler calls the audience to likewise engage in intercessory prayer for those who have died with the faith that the risen Jesus who will be with us always (28:20) will raise them from the "sleep" of death to life eternal.

Jesus' miraculous healing of two blind men (9:27-31) and his exorcism of a mute demoniac (9:32-34) present the audience with further models for their own supplicatory worship. They are called to pray to Jesus with the faith (9:28-29) that he can eliminate from their lives the evils, including their spiritual "blindness," that hinder their participation in worship. They may then celebrate (9:31, 33) his divine power over the devil, the ruler of demons (9:34), the power that can enable them to fulfill the scriptural pronouncement by which Jesus refused to worship the devil/Satan: "The Lord your God shall you worship and him alone shall you serve [Deut 6:13]" (Matt 4:10).

When the people of Gennesaret recognized Jesus, they and those from the surrounding region brought to him all who were sick (14:35), who then performed a noteworthy act of supplicatory worship, as they "beseeched/prayed" that they might only touch the tassel of his cloak. And as many as touched it were "healed/saved" (14:36), implying that they were not only healed of their sickness but saved from their sins. The members of the audience are thus encouraged to have the faith to pray to Jesus as the divine Son of God (14:33) who not only can heal their sicknesses but "will save" them from their sins (1:21; 9:1-8).

Jesus' healing of the daughter of the Canaanite woman (15:21-28) presents the audience with an outstanding model for their own supplicatory and intercessory worship. They are encouraged to have the great faith of the Canaanite woman that Jesus will provide for their own needs, as well as the needs of those for whom they pray, because of his divine compassion and power to provide an overabundance of salvific benefits. This unnamed Gentile woman reaffirms that "in his name the Gentiles will hope" (12:21), as she demonstrates for the audience that, regardless of their ethnic origin or gender, they may be confident that the compassionate Jesus will answer their prayers when they pray with faith for him to help them.

A man approached Jesus, "falling on his knees" in a posture for supplicatory worship (17:14), and voiced an intercessory prayer, "Lord, have mercy on my son" (17:15). In view of Jesus' previous prediction of the divine necessity for him to be killed (16:21), he will not be physically present much longer (17:17). Jesus answered the man's prayer, as he rebuked the demon causing his son's suffering so that it came out of him and he was healed "from that hour" (17:18)—from the time the man presented Jesus with his intercessory prayer of supplicatory worship. The members of the audience are to have the faith that the risen Jesus remains as "God with us" (1:23; 28:20), who can answer their supplicatory prayers of intercession (17:14–18).

After Jesus identified himself as the one with the unique divine power to walk on the sea (14:26–27), Peter asked Jesus to command him to come to Jesus on the water (14:28). When Jesus issued the command for him to come, Peter began to walk on the water and come to Jesus (14:29). But, seeing the strong wind and beginning to sink, he performed an act of supplicatory worship as he cried out, "Lord, save me!" (14:30). Peter received an immediate answer to his prayer as Jesus took hold of him and saved him from sinking, saying, "O you of little faith, why did you doubt?" (14:31). This recalls that at a previous storm on the sea Jesus similarly addressed the disciples as those of "little faith," before he calmed the storm (8:26) and thus answered their prayer, "Lord, save, we are perishing!" (8:25). Jesus' answer to these prayers of supplication by disciples provides a model for the audience, assuring them that Jesus has the divine power to likewise answer their prayers to be saved from any and all dangers symbolized by the chaotic sea.

Not everyone who cries out to Jesus as "Lord, Lord" in an act of supplicatory worship will enter into the kingdom of heaven at the final judgment, but only the one who does the will of his heavenly Father (7:21). Supplicatory worship alone will not suffice; it must be complemented by ethical worship. Despite the prophecies, exorcisms, and great deeds many may have done in the name of Jesus (7:22), he will confess to them that he never knew them and they will be dismissed as workers of lawlessness, those who failed to do God's will (7:23). For disciples and thus the Matthean audience to make sure that they will be known by Jesus at the final judgment they must do the will of his heavenly Father by doing the more abundant righteousness (5:20) Jesus has revealed to them, doing what is right and just in accord with the will of God, which pleases God as ethical worship.

The mother of the sons of Zebedee approached Jesus with her two sons and performed an act of petitionary worship, as she was "worshiping and asking something from him" (20:20). She requested that he command that her two sons sit in the places of preeminence in his kingdom (20:21). This inappropriate act of supplicatory worship reinforces for the audience Jesus' teaching to pray not for the accomplishment of one's own will, but rather that the will of the heavenly Father be done (6:9–10).

As Jesus and his disciples left Jericho, a large crowd followed him (20:29). When two blind men sitting by the way heard that Jesus was passing by, they performed an act of supplicatory worship, saying to him, "Have mercy on us, Lord, Son of David!" (20:30; cf. 9:27-31). In contrast to the unsympathetic crowd who wanted to silence the two blind men, Jesus had compassion on them in answer to their double prayer for mercy (20:30-31). He touched their eyes, and immediately they received their sight and "followed" him (20:34), thus joining the crowd who "followed" him (20:29), to his suffering, death, and resurrection in Jerusalem (20:17-19). In contrast to the inappropriate prayer of the mother for her two sons (20:20-23), the appropriate, intensified prayer of the two blind men presents the audience with a model for how they are to pray to Jesus for the insight to be able to "see" and properly "follow" him by imitating his self-sacrificial service for others (20:28).

In the parable of the wise and foolish maidens (25:1-13), after the bridegroom arrived, characterizing the final coming of Jesus (cf. 9:15), the wise maidens, who were ready, entered the wedding feast with him, symbolic of entering the kingdom of heaven, and then the door was locked (25:10). Later the foolish maidens came and performed an act of supplicatory worship, as they said, "Lord, Lord, open for us!" (25:11). But replying he said, "Amen I say to you, I do not know you!" (25:12). This recalls Jesus' previous warning that not everyone who says to him, "Lord, Lord," will enter the kingdom of heaven, only the one who does the will of his Father in heaven (7:21). The parable thus exhorts the audience to be ready for the unknown time of Jesus' final coming (25:13) by doing the will of God, so that they, like the wise maidens, may enter into the kingdom of heaven. The "will" of God includes especially extending to others the mercy that "I [God] will" as the ethical worship that complements ritualistic worship (9:13; 12:7).

Jesus as Teacher of Worship

Jesus as Teacher of Prayer

Jesus taught his disciples, as well as the Matthean audience, a model prayer for their communal worship (6:9-13), a prayer that accents a disposition of humble submission to God as the essence of authentic prayer. After addressing God as "our Father," they are to pray that his name be made holy (6:9), his kingdom come, and his heavenly will be done on earth (6:10). Having thus humbly submitted their own wills to God's will, they may then pray that God, who knows what they need (6:8), provide it for them (6:11), forgive their sins as they forgive those who sin against them (6:12), and deliver them from the evil one, the devil, so as not to be led into temptation (6:13; cf. 4:1-11). Finally, Jesus emphatically reaffirmed that they must forgive others in order to be forgiven by God (6:14-15).

Jesus taught that if his followers ask in prayer for the prudent discernment needed to correct the faults of others (7:3-6), it will be given them by God, for everyone who asks will receive, just as one who seeks finds, and to one who knocks it will be opened (7:7-8). Just as parents do not give bad things to their children, so even more the heavenly Father will surely give good things to those who ask for them in prayer (7:9-11). They are to pray to be able to correct the faults of others, just as they would want others to do for them; such love for one another sums up the meaning of the Law and the Prophets (7:12; cf. 5:20).

As Jesus told his disciples, although the "harvest" of people needing to be shepherded into the kingdom of heaven is large, the "workers" to help shepherd them are few (9:37). He then urged them to perform an act of supplicatory worship and ask the Lord of the "harvest" to send out "workers" to help shepherd his "harvest" of people (9:38). Jesus then provided a preliminary answer to their prayer, as he summoned his twelve disciples and gave them a share in his own divine authority over unclean spirits to cast them out and heal every disease and every sickness (10:1). Jesus thus taught the audience to pray that God will continue to provide workers to lead people into the kingdom of heaven.

If two of Jesus' followers agree on earth about anything for which they ask, especially regarding the restoration of a sinning fellow believer, Jesus taught that "what you pray for will be done for you" by his Father in heaven (18:18-19). Where two or three are gathered together in Jesus' name, whose name signifies that he is the one who will save his people from their sins (1:21), there he is in the midst of them (18:20). Communal prayer, especially for the repentance and restoration of sinners, is thus another way that the risen Jesus is present to the members of the audience as "God with us" (1:23; 28:20).

Jesus taught his disciples that "whatever you ask for in prayer, believing, you will receive" (21:22). By praying with faith in God, the audience, as a community of believers, can become God's "house of prayer" that the Jerusalem temple failed to become (21:13). Jesus' teaching that "he is not the God of the dead but of the living" (22:32b) reinforces that the sacrifices of dead animals (21:12) are not the authentic worship God wanted in the temple as God's "house of prayer." Authentic worship is giving to God what belongs to God (22:21)—the living human being, and worshiping the God of the living, who will raise believers to eternal life, just as he will raise the patriarchs who worshiped the God of the living, Abraham, Isaac, and Jacob, after he has raised Jesus from the dead (22:32).

Jesus asked the Jewish leaders if they have never read in the scriptures that the "stone," representative of the Son of God, Jesus, that the "builders," representative of the Jewish leaders of the temple, rejected by killing him has become the cornerstone of a new place for authentic prayer and worship. This has been done by the Lord God, who will raise Jesus from the dead, and "it is wonderful in our eyes" (21:42). This indicates to the audience that through his death and resurrection Jesus will become the foundational cornerstone of the church. Therefore the kingdom of God will be taken away from the Jewish leaders and given to a nation that will produce its "fruits" (21:43; cf. 21:18-19) of authentic worship, the church led by the disciples (16:18), as the community of those who pray with faith in God (21:21-22). It will become the place for the true and authentic worship of God, God's communal "house of prayer" (21:13), that the Jewish temple failed to become.

Jesus as Teacher of Ritualistic Worship

Jesus taught that when his followers fast as an act of ritualistic, ascetic worship, they are not to look gloomy like hypocritical Jews who neglect their appearance so that they may appear to people to be fasting. They have already received their human reward (6:16). They have drawn attention to themselves rather than to God as the object of true worship. When disciples, and thus the audience, fast, they are to attend to their appearance (6:17), so that they do not appear to people to be fasting. Their heavenly Father, who sees what they are doing in private, will reward them (6:18), as then their fasting will be pleasing to him as an act of authentic worship.

The disciples of John questioned Jesus why they and the Pharisees practice the ascetic worship of fasting but his disciples do not (9:14). Jesus responded by pointing out to them the inappropriateness for the wedding guests/his disciples to mourn/fast as long as the bridegroom/Jesus is with them (9:15a). With a reference to his being put to death, Jesus went on to declare that the days will come when he as the bridegroom will be taken away from them, and then they will fast (9:15b). This calls for the audience to celebrate in their liturgical worship the arrival of Jesus ("God with us") as the divine bridegroom of the messianic wedding feast of the kingdom of heaven, but also to practice the ascetic worship of fasting, as exemplified (4:2-4) and taught (6:16-18) by Jesus.

The command of the risen Jesus to make disciples of all the nations by baptizing them into the name of the Father and of the Son and of the Holy Spirit (28:19) reminds the audience that their own baptism was a ritual, sacramental act of worship by which they became beloved sons and daughters of God and thus brothers and sisters of Jesus. The brothers and sisters of Jesus are characterized as those who do the will of Jesus' heavenly Father (12:50), as taught and exemplified by Jesus. Equipped like Jesus with the Holy Spirit at their baptism, the members of the audience are enabled to do God's will, which includes resisting false worship for the true worship of God. They are also enabled by the Holy Spirit to make disciples of all the nations by baptizing them into the divine family, so that they make engage in the true worship not only of the divine Father but of Jesus, his divine beloved Son (3:16–18; 4:10; 17:5).

Jesus as Teacher of Ethical Worship

In the second set of four beatitudes (5:7–10) Jesus pronounced God's blessing upon those who help the unfortunate, especially those exemplified in the first set of four beatitudes (5:3–6), and promised them God's heavenly reward. Blessed are the merciful, those who exhibit compassion for the unfortunate as the ethical worship God desires (Hos 6:6), for they will be shown mercy by God (Matt 5:7). Blessed are "the clean of heart," those who help the unfortunate with the honesty, sincerity, and integrity required to truly worship God (Ps 15; 24:3–6), for they will see God (Matt 5:8) as the goal of their worship (Ps 42:3).

Jesus taught the need not just to avoid anger, but, more positively, to reconcile oneself with one's fellow human being. If someone comes to offer in cultic worship a sacrificial gift at the altar, and then remembers that someone has something against him (5:23), he is to leave the gift at the altar, go first to reconcile himself with the person, and then return to offer the gift (5:24). Jesus thus indicated the fundamental need for the ethical behavior, in this case, reconciliation, that is a precondition for and complements cultic worship. For cultic or liturgical worship to please God, it must be accompanied by the ethical worship God desires ("I desire mercy and not [simply] sacrifice" [Hos 6:6; cf. Matt 9:13; 12:7]).

Jesus taught that when his followers practice almsgiving, giving to the poor as an act of ethical worship sometimes equated with sacrificial worship in the biblical tradition, they are not to draw attention to themselves, in order that "they may be glorified" by people (6:2), thus making themselves an object of false doxological worship. Indeed, this would contradict Jesus' previous teaching for his followers to let people see their good deeds, so that "they may glorify" the heavenly Father (5:16) as an act of true doxological worship. If they perform their almsgiving privately and in a way that does not draw attention to themselves, it will amount to ethical worship pleasing to God, who will reward them accordingly (6:3-4).

When Jesus and his disciples shared table fellowship with Matthew and many other tax collectors and public sinners (9:10), the Pharisees objected (9:11), since such people were considered ritually unclean for failing to observe the cultic food regulations, which gave meals a worship dimension. Jesus replied that those who are "sick" need a physician (9:12). He then taught the Pharisees, as well as the audience, to go and learn the meaning of the divine scriptural pronouncement, "Mercy I desire and not [simply] sacrifice" (Hos 6:6), for Jesus did not come to call the righteous but sinners to repentance (Matt 9:13). Jesus thus extended to sinners, as those who are spiritually "sick," the healing mercy God desires as the ethical worship that complements ritualistic worship.

Jesus taught the importance of the heart for authentic worship (15:8-9), as he urged the crowd to hear and understand (15:10) that "not what enters into the mouth defiles a person, but what comes out of the mouth, this defiles a person" (15:11), thus preventing authentic worship. He explained that "the things that come out of the mouth come from the heart, and these things defile a person" (15:18). For from the heart come the kinds of behavior that transgress the commandments of God—evil thoughts, murder, adultery, sexual immortality, theft, false witness, blasphemy (15:19). Eating with unwashed hands does not defile a person (15:2), but the evil things that come from the heart are what defile a person (15:20), as they break the very commandments of God, the obedience of which God wants as authentic ethical worship.

To the first and greatest commandment that "you shall love the Lord your God" whole-heartedly (22:37-38), Jesus added a second like it: "You shall love your neighbor as yourself [Lev 19:18]" (Matt 22:39). But Jesus had already extended the commandment to love your neighbor to include loving your enemy and thus be "perfect," completely inclusive in loving all human beings, like the heavenly Father (5:43-48). For the audience to become God's household of authentic worship that the Jerusalem temple failed to be (21:13) they are not only to pray to God with faith (21:21-22) and confess their whole-hearted love of God in liturgical worship, but also to practice the ethical worship of loving all of their fellow human beings.

In contrast to the scribes and Pharisees, who exalt themselves and seek to be served and honored as great ones by human beings (23:5-10), the greatest among the followers of Jesus will be their "servant" (23:11), and whoever will exalt himself will be humbled by God, but whoever "will humble himself" will be exalted by God (23:12). This recalls Jesus' previous teaching that whoever "will humble himself" like a child is the greatest in the kingdom of heaven (18:4). And it recalls that whoever wishes to be great among his disciples will be their "servant" (20:26). Jesus himself provides the model for this. As the Son of Man, he did not come "to be served" but "to serve" and to give his life as a ransom for many (20:28), an act of self-sacrificial worship. Similarly, the followers of Jesus are to humble themselves, like Jesus who is "humble" in heart (11:29), and serve one another as an act of ethical self-sacrificial worship for which they will be exalted by God.

In the climactic parable of universal judgment (25:31–46) Jesus teaches the audience to be ready for the unknown time of his final coming (25:13) by attending to the provocative way that he is still with them in the "least brothers" with whom he identifies himself (25:40, 45). The members of the audience are urged to become righteous "sheep" rather than condemned "goats" (25:31–33, 41) by extending to Jesus' needy least brothers the mercy God desires as ethical worship (9:13; 12:7). This includes such compassionate practices as feeding the hungry, giving drink to the thirsty, welcoming strangers, clothing the naked, caring for the sick, and visiting prisoners (25:35–40).

But the audience may find themselves in the situation of being needy "least brothers" of Jesus, as disciples, "these little ones" (10:42; 18:6, 10, 14), who humble themselves like a child, believe in Jesus, and do the will of his Father as "brothers" in the true family of Jesus (12:49–50). They may take the risk of becoming Jesus' "least brothers" as his disciples, since they can be assured that there will be righteous "sheep" who will take care of them and be rewarded with entrance into the kingdom of heaven for doing so (25:34). They are to be encouraged, then, that becoming needy "least ones" and enduring the hardships of discipleship amounts to ethical worship pleasing to God, since Jesus, "God with us" (1:23; 28:20), identifies himself with "these least brothers of mine" (25:40, 45).

Jesus as Worshiper

The Praying of Jesus

As the second of his three temptations (4:1–11), the devil took Jesus to the holy city of Jerusalem and stood him on the pinnacle of the temple (4:5), a place associated with both prayer and protective refuge. The devil enticed Jesus to demonstrate his status as the Son of God by throwing himself down

(4:6a). The devil cleverly quoted from a psalm used in temple worship to celebrate God's promise of protection particularly for the Davidic Christ: "He will command his angels concerning you and on their hands they will lift you up, lest you strike your foot against a stone [Ps 91:11–12]" (4:6b). Jesus overcame the devil's temptation by appealing to another scriptural word of God: "You shall not test the Lord your God [Deut 6:16]" (4:7). With this second temptation Jesus models for the audience how authentic prayer refrains from trying to manipulate God for one's personal benefit.

Again, the devil took Jesus to a very high mountain and showed him all the kingdoms of the world and their glory (4:8). He tempted him with the diabolical promise, "All these things I will give you, if you fall down and worship me" (4:9). Jesus overcame this third temptation by again appealing to a scriptural word of God: "The Lord your God shall you worship and him alone shall you serve [Deut 6:13]" (4:10). With this third final and climactic temptation Jesus models for the audience how authentic worship and prayer must be centered totally on God alone and thus excludes giving oneself over to and making life's priority the pursuit of worldly power, prestige, and wealth, which amounts to the worship of false gods and/or the devil.

Jesus taught his disciples and thus the audience to pray that the will of their heavenly Father may be done on earth (6:9–10). He later performed a prayer of laudatory worship, praising his heavenly Father for the accomplishment of his gracious will: "I praise you, Father, Lord of heaven and earth, that you have hidden these things from the wise and intelligent, but have revealed them to the childlike. Yes, Father, such has been your good pleasure" (11:25–26). Those in the audience are to become the "childlike" to enter into the kingdom of heaven (18:3–4), disciples who as "little ones" (10:42) are humble recipients of divine revelation. They are invited to join Jesus in praising his Father, whose true character Jesus, to whom his Father has handed over everything, has revealed to them (11:27).

After Jesus forced the disciples to embark in the boat and precede him to the other side of the Sea of Galilee, while he dismissed the crowds (14:22) who had been miraculously fed (14:13–21), he went up the mountain by himself to pray (14:23), thus performing an act of worship placing him in communion with God. As a result of his prayer, Jesus came to his disciples and revealed to them his unique divine power to walk on the sea (14:25), thus treading down the stormy waters of chaos (14:24) and making the sea crossable for his disciples, demonstrating that he has an absolute divine power to save people from all evils.

Children were brought to Jesus as an implicit act of supplicatory worship for him to lay his hands on them and pray, but the disciples rebuked them (19:13). Jesus, however, said, "Allow the children and do not prevent them to come to me, for the kingdom of heaven belongs to such as these" (19:14). He then placed his hands on them and presumably prayed for them in answer to the supplicatory gesture that he do so (19:13). Jesus here not only reaffirmed his appeal that "unless you become like children, you will not enter into the kingdom of heaven" (18:3), but presents the audience with a model of praying for children as those in need of and worthy of God's blessing and thus of participation in communal worship.

At Gethsemane Jesus prayed, "My Father, if it is possible, let this cup pass from me" (26:39a). The dramatic tension between the divine necessity that Jesus suffer and die and his quite human dread of the kind of suffering and death he was to undergo (26:37–38) was resolved through the very process of his praying as Jesus uttered the words "but not as I will but as you will!" (26:39b). By so praying, he exemplified the key characteristic of his new "family" of followers: "whoever does the will of my Father in heaven is my brother and sister and mother!" (12:50). For those he calls to follow him on his way to suffering and death, Jesus demonstrated what it means to think "the things of God" rather than the "things of human beings" (16:23) and to "deny oneself" (16:24) in order to take up one's cross and follow him—namely, to deny one's own will in favor of God's sovereign and salvific will.

When Jesus prayed the first time at Gethsemane, he left open that it might be "possible" that his Father's will correspond to his own will not to drink the cup of suffering and death (26:39). But in his second prayer, "My Father, if it is not possible that this cup pass without my drinking it, your will be done!" (26:42), he realized that "it is not possible" for him to escape drinking the "cup," and without any further mention of his own will totally resigned himself to the will of God. His second prayer thus enabled Jesus to accept his Father's will even more fully and absolutely. With an exact echo of the "Our Father" prayer he taught his disciples, "your will be done" (6:10), Jesus not only exemplified how to pray but makes it possible for the disciples and the audience to accept and accomplish God's will on the basis and strength of his prayer.

While on the cross Jesus cried out in a loud voice, "My God, My God, why have you forsaken me? [Ps 22:1]" (Matt 27:46). Having endured God's silent abandonment, symbolized by the dismal darkness (27:45) God caused instead of rescuing him from an excruciating death at the hands of reviling accusers (27:39–44), Jesus prayed for the reason "why" or "for what purpose" God has forsaken him. Although indicative of his experience of intense anguish as he dies radically alone and without divine intervention, Jesus' cry is not one of despair but is a lamentful prayer, uttered with complete confidence and total trust in his God, whom he addressed twice as "my

God." With confidence in his Father's sovereign plan for him, he prayed for God to refute the ridicule of his trust as God's Son (27:43) by disclosing the divine purpose of his death.

In response to Jesus' death and as a beginning to the answer of his prayer as to "why" God abandoned him to death (27:46), the veil hanging in the temple sanctuary "was split" by God (divine passive) in two pieces "from top to bottom" (27:51). This destruction of the sanctuary veil, symbolic of the temple cult, indicated the termination of the old temple sanctuary that Jesus had judged inadequate as the place of authentic prayer and worship (21:12-17) and pointed to the advent of a new, superior sanctuary. By his death in apparent weakness, Jesus demonstrated his power to destroy the old temple sanctuary and opened the way for his rebuilding of a new one for authentic prayer and worship—the community of his followers.

The Ritualistic Worship of Jesus

Jesus' act of ritualistic worship in being baptized by John to fulfill all righteousness (3:13-15) provides the members of the audience with a foundational model for their own Christian sacramental baptism. At his baptism Jesus was empowered with the Holy Spirit of God and declared God's beloved Son by his heavenly Father (3:16-17). The members of the audience have been baptized "into the name of the Father and of the Son and of the Holy Spirit" (28:19). The baptism of Jesus reminds them how their own baptism was in the Holy Spirit, which enables them to practice the ethical behavior, to "produce the fruit" (3:8) of good works and to fulfill all the righteousness (3:15), that God desires for entrance into the kingdom of heaven (5:20). Their ethical worship is to complement their sacramental baptism as an act of ritual worship.

While the disciples and Jesus were eating the Passover meal, Jesus, as the host of the meal, performed the ritualistic worship of taking bread, blessing or thanking God for it, breaking it for distribution, and giving it to his disciples (26:26). In the ritual of the Passover meal the role of the host was to pronounce the traditional symbolic interpretations upon the various elements of the meal. This enabled the participants not only to commemorate but to actually share in and sacramentally relive the salvific experience of the original Passover meal, when God liberated his people from slavery in the exodus from Egypt and gave them the hope of future and final salvation. In his last Passover meal with his disciples, Jesus, as their Teacher (26:18), Lord (26:22), and host, transformed the meaning of this meal for them as he placed a new symbolic interpretation upon the bread and wine. He thereby instituted the sacrament of the Eucharist, enabling the audience not only to commemorate but to relive the salvific experience of Jesus' last meal, which anticipated his self-sacrificial death.

After the body of the lamb was served at the Passover meal, Jesus directed the disciples to take and eat the bread he has blessed and broken for them, which he designated as the symbolic and sacramental equivalent of his body: "This is *my* body" (26:26). By giving them the Passover bread, which is his body destined for his self-sacrificial death, to eat, Jesus enabled his disciples at this meal, and the audience in the sacramental meal of the Eucharist, to share in his death as the salvific event that climaxes all of the past saving deeds of God for his people that the Passover celebrated. Those who eat the bread that has become the very body of Jesus are united in a special table fellowship with him and thus share in the salvific effect of his death as an act of self-sacrificial worship (20:28).

The ritual gestures of taking, blessing, breaking, and giving that Jesus performed in offering the bread that is his body (26:26) recall the identical gestures he used in both of his previous miraculous meals with the crowds (14:13–21; 15:32–39). The pattern Jesus established by these gestures in the miraculous meals concluded with his disciples distributing the bread to the crowds (14:19; 15:36). This pattern implies that when the disciples take the Passover bread/body that Jesus gives them, they are not only to feed themselves but to again distribute it to the people in future celebrations of this new Passover meal. By instituting the Eucharist at his last meal with his disciples, Jesus has enabled them, as well as the audience, to feed, satisfy, and unify other people with him and his saving, self-sacrificial death.

As the commemoration of Jesus' new and unique Passover meal, the sacramental meal of the Eucharist, which includes the drinking of the wine/blood of Jesus, celebrates the divine forgiveness of sins that the blood of the salvific sacrificial death of Jesus makes available for all peoples (26:27–28). The sacramental celebration of the Eucharist not only commemorates and makes present for its participants the past saving events of Jesus' life, death and resurrection, but also anticipates the future, final, and festive "wedding" banquet that Jesus, the divine "bridegroom" (9:15; 22:2), will share with all of his followers in the kingdom of heaven (26:29).

The Ethical Worship of Jesus

Jesus performed an act of ethical worship when he extended mercy to tax collectors and sinners by sharing meal fellowship with them (9:10–11). He then directed the Pharisees, as well as the audience, to go and learn the meaning of the scriptural pronouncement, "Mercy I desire and not [simply] sacrifice" (Hos 6:6), for Jesus did not come to call the righteous but sinners to repentance (Matt 9:13). Jesus thus extended to sinners, as those who are spiritually "sick" (9:12), the healing mercy God desires as the ethical worship that complements cultic worship.

The controversy between Jesus and the Pharisees over proper worship on the Sabbath (12:1–8) provides the audience with a model for their own worship. In compassionately allowing his disciples to satisfy their hunger as an act of priestly worship appropriate on the Sabbath (12:1–4), Jesus demonstrated that he is "Lord" of the Sabbath (12:8). He gave them the rest and refreshment that the Sabbath anticipates by extending to them the mercy God desires as the ethical worship that complements cultic worship (12:7a). As something greater than the sacrificial worship of the temple (12:6), the mercy embodied and actualized by Jesus for his disciples rendered them as innocent as the priests who conduct sacrificial worship in the temple on the Sabbath (12:5, 7b). This reinforces Jesus' invitation for the audience to learn from him to extend to others the mercy God desires as their ethical worship (12:7; 9:13).

Final Summary

To summarize and conclude, the Gospel of Matthew encourages and inspires its audience to practice the true, authentic, and holistic worship required for believers in Jesus to live in the kingdom of heaven. In accord with all that Jesus taught and exemplified regarding authentic worship, they are invited to complement their worship of God (4:10) by worshiping and praying to Jesus as God's beloved Son (3:17; 17:5), who represents "God with us" (1:23; 28:20). And they are invited to complement their ritualistic worship, especially the baptism (3:13–17; 28:19) and Eucharist (26:26–28) instituted for them by Jesus, with an ethical worship that extends to others, especially to disciples (10:40–42), children (18:5), and "the least ones" with whom Jesus identifies himself (25:40, 45), the mercy God desires for a holistic worship (9:13; 12:7). Indeed, a compassionate mercy toward all is the distinctive and noteworthy hallmark that characterizes the theme of worship in the kingdom of heaven according to the Gospel of Matthew.

Bibliography

Angel, Andrew R. "*Crucifixus Vincens*: The 'Son of God' as Divine Warrior in Matthew." *CBQ* 73 (2011) 299–317.
Avalos, Hector. "Blindness." *EDB* 193.
Balz, Horst. "ἔξεστιν." *EDNT* 2.5–6.
———. "οὐαί." *EDNT* 2.540.
Beilner, Wolfgang. "σάββατον." *EDNT* 3.219–22.
Borchert, Gerald L. *Worship in the New Testament: Divine Mystery and Human Response*. St. Louis: Chalice, 2008.
Boxall, Ian. *Discovering Matthew: Content, Interpretation, Reception*. London: SPCK, 2014.
Bühner, Jan-Adolf. "σκηνή." *EDNT* 3.251–52.
Burer, Michael H. *Divine Sabbath Work*. BBRSup 5. Winona Lake, IN: Eisenbrauns, 2012.
Byrne, Brendan. *Lifting the Burden: Reading Matthew's Gospel in the Church Today*. Collegeville, MN: Liturgical, 2004.
Carter, Warren. "The Crowds in Matthew's Gospel." *CBQ* 55 (1993) 54–67.
———. "Matthew 4:18–22 and Matthean Discipleship: An Audience-Oriented Perspective." *CBQ* 59 (1997) 58–75.
Carter, Warren and John Paul Heil. *Matthew's Parables: Audience-Oriented Perspectives*. CBQMS 30. Washington: Catholic Biblical Association, 1998.
Charette, Blaine. *The Theme of Recompense in Matthew's Gospel*. JSNTSup 79. Sheffield: JSOT Press, 1992.
Clements, E. Anne. *Mothers on the Margin?: The Significance of the Women in Matthew's Genealogy*. Eugene, OR: Pickwick, 2014.
Donaldson, Terence L. *Jesus on the Mountain: A Study in Matthean Theology*. JSNTSup 8. Sheffield: JSOT Press, 1985.
———. "The Law That Hangs (Matthew 22:40): Rabbinic Formulation and Matthean Social World." *CBQ* 57 (1995) 689–709.
Eubank, Nathan. "Storing Up Treasure with God in the Heavens: Celestial Investments in Matthew 6:1–21." *CBQ* 76 (2014) 77–92.
———. "What Does Matthew Say about Divine Recompense?: On the Misuse of the Parable of the Workers in the Vineyard (20.1–16)." *JSNT* 35 (2013) 242–62.
France, R. T. *The Gospel of Matthew*. NICNT. Grand Rapids: Eerdmans, 2007.

Gerhardsson, Birger. *The Testing of God's Son (Matt 4:1–11 & Par)*. ConBNT 2/1. Lund: Gleerup, 1966.

Gibbs, Jeffrey A. "Israel Standing with Israel: The Baptism of Jesus in Matthew's Gospel (Matt 3:13–17)." *CBQ* 64 (2002) 511–26.

Giesen, Heinz. "σκανδαλίζω." *EDNT* 3.248.

Goodwin, Mark. J. *Paul: Apostle of the Living God*. Harrisburg, PA: Trinity Press International, 2001.

Gullotta, Daniel N. "Among Dogs and Disciples: An Examination of the Story of the Canaanite Woman (Matthew 15:21–28) and the Question of the Gentile Mission within the Matthean Community." *Neot* 48 (2014) 325–40.

Gundry, Robert H. *Matthew: A Commentary on His Literary and Theological Art*. Grand Rapids: Eerdmans, 1982.

Harrington, Hannah K. "Clean and Unclean." *NIDB* 1.681–89.

Hegermann, Harald. "διαθήκη." *EDNT* 1.299–301.

Heil, John Paul. "The Blood of Jesus in Matthew: A Narrative-Critical Perspective." *PRSt* 18 (1991) 117–24.

———. *The Book of Revelation: Worship for Life in the Spirit of Prophecy*. Eugene, OR: Cascade, 2014.

———. *The Death and Resurrection of Jesus: A Narrative-Critical Reading of Matthew 26–28*. Minneapolis: Fortress, 1991.

———. "The Double Meaning of the Narrative of Universal Judgment in Matthew 25.31–46." *JSNT* 69 (1998) 3–14.

———. "Ezekiel 34 and the Narrative Strategy of the Shepherd and Sheep Metaphor in Matthew." *CBQ* 55 (1993) 698–708.

———. *The Gospel of John: Worship for Divine Life Eternal*. Eugene, OR: Cascade, 2015.

———. *Jesus Walking on the Sea: Meaning and Gospel Functions of Matt 14:22–33, Mark 6:45–52 and John 6:15b–21*. AnBib 87. Rome: Biblical Institute, 1981.

———. *1–3 John: Worship by Loving God and One Another to Live Eternally*. Eugene, OR: Cascade, 2015.

———. *The Letter of James: Worship to Live By*. Eugene, OR: Cascade, 2012.

———. *The Letters of Paul as Rituals of Worship*. Eugene, OR: Cascade, 2011.

———. "The Narrative Roles of the Women in Matthew's Genealogy." *Bib* 72 (1991) 538–45.

———. *1 Peter, 2 Peter, and Jude: Worship Matters*. Eugene, OR: Cascade, 2013.

———. "Reader-Response and the Narrative Context of the Parables about Growing Seed in Mark 4:1–34." *CBQ* 54 (1992) 271–86.

———. "Significant Aspects of the Healing Miracles in Matthew." *CBQ* 41 (1979) 274–87.

———. *The Transfiguration of Jesus: Narrative Meaning and Function of Mark 9:2–8, Matt 17:1–8 and Luke 9:28–36*. AnBib 144. Rome: Editrice Pontificio Istituto Biblico, 2000.

———. *Worship in the Letter to the Hebrews*. Eugene, OR: Cascade, 2011.

Huizenga, Leroy Andrew. "Obedience unto Death: The Matthean Gethsemane and Arrest Sequence and the Aqedah." *CBQ* 71 (2009) 507–26.

Huys, M. "Turning the Tables: Jesus' Temple Cleansing and the Story of Lycaon." *ETL* 86 (2010) 137–61.

Jolley, Marc A. "Fear." *EDB* 457.

Kellermann, Ulrich. "Ἡρῴδης." *EDNT* 2.122–23.

Lee, Dorothy A. "The Faith of the Canaanite Woman (Mt. 15:21–28): Narrative, Theology, Ministry." *Journal of Anglican Studies* 13 (2015) 12–29.

Lentzen-Deis, Fritzleo. *Die Taufe Jesu nach den Synoptikern: Literarkritische und gattungsgeschichtliche Untersuchungen*. Frankfurter Theologische Studien 4. Frankfurt: Knecht, 1970.

Martin, Michael Wade. "The Poetry of the Lord's Prayer: A Study in Poetic Device." *JBL* 134 (2015) 347–72.

Mbabazi, Isaac K. *The Significance of Interpersonal Forgiveness in the Gospel of Matthew*. Eugene, OR: Pickwick, 2013.

McDonald, P. M. "'I Am with You Always, to the End of the Age': Presence in the Gospel according to Matthew." *PIBA* 28 (2005) 66–86.

Metzger, Bruce Manning. *A Textual Commentary on the Greek New Testament: Second Edition*. Stuttgart: Deutsche Bibelgesellschaft, 1994.

Meyer, Ben F. "Many (=All) Are Called, but Few (=Not All) Are Chosen." *NTS* 36 (1990) 89–97.

Morris, Leon. *The Gospel according to Matthew*. Pillar New Testament Commentary. Grand Rapids: Eerdmans, 1992.

Nicklas, Tobias. "Versöhnung mit Israel im Matthäusevangelium?" *BL* 88 (2015) 17–24.

Nolland, John. *The Gospel of Matthew: A Commentary on the Greek Text*. NIGTC. Grand Rapids: Eerdmans, 2005.

Nützel, Johannes M. "γόνυ." *EDNT* 1.257–58.

Osborne, Grant R. *Matthew*. Exegetical Commentary on the New Testament. Grand Rapids: Zondervan, 2010.

Ottenheijm, Eric. "The Shared Meal—a Therapeutical Device: The Function and Meaning of Hos 6:6 in Matt 9:10–13." *NovT* 53 (2011) 1–21.

Park, Eugene Eung-Chun. "Rachel's Cry for Her Children: Matthew's Treatment of the Infanticide by Herod." *CBQ* 75 (2013) 473–85.

Perrin, Nicholas. *Jesus the Temple*. Grand Rapids: Baker Academic, 2010.

Peterson, David. *Engaging with God: A Biblical Theology of Worship*. Downers Grove, IL: InterVarsity, 1992.

Popkes, Wiard. "δεῖ." *EDNT* 1.279–80.

Powell, Mark Allan. "Do and Keep What Moses Says (Matthew 23:2–7)." *JBL* 114 (1995) 419–35.

———. "Expected and Unexpected Readings of Matthew: What the Reader Knows." *AsTJ* 48 (1993) 31–51.

———. *God With Us: A Pastoral Theology of Matthew's Gospel*. Minneapolis: Fortress, 1995.

———. "The Magi as Kings: An Adventure in Reader-Response Criticism." *CBQ* 62 (2000) 459–80.

———. "The Magi as Wise Men: Re-examining a Basic Supposition." *NTS* 46 (2000) 1–20.

———. "Matthew's Beatitudes: Reversals and Rewards of the Kingdom." *CBQ* 58 (1996) 460–79.

———. "Neither Wise Nor Powerful: Reconsidering Matthew's Magi in Light of Reader Expectations." *Trinity Seminary Review* 20 (1998) 19–31.

———. "Toward a Narrative-Critical Understanding of Matthew." *Int* 46 (1992) 341–46.

———. "A Typology of Worship in the Gospel of Matthew." *JSNT* 57 (1995) 3–17.

Rebell, Walter. "ὡσαννά." *EDNT* 3.509.
Resseguie, James L. *Narrative Criticism of the New Testament: An Introduction*. Grand Rapids: Baker Academic, 2005.
Schenk, Wolfgang. "ζυγός." *EDNT* 2.104.
———. "προσφέρω." *EDNT* 3.177–78.
Schneider, Sebastian. "Barmherzigkeit *und* Zorn! Überlegungen zum Gleichnis vom unbarmherzigen Knecht (Mt 18,23–35)." *BZ* 59 (2015) 161–78.
Staudinger, Ferdinand. "ἐλεημοσύνη." *EDNT* 1.428–29.
Thiselton, Anthony C. "Oath." *NIDB* 4.309–12.
Tipei, John Fleter. *The Laying On of Hands in the New Testament: Its Significance, Techniques, and Effects*. Lanham, MD: University Press of America, 2009.
Turner, David L. *Matthew*. BECNT. Grand Rapids: Baker Academic, 2008.
Van der Horst, P. W. "Once More: The Translation of *hoi de* in Matthew 28.17." *JSNT* 27 (1986) 27–30.
Viljoen, François P. "Hosea 6:6 and Identity Formation in Matthew." *AcT* 34 (2014) 214–37.
Weaver, Dorothy J. *Matthew's Missionary Discourse: A Literary Critical Analysis*. JNSTSup 38. Sheffield: JSOT Press, 1990.
Wilson, Walter T. *Healing in the Gospel of Matthew: Reflections on Method and Ministry*. Minneapolis: Fortress, 2014.
Wimmer, Joseph F. *Fasting in the New Testament: A Study in Biblical Theology*. New York: Paulist, 1982.
Zmijewski, Josef. "νηστεύω." *EDNT* 2.465–67.

Scripture Index

OLD TESTAMENT

Genesis
1:26–27 (LXX)	114
1:27	95
2:24	95
12:3	6
12:8	6
13:4	6
21:23	6
22:12	13
26:25	6
33:20	6
38:14–25	5
38:26	5

Exodus
3:6	115
3:12	8n7
4:22	8, 10, 14, 18
4:23	8, 8n7, 10
6:6	134, 152
7:16	8n7
7:26	8n7
8:16	8n7
9:1	8n7
9:13	8n7
10:3	8n7
10:7	8n7
10:8	8n7
10:11	8n7
10:24	8n7
10:26	8n7
12	136
12:1–13	134, 152
12:9	137, 153
12:14 (LXX)	135, 152
12:31	8n7
12:46	137, 153
15:13 (LXX)	134, 152
17:2	15, 19
17:7	19
20:7	24
20:12	72
20:12–16	97
20:13–16	73
20:13	24, 31
20:14	24
20:17	24
21:17	72
21:32	136
24:3–8	138, 153
24:8	138, 153
24:9–11	138, 153
24:12	21
24:13	21
24:15	21
30:11–16	84
34:21	51

Leviticus
4:7	139
4:18	139
4:25	139
4:30	139
4:34	139

Leviticus (continued)

11:4	121
11:41–44	121
14:1–9	35
15:25–30	39
19:12	24
19:18	24, 97, 117, 168
20:9	72
24:5–9	52
24:20	24
27:30–33	121

Numbers

6:2–8	9
6:8	9
9:12	137, 153
14:22	15, 19
15:37–41	39
18:8–32	121
19:11–22	122
21:5–6	14, 18
24:17	7
25:1–3	15, 19
27:17	42
28:9–10	52

Deuteronomy

4:16 (LXX)	114
5:16–20	97
5:16	72
5:17–20	73
5:17	24, 31
5:18	24
5:21	24
6:5	117
6:13	3, 15, 19, 41, 44, 47, 59, 162, 170
6:16	15, 19, 170
8:1–6	14, 18
8:3	14, 18, 19, 21
14:22–29	121
15:11	135
19:15	86
24:1–5	24
24:1–4	95
25:5–6	115
29:24–25	15, 19
32:5 (LXX)	83
34:5–6	81

Joshua

2:11	6

Judges

13:5	9
13:7	9

Ruth

1:16	6

1 Samuel

21:2–7	52

2 Samuel

5:2	7
5:8	40
5:8 (LXX)	107
7:1–17	5
7:12	5
7:14	8, 10
11	6

1 Kings

1:8	12
11	8, 10

2 Kings

2:11	81
5:7	34–35
22:17	42

2 Chronicles

36:11–16	23, 31

Psalms

2:7	8, 10, 13
8:3	108, 129, 160
15	22, 30, 73, 90, 167
18:17	70
22:1	146, 156, 171
24:3–6	22, 30, 73, 90, 167
37:11	22

41:6 (LXX)	141
41:12 (LXX)	141
42:5 (LXX)	141
42:3	22, 30, 73, 90, 167
65:8	36, 45
69:2–4	70
69:14–16	70
69:22	147
77:20	70
78:18	15, 19
89:10	36, 45
89:27	8, 10
91:11–12	15, 170
106:14	15, 19
110:1	118
113–18	140n18
116:1–9	140n18
117:22–23 (LXX)	111
117:26 (LXX)	123
118:25–26	106, 160
144:7	70
148:1 (LXX)	106, 106n34

Job
9:8	70

Wisdom
14:1–4	70, 70n7
14:1–2	70n7
14:3–4	70n7

Hosea
6:6	2, 22, 24, 30, 31, 38, 44, 47, 51, 52, 56, 64, 65, 73, 90, 101, 105, 167, 168, 174
11:1	8, 10, 14, 18
11:2	8, 10

Amos
3:7	111

Micah
5:1	7

Joel
1:11 (LXX)	110

Jonah
2:1	77
2:2–11	78

Zechariah
9:9	105
9:11	139n13
11:12	136

Malachi
3:23–24	12

Isaiah
4:3	9
5:1–7	110
6:9–10	57
7:14	1
8:23–9:1	16
8:23	9
11:1–9	5
11:1	9
29:13	72, 90, 117
35:5	40
40:3	12
41:8	13
42:1–4	54–55
42:1	13
43:16	70
53:4	36, 45
54:5–6	39, 46
55:10–11	57
56:7	107
60:6–7	7, 10
61:1	22
61:2–3	22
62:4–5	39, 45
62:11	105

Jeremiah
7:11	107
23:5	5
25:4 (LXX)	111
31:15	8, 11

Jeremiah (continued)

31:31–34	139n13
32:17–41	139n13
38:20	13

Ezekiel

17:23 (LXX)	60n34
31:5–6 (LXX)	60n34
34:1–22	7
34:5–6	42
34:23	5, 7

Daniel

4:10–12	60n34
4:20–21	60n34
7:9	81
7:13–14	37
7:14 (LXX)	150
10:6	81
12:3	61, 66

NEW TESTAMENT

Matthew

1–2	4, 5–11
1	5–6
1:1	5, 6, 8, 9, 10, 40, 52, 55, 63, 159
1:2–3	7
1:2	6
1:3	5
1:5	6, 7, 9, 10, 16, 74, 159
1:6	5, 6
1:11	6, 8
1:16–18	159
1:16–17	6
1:18	6, 9, 10, 11, 13, 159
1:20	6, 9, 10, 11, 13, 87, 159
1:21	6, 7, 9, 10, 11, 12, 13, 15, 16, 17, 19, 20, 37, 40, 45, 54, 72, 87, 139, 148, 157, 162, 165
1:23	1, 2, 3, 6, 7, 8, 9, 10, 11, 12, 13, 16, 21, 35, 36, 37, 44, 45, 47, 54, 63, 84, 85, 87, 93, 126, 127, 132, 133, 135, 151–52, 158, 159, 161, 163, 165, 169, 174
1:25	9, 11
2	7–9
2:1–12	6, 10, 55
2:1–4	105
2:1–2	10
2:1	7, 13n1, 159
2:2	2, 3, 7, 8, 10, 11, 12, 16, 19, 34, 69, 87, 106, 146, 159, 161
2:3	7, 106
2:4	7, 10, 16, 19, 78, 91, 159
2:6	7, 8, 9, 10, 11, 16, 17, 42–43, 69
2:8	7, 146
2:9	7
2:10–11	8, 11, 23, 30, 31
2:10	7, 149
2:11	2, 3, 7, 10, 13n1, 16, 34, 69, 71, 74, 78, 81, 90, 91, 96, 105, 141, 149, 154, 159, 161
2:13	8
2:14	8
2:15	8, 9, 10, 11, 13, 16, 19, 22, 30, 36, 45, 63
2:16–18	22
2:16	8, 11, 108
2:17	8
2:18	8, 11
2:19–21	9
2:22	9
2:23	9, 11
3–4	4, 12–20
3	12–14
3:1	12, 13n1
3:2	3, 12, 13, 16, 18, 19, 43, 49, 57
3:3	12
3:4	12
3:5	12, 17, 18
3:6	12, 13, 13n1, 18
3:7–8	122
3:7	12, 13, 18, 77
3:8	13, 14, 18, 57, 59, 65, 113, 131, 172

3:9	6, 10, 12, 18, 74	4:17	3, 16, 17, 20, 21, 38, 43, 49, 57, 62
3:10	13, 18, 29	4:18–22	17, 19, 21, 38, 80
3:11	13, 18, 48, 55, 150	4:19	17, 20, 50, 57, 62, 64, 66, 79, 91
3:12	13, 18, 48, 60, 125	4:21	102
3:13–17	2, 174	4:23	17, 19, 41, 42, 47, 48, 151
3:13–15	172	4:24	17, 20, 36, 41, 45, 71, 96
3:13	13, 13n1	4:25	17, 20, 21, 34
3:14	13	5–7	4, 21–33, 34, 42
3:15	13, 14, 18, 172	5:1–16	21–23
3:16–18	151, 157, 167	5:1	21, 30, 75
3:16–17	14, 15, 18, 55, 172	5:2	21
3:16	13, 14, 54, 55, 150	5:3–16	23n4
3:17	13, 14, 22, 30, 36, 45, 54, 63, 81, 111, 118, 141, 148, 150, 152, 154, 157, 158, 174	5:3–10	22–23, 30
		5:3–6	22, 30, 167
		5:3	22, 30
4:1–11	3, 14–16, 17, 19, 26, 32, 37, 165, 169	5:4	22
		5:5	22
4:1–4	17	5:6	22, 70, 89
4:1	14, 55, 77, 150	5:7–10	22, 30, 167
4:2–11	55	5:7	22, 30, 167
4:2–4	39, 46, 63, 67, 166	5:8	22, 30, 73, 90, 167
4:2	14, 19, 26, 49	5:9	22, 30
4:3	14, 63, 71, 77	5:10–12	58, 59, 66, 107
4:4	14, 19, 21	5:10	22, 23, 30
4:5–7	17	5:11–12	122
4:5–6	71	5:11	23, 30, 80
4:5	15, 169	5:12	23, 25, 29, 30–31, 100, 149
4:6	15, 19, 63, 77, 169–70	5:13	23, 31
4:7	15, 19, 170	5:14–16	23, 31
4:8–10	17, 36, 44, 45, 58, 59, 62, 66	5:14	23, 27, 31, 32
4:8–9	3, 19, 59	5:16	2, 23, 25, 27, 31, 32, 38, 46, 50, 64, 75, 134, 135, 152, 160, 168
4:8	15, 170		
4:9	15, 81, 141, 154, 170	5:17–48	23–25
4:10	3, 15, 19, 21, 27, 32, 41, 42, 44, 47, 49, 55, 56, 59, 79, 150, 151, 157, 162, 167, 170, 174	5:17	23–24, 31
		5:18	24
		5:19	24
		5:20	24, 25, 28, 29, 30, 31, 33, 49, 51, 58, 64, 85, 97, 113, 126, 131, 133, 163, 165, 172
4:11	15, 36		
4:12–25	16–17		
4:12	16		
4:13	16	5:21–7:29	49
4:14	16	5:21–7:12	28
4:15–16	16, 55	5:21–48	97
4:15	9, 75		
4:16	16, 17, 23, 31		

Matthew (continued)

Reference	Pages
5:21	24, 31
5:22	24, 31
5:23–24	2, 3, 49, 96
5:23	24, 31, 167
5:24	24, 31, 56, 59, 65, 66, 167
5:27–30	24
5:29–30	86
5:31–32	24, 96, 127
5:33–37	24, 120–21
5:34–35	68
5:35	87
5:37	58, 68
5:38–42	24
5:43–48	24, 117, 131, 168
5:43–47	98, 128
5:43–44	124
5:44	24
5:45	25, 31, 84, 113
5:46	25, 31
5:47	25, 31
5:48	25, 31, 97, 128
6:1–18	25–26
6:1	25, 100, 119
6:2	25, 31–32, 167
6:3–4	25, 32, 168
6:4	80
6:5–15	2
6:5	26, 119
6:6–13	151, 157
6:6	26, 80
6:7	26
6:8	26, 32, 164
6:9–13	26, 32, 164
6:9–10	50, 64, 70, 103, 163, 170
6:9	26, 32, 120, 164
6:10	26, 32, 56, 61, 65, 66, 79, 86, 92, 93, 143, 150, 155, 171
6:11	26, 32, 164
6:12	26, 32, 38, 45, 55, 88, 89, 94, 139, 165
6:13	26, 32, 58, 59, 60, 65, 66, 142, 165
6:14–15	26, 32, 38, 45, 55–56, 88, 89, 94, 139, 165
6:16	26, 166
6:16–18	2, 39, 46, 63, 67, 166
6:17	26, 32, 166
6:18	26, 32, 80, 166
6:19–34	27
6:19–21	59, 62, 66, 101
6:19	27
6:20	27, 32, 98, 128
6:21	27, 32, 73, 90, 98, 128
6:22	27, 32
6:23	27, 101
6:24	27, 32, 43, 59, 62, 66, 73, 90, 98, 101, 128, 136
6:25–34	59
6:25	27, 43
6:26	27, 53, 99
6:27	27
6:28–29	27
6:30	27, 74, 77, 83, 149
6:31	27, 32
6:32	27, 32
6:33	27, 32, 43, 59, 99
6:34	27, 32
7:1–12	28
7:1–2	28
7:3–6	165
7:3–5	28, 33
7:6	28, 33
7:7–8	28, 33, 62, 66, 87, 93, 165
7:7	29
7:8	29, 109
7:9–11	28, 33, 165
7:11	68
7:12	28, 33, 117, 165
7:13–29	28–30
7:13	28, 51, 64
7:14	28, 97, 113, 131
7:15–16	29
7:17–18	29
7:19	29
7:20	29
7:21	29, 33, 56, 61, 65, 66, 86, 87, 93, 125, 132, 163, 164
7:22	29, 33, 125, 163
7:23	29, 61, 66, 122, 125, 163
7:24–27	29–30
7:24	122

7:28	4, 30, 116, 131	8:33	37
7:29	30, 42, 110, 116, 131, 151, 157	8:34	37, 45, 71
		9:1–8	38, 45, 72, 162
8–10	4, 34–47	9:1	37
8:1–9:35	34–47	9:2	37, 38, 41, 46, 48, 63, 96, 139
8:1–4	44		
8:1	34	9:3–4	57
8:2–3	48	9:3	37
8:2	34, 39, 48, 50, 63, 64, 71, 74, 87, 90, 161	9:4	37
		9:5	37, 48, 139
8:3–4	161	9:6–7	37
8:3	35	9:6	38, 46, 110, 139, 150
8:4	35, 48, 63, 96	9:8	2, 38, 46, 48, 50, 63, 64, 75, 110, 139, 150, 160
8:5–13	6, 10, 45, 55		
8:5–6	48, 50, 63, 64	9:9–13	39, 46
8:5	35, 37, 71, 161	9:9	38, 39, 46
8:6	35, 161	9:10–13	2, 86
8:7	35	9:10–11	173
8:8	35, 36, 45	9:10	38, 110, 168
8:9	35	9:11	38, 57, 168
8:10	35, 74, 109, 130, 161	9:12	38, 168, 174
8:11–12	35	9:13	2, 24, 31, 38, 39, 42, 44, 46, 47, 49, 51, 53, 55, 56, 57, 59, 63, 64, 65, 66, 73, 84, 85, 86, 88, 90, 93, 98, 101, 102, 105, 107, 110, 113, 119, 121, 122, 124, 125, 126, 128, 129, 132, 145, 151, 158, 164, 167, 168, 169, 174
8:11	69, 70, 76, 89, 91		
8:13	35, 74, 83, 92, 109, 130, 161		
8:14–15	45		
8:14	36		
8:16	36, 41, 43, 45, 48, 63, 96		
8:17	36, 42, 45, 48, 63		
8:18–19	36		
8:20	36		
8:21	36	9:14	39, 46, 166
8:22	36	9:15	39, 46, 49, 84, 124, 135, 140, 154, 164, 166, 173
8:23–24	45		
8:23	36	9:16–17	39, 46, 62, 67
8:24	36	9:18	2, 39, 40, 46, 48, 50, 63, 64, 71, 74, 87, 90, 162
8:25	36, 37, 40, 45, 71, 90, 163		
		9:19	39
8:26	36, 45, 71, 74, 77, 83, 90, 149, 163	9:20	39, 72
		9:21	39, 72
8:27	36, 37, 45, 71	9:22	39
8:28–34	37, 43, 45	9:23	40, 46
8:28	37	9:24–25	162
8:29–31	37, 45	9:24	40, 46
8:29	37, 63, 71, 90	9:25	40, 46, 48
8:30–31	37	9:26	40, 46
8:31	71	9:27–31	41, 46, 103, 162, 164
8:32	37		

Matthew *(continued)*

9:27–30	48
9:27	5, 10, 40, 48, 50, 52, 55, 63, 64, 74, 83, 88, 92, 107, 118
9:28–29	41, 47, 162
9:28	40, 109, 130
9:29–30	107
9:29	40, 109, 130
9:30	40
9:31	40, 41, 47, 162
9:32–34	41, 46, 162
9:32–33	48, 55
9:32	41, 48, 63, 96
9:33–34	57
9:33	41, 43, 47, 48, 63, 75, 162
9:34	41, 43, 47, 49, 55, 162
9:35—10:42	41–44
9:35	41, 42, 47, 48, 151
9:36—11:1	4
9:36–38	42, 47
9:36	41, 43, 69, 74, 87
9:37–38	59, 65, 125
9:37	42, 47, 57, 165
9:38	42, 43, 47, 62, 67, 165
10:1	42, 47, 83, 92, 125, 151, 157, 165
10:2–4	42, 80
10:2	74, 102
10:4	135
10:5–6	74
10:5	42
10:6	42, 54, 55, 57
10:7–8	125, 151, 157
10:7	43, 57, 58–59, 62
10:8	43, 44, 83, 92
10:9	43, 127, 133
10:10	43, 57, 127, 133
10:11–13	127, 133
10:11	43
10:12	43
10:13	43
10:14–15	43
10:14	57
10:16–25	59, 138, 142
10:16–24	43
10:16–23	127, 133
10:16	122
10:17	122
10:22	59, 124, 147
10:23	59, 122
10:24–25	60
10:25	43, 67
10:28	44, 122
10:29–31	44
10:31	53
10:32–33	44, 47
10:34–37	44, 47
10:38	140
10:39	147
10:40–42	174
10:42	126, 133, 169, 170
11:15	49
11:16–23	57
11:16–19	50
11:16–17	49
11:18	49
11:19	49
11:20–24	50, 64
11:20	49, 64
11:21	49, 64, 120
11:23	50, 64
11:25–12:50	50–56
11:25–27	71, 90
11:25–26	2, 50, 64, 70, 170
11:25	50, 51, 62, 64, 108, 129
11:27	50, 51, 52, 63, 64, 70, 78, 85, 93, 105, 111, 118, 150, 170
11:28–29	51, 52, 53–54
11:28	51, 64, 119, 132
11:29	51, 52, 64, 73, 84, 90, 93, 105, 119, 120, 132, 169
11:30	51, 64, 132
12:1–14	2
12:1–8	53, 64, 174
12:1–4	53, 64, 174
12:1	51
12:2	52, 53
12:3	52
12:4	52
12:5	52, 53, 65, 174

12:6	2, 5, 52, 52n15, 53, 65, 84, 85, 93, 107, 124, 129, 145, 156, 174	12:50	56, 65, 86, 93, 125, 141–42, 151, 154, 157, 167, 171
12:7	2, 24, 31, 52, 52n15, 53, 54, 55, 56, 57, 59, 63, 65, 66, 73, 84, 85, 86, 88, 90, 93, 98, 101, 102, 105, 107, 119, 121, 122, 124, 125, 126, 128, 129, 132, 145, 151, 158, 164, 167, 169, 174	13:1–58	56–63
		13:1–53	4, 63
		13:1–9	65
		13:1	56, 57
		13:2	57
		13:3–9	56
		13:3–8	125
		13:3	57, 125
12:8	52, 53, 174	13:4–7	57
12:9	53	13:4	58
12:10–13	54	13:5–6	58
12:10	53	13:7	59
12:11	53	13:8	57, 59, 65, 125
12:12	53	13:9	57
12:13	53	13:10	57
12:14	53, 54, 57, 113, 117	13:11	57, 58, 62, 67, 125
12:15	54	13:12	125, 132
12:16	54	13:13–15	57
12:17	54	13:13–14	58
12:18–21	54	13:13	59, 65
12:18	54, 55, 121	13:14	59, 65
12:19	54	13:15	58
12:20	54, 121	13:16–18	58
12:21	54, 55, 74, 91, 162	13:16–17	57
12:22–23	55	13:18–23	58, 125
12:22	55, 96	13:19–23	60
12:23–24	57	13:19	58, 59, 60, 61, 65
12:23	55	13:20–21	59, 65, 66
12:24–28	56	13:20	58
12:24	55	13:21	58
12:25–27	55	13:22	59, 65, 66
12:28	55	13:23	59, 62, 65, 67, 73, 125
12:29	55	13:24–30	60, 66
12:31–32	56	13:24	60, 61
12:34	73, 122	13:25	60
12:35	62, 67	13:27	60, 62, 67, 100
12:38–45	57	13:28–30	61
12:38	77	13:28	60
12:39	77	13:29	60
12:40	77, 78, 91	13:30	60, 125
12:46–50	57, 63	13:31–32	66
12:46–48	56, 65	13:31	60
12:49–50	57, 61, 66, 126, 133, 169	13:32	60
12:49	56, 65	13:33	60, 66
		13:36–43	61, 66

Matthew (continued)

Reference	Pages
13:37–38	61
13:38	61, 66, 84
13:40	61
13:41–43	61
13:41	61, 66, 122
13:42	61, 66
13:43	61, 62, 66
13:44	61, 66, 73, 90
13:45–46	61, 66
13:47–50	62, 66
13:48	62
13:49	62
13:50	62, 66
13:51–53	62, 67
13:51	62, 67
13:52	62, 67, 122
13:53	4
13:54–56	63
13:54	106
13:55–56	63
13:57	63, 81, 106
13:58	63
14–18	4, 68–94
14	68–72
14:1–12	69, 89
14:1	68
14:3–4	68
14:5	68
14:6–8	68
14:6	68, 69
14:7	68
14:8–9	68
14:9	68, 69
14:12	69
14:13–21	69, 70, 71, 74, 76, 77, 89, 90, 91, 137, 170, 173
14:14	68, 74, 75, 87
14:15–21	75
14:15	69, 74
14:16	69
14:17	76
14:19	2, 69, 74, 76, 89, 137, 173
14:20–21	76
14:20	69, 70, 76, 89, 91, 137
14:21	69
14:22	70, 170
14:23	70, 71, 90, 151, 157, 170
14:24	70, 170
14:25	70, 170
14:26–27	70, 82, 89, 92, 163
14:28–31	78, 159
14:28	70, 89, 163
14:29	70, 89, 163
14:30–31	78
14:30	70, 89, 163
14:31	70–71, 74, 77, 83, 89, 149, 163
14:32	71, 78, 90, 91
14:33	2, 8, 10, 71, 72, 74, 76, 78, 90, 91, 118, 148, 148n29, 149, 157, 159, 161, 162
14:34	71
14:35	71, 96, 162
14:36	71–72, 162
15	72–76
15:1–20	73, 90
15:1	72, 90
15:2	72, 90, 168
15:3	72, 90
15:4	72, 73, 90
15:5	72, 90
15:6	72, 90
15:7	72, 90
15:8–9	72, 90, 168
15:8	89, 94, 98, 117, 128
15:9	117
15:10	73, 168
15:11	73, 168
15:12–14	73
15:15–17	73
15:18	73, 168
15:19	73, 168
15:20	73, 168
15:21–28	74, 91, 162
15:21	73, 75
15:22–28	6, 10
15:22	5, 10, 74, 83, 88, 92, 109, 118, 130
15:23	74
15:24	74
15:25	2, 74, 87
15:26	74
15:27	74

SCRIPTURE INDEX

15:28	74, 83, 92, 109, 130	16:27	80
15:29–31	75	16:28	80, 82, 92
15:29	75, 95	17:1–2	82, 92
15:30	75, 95	17:1	80–81, 83, 92, 140, 154
15:31	2, 75, 160	17:2	81, 160
15:32–39	76, 77, 91, 137, 173	17:3–4	160
15:32	75, 87	17:3	81, 82, 92
15:33	75, 76, 91	17:4	81, 82, 92
15:34	76	17:5	81, 82, 83, 84, 92, 111, 118, 141, 148, 152, 154, 157, 158, 160, 167, 174
15:35	76		
15:36	2, 76, 137, 173	17:6	81, 92, 141, 154, 160
15:37–38	76	17:7	82, 92
15:37	76, 91, 137	17:8	82, 92
15:39	76	17:9	82
16:1–17:23	77–84	17:10	82
16:1	77, 95, 115, 117	17:11	82
16:2–3	77	17:12	82
16:4	77	17:13	82
16:5	77	17:14–18	84, 163
16:6	77, 115	17:14	83, 92, 146, 162
16:7	77	17:15	83, 88, 92, 146, 162
16:8	77, 83, 149	17:16	83, 92
16:9–10	77	17:17	83, 92, 162–63
16:11	78, 115	17:18	83, 92, 163
16:12	78, 115	17:19–20	83
16:13–14	78	17:19	83
16:13	8, 10	17:20	83, 109, 141, 142, 149, 154, 155
16:14	78, 91, 106		
16:15	78, 91	17:22–23	103, 111
16:16	78, 79, 82, 91, 92, 118, 148, 157, 160, 161	17:22	83, 95, 102, 144
		17:23	77, 83, 88, 102, 145
16:17	78	17:24—19:1	4
16:18	78, 111, 130, 166	17:24—18:35	84–89, 95
16:19	78–79	17:24–27	85, 92
16:20	79, 82, 92	17:24–25	84
16:21–22	103	17:25–26	84, 92
16:21	77, 79, 81, 82, 83, 91, 92, 102, 104, 108, 109, 111, 145, 160, 162	17:25	84
		17:26	84
16:22	79, 91, 102	17:27	84, 85, 86, 92
16:23	79–80, 91, 142, 155, 171	18:1–10	86, 93
16:24–26	80	18:1–4	86
16:24–25	98, 128	18:1	85, 93
16:24	79, 104, 140, 142, 155, 171	18:2	85, 93
		18:3–4	170
16:25	80, 99, 103, 104, 128, 147	18:3	85, 93, 97, 127, 171
		18:4	85, 93, 120, 169
16:26	80		

Matthew *(continued)*

18:5	2, 85, 86, 93, 152, 158, 174
18:6	86, 126, 133, 169
18:7	86, 120
18:8–9	86, 97
18:10	86, 126, 133, 169
18:12–13	86, 93
18:14	86, 93, 126, 133, 169
18:15	86
18:16	86
18:17	86
18:18–19	86, 93, 165
18:19–20	2, 3, 142, 152, 155, 158
18:19	109, 124, 130
18:20	87, 93, 124, 152, 158, 165
18:21–22	87
18:21	88, 93
18:22	87, 88, 93
18:23–24	88, 93
18:23	87, 112
18:24	87
18:25	87
18:26	87, 88, 89, 94
18:27	87, 88, 93
18:28	88
18:29	88
18:30	88
18:31	88
18:32–33	89
18:32	88
18:33	88, 93
18:34	88
18:35	88, 93
19–25	4, 95–133
19–20	95–104
19:1	4, 95
19:2	95
19:3–9	96, 127
19:3	95, 117, 127
19:4	95
19:5	95
19:6	95
19:7	95, 127
19:8	95, 127
19:9	96, 127
19:10–11	127
19:10	96
19:11	96
19:12	96, 127
19:13	96, 97, 127, 151, 158, 170, 171
19:14	97, 170–71
19:15	97
19:16–22	99
19:16–17	97
19:16	97, 98, 128, 135
19:17	97, 98, 101, 128
19:18–19	97
19:19	98, 117, 131
19:20	97
19:21	97, 98, 128, 135
19:22	98, 128
19:23	99
19:24	99
19:25–26	147
19:25	99
19:26	99, 141, 154
19:27	99
19:28	99
19:29	99
19:30	100, 101, 103, 128
20:1–16	128
20:1	100, 110
20:2	100
20:3	100
20:4	100
20:5	100
20:6	100
20:7	100
20:8–12	101
20:8	100
20:9	100
20:10	100, 101n21
20:11	101, 110
20:12	101
20:13	101
20:14	101, 101n21
20:15	101, 101n21
20:16	101, 103, 128
20:17–19	103, 104, 128, 164
20:17	102
20:18–19	111
20:18	102, 108, 144, 160
20:19	77, 102, 145

20:20–23	103, 104, 128–29, 138, 164	21:14	40, 107, 108
20:20	2, 102, 140, 154, 163	21:15	5, 10, 108, 118, 129, 160
20:21	102, 104, 163	21:16	108, 129, 160
20:22–23	141	21:17–22	112
20:22	102	21:17	108, 130
20:23	103, 138	21:18–19	166
20:24	103, 128	21:18	108, 130
20:25	103, 106, 128, 160	21:19	108, 111, 130
20:26	103, 120, 128, 169	21:20	108–9
20:27	103, 128	21:21–22	5, 111–12, 115, 116, 118, 130, 131, 142, 155, 166, 168
20:28	103, 104, 106, 120, 128, 129, 134, 137, 139, 147, 152, 153, 160, 164, 169, 173	21:21	109, 116, 130
		21:22	109, 109n41, 123, 130, 141, 145, 150, 154, 165
20:29	103, 104, 128, 164	21:23	109, 110, 150, 151, 157
20:30–31	5, 10, 104, 107, 118, 128, 164	21:24	110
		21:25	110
20:30	103, 106, 164	21:26	110, 112
20:31	103–4, 106	21:27	110
20:32	104	21:28–32	110, 112, 113
20:33–34	107	21:31	110
20:33	104	21:32	110
20:34	104, 128	21:33–46	112
21–23	104–23	21:33–43	112
21:1–3	104	21:33	100, 110, 112
21:1	105, 129	21:34	111, 112
21:4	105	21:35–36	112
21:5	105	21:35	111
21:6	105, 129	21:36	111, 112
21:7	106, 129, 160	21:37	111
21:8	106, 129	21:38–39	111
21:9	5, 10, 106, 108, 116, 118, 123, 129, 131, 160	21:40	111
		21:41	111, 112, 114
21:10–11	122	21:42–43	112
21:10	106	21:42	111, 115, 123, 130, 145, 166
21:11	106, 107, 116, 129, 131		
21:12–17	147, 156, 172	21:43	111, 130, 166
21:12–13	108, 109, 112, 116, 119, 123, 130, 131, 150	21:45	112
		21:46	112, 116, 131
21:12	107, 112, 115, 129, 131, 165	22:1–14	130
		22:1	112
21:13	3, 5, 107, 108, 109n41, 111, 112, 114–15, 116, 118, 123, 129, 130, 131, 145, 160, 165, 166, 168	22:2	112, 140, 154, 173
		22:3–4	112
		22:5	112
		22:6	112
21:14–16	112, 150	22:7	112
21:14–15	109–10	22:8	112–13

SCRIPTURE INDEX 191

Matthew (continued)

Reference	Pages
22:9	113
22:10	113
22:11–12	113, 130
22:13	113, 130
22:14	113, 131
22:15	113, 117
22:16	113, 114, 119, 151, 157
22:17	114
22:18	114
22:19	114
22:20	114
22:21	114, 116–17, 118, 119, 123, 131, 165
22:23–28	115, 116
22:23	115
22:24	115, 119
22:25	115
22:26	115
22:27	115
22:28	115
22:29	115
22:30	115–16
22:32	116, 117, 118, 119, 123, 131, 165, 166
22:33	116, 131
22:34–40	151, 158
22:34–35	118
22:34	117
22:35–36	117
22:36–40	123–24
22:36	119
22:37–40	118–19
22:37–38	117, 131, 168
22:37	117, 124
22:38	117
22:39	117, 124, 131, 168
22:40	117, 131
22:41	118
22:42–45	120
22:42	118
22:43	118
22:44	118
22:45	118, 124
22:46	118
23:1	118, 132
23:2	118, 132
23:3	119, 132
23:4	119, 132
23:5–10	120, 168
23:5	119
23:6	119
23:7	119
23:8	119
23:9	120
23:10	120
23:11	120, 168
23:12	120, 169
23:13	120
23:15	120
23:16–20	120
23:16	120
23:21–22	120
23:23	2, 54, 55, 120, 121, 122, 151, 158
23:24	121
23:25	120, 121
23:26	121
23:27	120, 122
23:28	122
23:29–39	107
23:29–32	122
23:29	120
23:30–31	81
23:33	122
23:34	122
23:35	122
23:36	122
23:37	122–23
23:38	123, 147
23:39	123
24–25	4, 123–27
24:1–2	147
24:1	123, 144
24:2	123, 144
24:3	124
24:4	124
24:5	124
24:9–13	138, 142
24:11	124
24:12	124
24:13	124, 147
24:22	147
24:23	124
24:24	124
24:27–30	124

24:36–44	141, 154	26:36–46	2
24:36	141, 154	26:26–30	2
24:42	141, 142, 154, 155	26:26–29	3
24:44	141, 154	26:26–28	2, 174
25:1–13	124–25, 132, 164	26:26–27	76
25:10	125, 164	26:26	69, 136, 137, 138, 152, 153, 172, 173
25:11	125, 132, 164	26:27–28	173
25:12	125, 164	26:27	138, 141, 153
25:13	125, 126, 132, 141, 142, 154, 155, 164, 169	26:28	138, 139, 139n15, 147, 153
25:14–30	125, 132	26:29	70, 76, 89, 91, 139, 153, 173
25:16–17	125	26:30	140
25:18	125	26:31–32	140
25:21	126, 132	26:31	144, 156
25:23	126, 132	26:32	149, 157, 161
25:24	125	26:33	140
25:25	125	26:34	140
25:26	125	26:35	140, 143
25:29	126, 132	26:36–44	151, 158
25:31–46	126, 132, 169	26:36	140, 144, 154, 156
25:31–33	126, 132, 169	26:37–38	171
25:34	126, 127, 133, 169	26:37	140, 154
25:35–40	126, 132, 169	26:38	141, 142, 143, 144, 154, 155, 156
25:40	2, 126, 127, 132, 133, 135, 152, 158, 169, 174	26:39	141, 142, 143, 154, 155, 171
25:41–46	126, 132	26:40	142, 143, 155
25:41	169	26:41	142, 143, 155
25:45	2, 126, 127, 132, 133, 135, 152, 158, 169, 174	26:42	143, 155, 171
26–28	4, 134–58	26:43	143
26:1–56	134–44	26:44	143
26:1	4	26:45	143–44, 156
26:2	134, 136, 144, 158	26:46	144, 156
26:6	134, 160	26:47–50	144, 156
26:7	134, 135, 160	26:56	144, 156
26:8	134, 135	26:57—27:54	144–48
26:9	135	26:59–60	144, 156
26:10	134, 135	26:60–61	145
26:11	135	26:61	144, 145, 147, 148, 156, 157, 161
26:12	134, 135–36, 137, 152, 153, 160	26:63–64	148
26:13	135, 152, 160	27:25	139n15
26:14	135	27:27	145
26:15	135, 136	27:28	145
26:17	136	27:29	146
26:18	136, 153, 172	27:36	148, 160
26:21	139, 153		
26:22	136, 153, 172		

Matthew (continued)

27:37	148
27:39–44	146, 171
27:40–43	147
27:40	147, 148, 157, 161
27:46–53	2
27:46	147
27:43	146, 156, 172
27:45	146, 171
27:46	146, 147, 156, 171, 172
27:47	146, 148
27:49	147
27:50	147
27:51–53	148, 160
27:51	147, 148, 156, 157, 161, 172
27:52	147
27:53	147
27:54	8, 10, 148, 148n29, 149, 157, 160
27:55—28:20	149–52, 152n38
27:55–56	149
28:7	149, 161
28:8	149, 161
28:9	2, 149, 157, 161
28:11–15	149
28:16–17	3
28:16	149, 157, 161
28:17	2, 149, 149n33, 157, 161
28:18	150
28:19–20	6, 10
28:19	2, 3, 13, 14, 18, 150, 157, 167, 172, 174
28:20	2, 3, 151, 157, 158, 162, 163, 165, 169, 174

Mark

2:12	41n21

Author Index

Angel, Andrew R., 148n29
Avalos, Hector., 40n18

Balz, Horst., 95n1, 120n77
Beilner, Wolfgang., 52n13, 53n17
Borchert, Gerald L., 1n1
Boxall, Ian., 1n1, 4n7
Bühner, Jan-Adolf., 81n45
Burer, Michael H., 53n16
Byrne, Brendan., 6n1, 6n2, 7n4, 9n9, 9n11, 14n3, 15n6, 16n7, 24n5, 25n8, 27n14, 28n17, 30n20, 34n1, 36n6, 38n12, 40n15, 40n16, 42n23, 48n1, 49n5, 50n7, 50n8, 51n11, 53n19, 54n20, 54n21, 54n22, 56n26, 58n28, 60n33, 62n43, 69n5, 70n6, 71n8, 71n10, 73n14, 73n16, 73n17, 75n21, 75n25, 76n29, 79n38, 79n39, 80n41, 80n42, 81n46, 82n47, 82n49, 84n55, 84n56, 85n60, 87n67, 89n71, 96n4, 96n5, 97n8, 98n11, 99n13, 102n23, 103n26, 104n29, 107n36, 109n41, 112n48, 113n52, 114n55, 115n60, 116n62, 116n64, 118n69, 118n71, 118n72, 119n75, 121n81, 123n87, 124n89, 126n92, 126n93, 135n4, 139n16, 140n17, 145n22, 146n24, 146n25, 148n30, 151n36, 151n37

Carter, Warren., 17n8, 17n9, 63n44, 89n71, 110n44, 125n90, 126n92, 127n94
Charette, Blaine., 113n52
Clements, E. Anne., 6n3

Donaldson, Terrence L., 81n43, 117n68

Eubank, Nathan., 25n9, 102n23

France, R. T., 4n7, 7n4, 22n1, 23n2, 23n3, 27n15, 44n28, 51n12, 55n24, 61n36, 61n39, 69n3, 75n24, 76n27, 77n32, 78n35, 85n61, 86n63, 87n65, 96n2, 98n10, 100n18, 103n26, 103n27, 105n30, 106n34, 106n34, 108n38, 109n39, 111n46, 111n47, 113n50, 113n51, 115n59, 116n64, 117n65, 117n67, 121n82, 123n86, 124n88, 138n11, 147n27, 148n28, 150n35

Gerhardsson, Birger., 14n4
Gibbs, Jeffrey., 13n2
Giesen, Heinz., 84n58
Goodwin, Mark J., 78n34
Gullotta, Daniel N., 75n21
Gundry, Robert H., 61n38, 62n40

Harrington, Hannah K., 72n12
Hegermann, Harald., 139n14

AUTHOR INDEX

Heil, John Paul., 1n2, 6n3, 7n5, 35n3, 36n6, 58n31, 63n44, 71n10, 78n35, 81n44, 81n45, 82n48, 89n71, 107n37, 110n44, 125n90, 126n92, 127n94, 139n13, 144n21, 148n30, 152n38
Huizenga, Leroy Andrew., 144n20
Huys, M., 107n35

Jolley, Marc., 42n26

Kellermann, Ulrich., 8n8

Lee, Dorothy A., 75n21
Lentzen-Deis, Fritzleo., 13n2

Martin, Michael Wade., 26n11
Mbabazi, Isaac K., 26n12
McDonald, P. M., 152n38
Metzger, Bruce Manning., 112n49, 120n78
Meyer, Ben F., 113n51
Morris, Leon., 4n7, 16n7, 37n7, 38n8, 39n13, 39n14, 42n22, 52n14, 53n18, 56n25, 63n45, 72n12, 74n18, 75n23, 77n30, 80n40, 87n66, 98n12, 100n17, 101n20, 102n23, 113n53, 114n57, 120n77, 121n80, 122n83

Nicklas, Tobias., 139n15
Nolland, John., 4n7, 14n5, 22n1, 24n6, 29n19, 34n2, 36n5, 37n7, 38n9, 48n2, 49n4, 50n6, 51n9, 55n23, 55n24, 56n25, 61n37, 63n44, 63n46, 71n10, 72n12, 73n15, 74n19, 75n20, 75n23, 77n32, 78n33, 79n36, 84n58, 85n59, 85n62, 87n65, 97n7, 98n10, 100n19, 103n26, 104n28, 105n30, 105n32, 121n81, 123n85, 134n2, 135n6, 136n7, 137n9, 149n32, 151n36, 152n38
Nützel, Johannes M., 83n52

Osborne, Grant R., 4n7, 25n8, 25n10, 26n11, 26n13, 29n18, 40n17, 41n20, 42n24, 43n25, 44n27, 49n3, 50n6, 51n10, 54n22, 56n26, 57n27, 58n30, 60n32, 60n35, 62n41, 69n2, 69n4, 72n11, 72n13, 75n22, 76n26, 76n28, 77n30, 79n36, 79n39, 81n46, 83n51, 83n53, 83n54, 85n59, 87n68, 88n70, 96n3, 96n5, 97n9, 98n12, 99n14, 99n16, 102n25, 103n26, 105n32, 106n33, 107n35, 107n37, 109n39, 109n40, 109n42, 110n43, 110n45, 113n54, 114n56, 114n57, 115n61, 116n63, 117n66, 118n70, 121n80, 122n84, 123n86, 134n1, 135n3, 136n8, 137n10, 138n12, 139n16, 143n19, 146n23, 146n25, 146n26, 149n31, 149n32, 150n34, 150n35

Ottenheijm, Eric., 39n12

Park, Eugene Eung-Chun., 9n9
Perrin, Nicholas., 3n4
Peterson, David., 1n1, 1n3
Popkes, Wiard., 79n37
Powell, Mark Allan., 1n1, 3n5, 3n6, 7n4, 23n4, 118n74
Rebell, Walter., 106n34
Resseguie, James L., 3n5

Schenk, Wolfgang., 51n10, 96n6
Schneider, Sebastian., 89n71
Staudinger, Ferdinand., 25n10

Thiselton, Anthony C., 68n1
Tipei, John Fleter., 97n7
Turner, David L., 4n7, 23n3, 28n16, 38n10, 53n19, 62n42, 71n9, 71n10, 76n29, 77n31, 79n36, 79n37, 82n50, 83n53, 84n57, 86n64, 99n15, 101n22, 102n24, 105n31, 106n33, 106n34, 107n37, 110n44, 115n58, 118n73, 120n79, 122n84, 135n5, 136n7

Van der Horst, P. W., 149n33

Viljoen, François P., 39n12

Weaver, Dorothy J., 58n29
Wilson, Walter T., 35n4, 40n19

Wimmer, Joseph F., 14n5

Zmijewski, Josef., 14n5